THE GELLI ARTS®
PRINTMAKER'S HANDBOOK

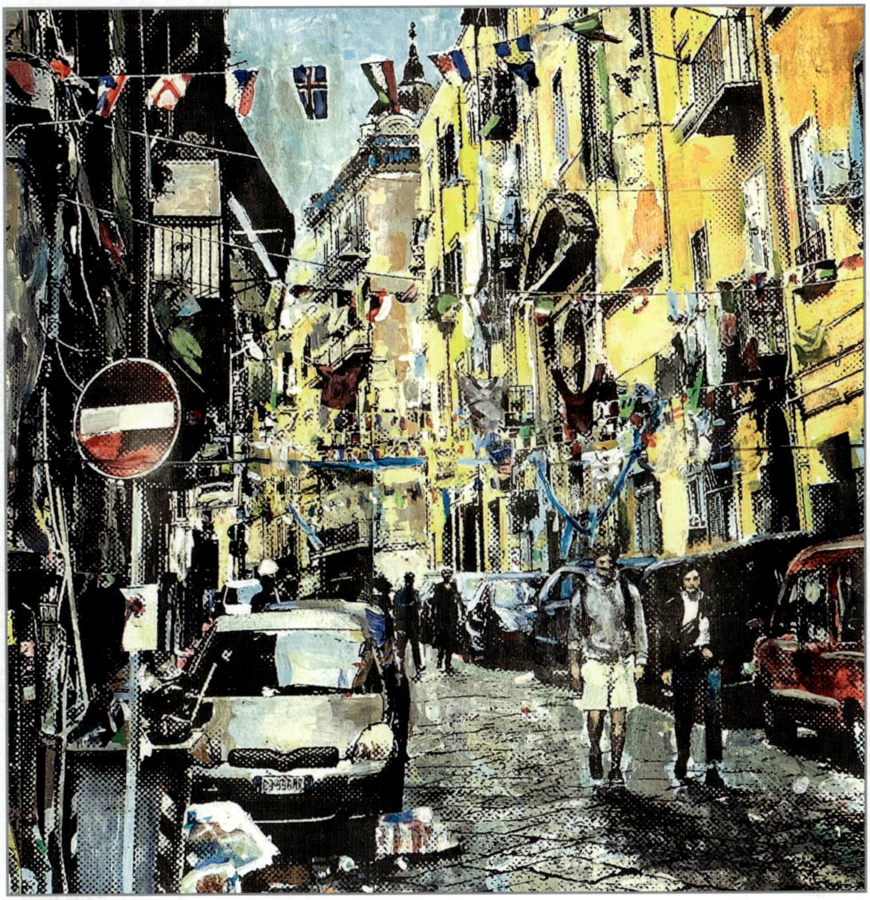

The Gelli Arts® Printmaker's Handbook:
Exploring Image Transfers and Layering Techniques
for Creating Incredible Art with Gel Plates

Jessica Russo Scherr

Editor: Kelly Reed
Project manager: Lisa Brazieal
Marketing Manager: Koryn Olage
Copyeditor: Linda Laflamme
Interior layout: Kim Scott/Bumpy Design
Cover design: Amy DeGrote and Aren Straiger
Cover image: Jessica Russo Scherr

ISBN: 979-8-88814-387-2

1st Edition (2nd printing)

© 2025 Jessica Russo Scherr

All photographs © Jessica Russo Scherr

Gelli Arts® is a registered trademark owned by Gelli Arts LLC, who has granted permission to include their trademark in this publication.

Rocky Nook Inc.
1010 B Street, Suite 350
San Rafael, CA 94901
USA

Represented in the E.U. by:
Rheinwerk Verlag GmbH
Rheinwerkallee 4
53227 Bonn
Germany
service@rheinwerk-verlag.de

www.rockynook.com

Distributed in the UK and Europe by Publishers Group UK
Distributed in the U.S. and all other territories by Publishers Group West

Library of Congress Control Number: 2025933394

This book is printed on acid-free paper.

Printed in Korea.

THE GELLI ARTS®
PRINTMAKER'S HANDBOOK

EXPLORING IMAGE TRANSFERS AND
LAYERING TECHNIQUES FOR CREATING
INCREDIBLE ART WITH GEL PLATES

JESSICA RUSSO SCHERR

rockynook

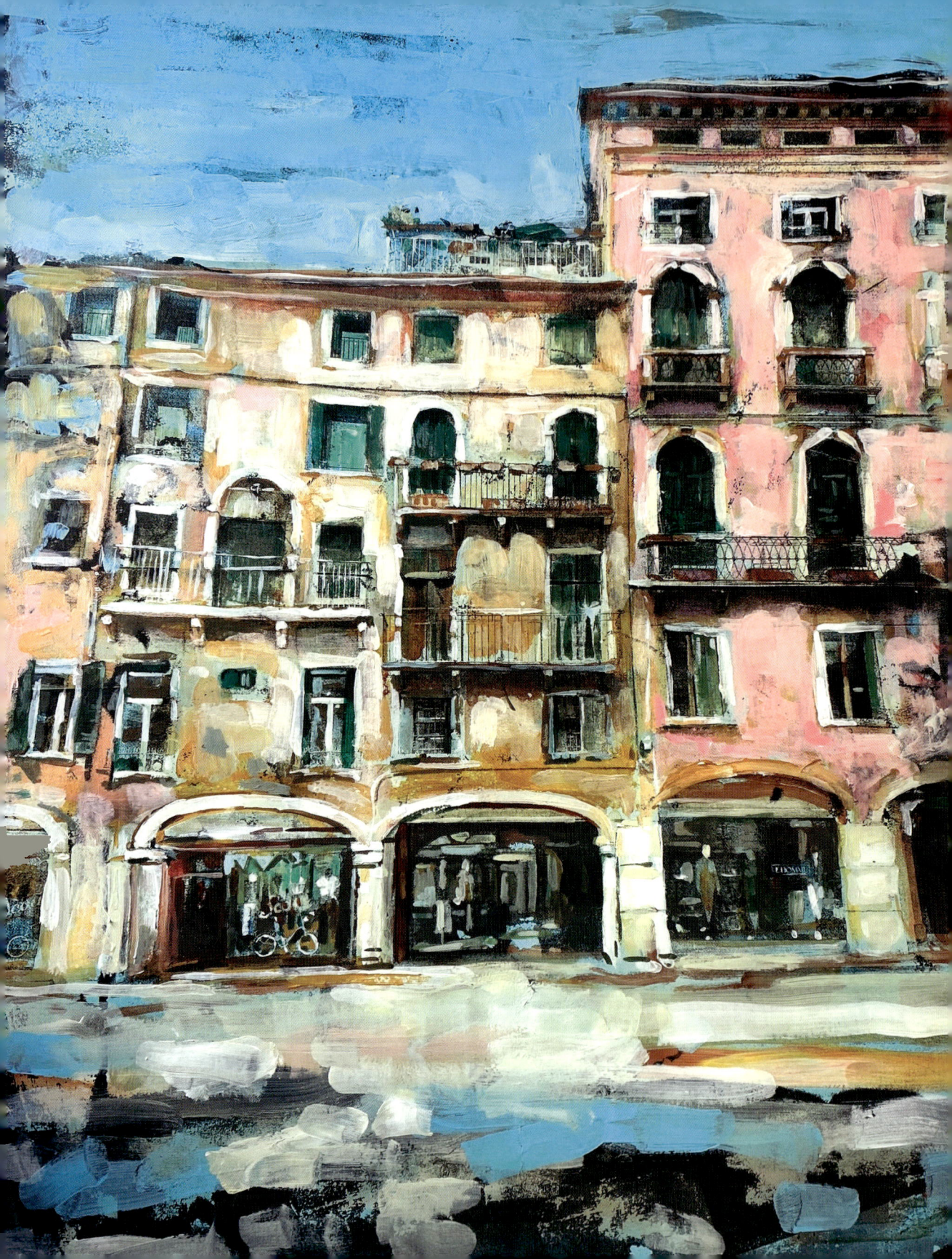

TABLE OF CONTENTS

1. INTRODUCTION   1

2. TOOLS & TERMS OF THE TRADE   9

3. WHAT IS IT & HOW IT WORKS   21

4. MAKING COLORS WORK FOR YOU   27

5. LAYER UPON TEXTURED LAYER   33

6. THE PERFECT TRANSFER   43

7. GETTING YOUR PHOTOS PRINT READY   53

8. REVERSE PAINTING   65

9. THE JOY OF ADDITIVE PAINTING   77

10. MAGAZINE TRANSFERS   85

11. BEYOND BLACK IMAGE TRANSFERS   91

12. LAYERED TRANSFERS   101

13. IMPOSSIBLE POSSIBLE WITH DIGITAL COLLAGE   111

14. CHARCOAL TRANSFERS   119

15. PRINTMAKING THAT FEELS LIKE PAINTING   127

16. COLLAGE AS REVERSE PAINTING   139

17. MASTERING MISHAPS   149

18. CREATIVE WAYS TO USE YOUR GEL PRINTS   157

ART TEACHER'S GUIDE   168

ACKNOWLEDGMENTS   170

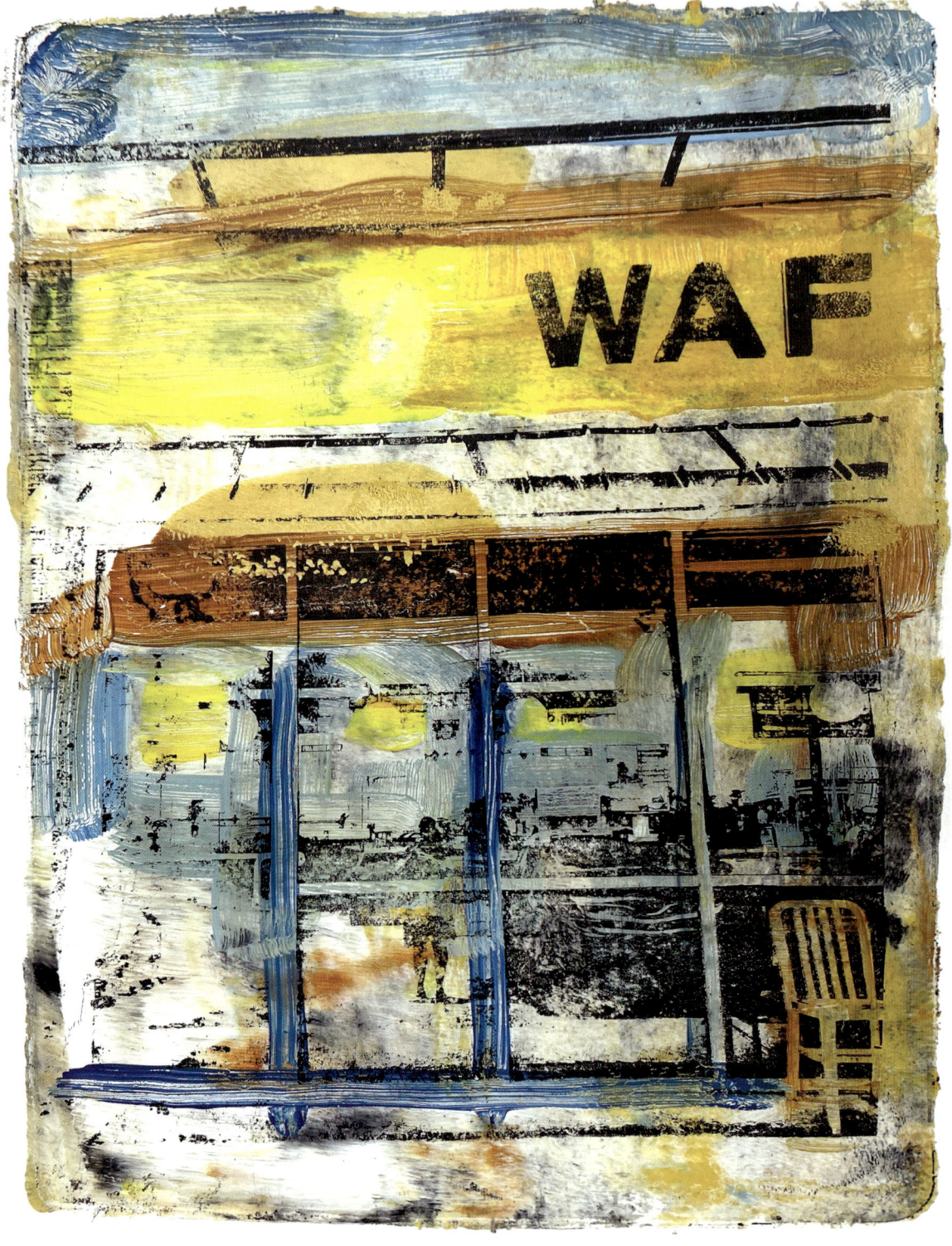

I
INTRODUCTION

If you're anything like me, your first go at gel printing may not have gone quite as planned. I started using my gel plate with curiosity and the misguided confidence that I could figure it out quickly. Instead, I ended up with a pile of prints that ranged from "meh" to "what happened here?" Over time, I developed techniques that made the process more predictable while still leaving room for happy accidents. That balance between control and spontaneity is what I hope to guide you through in this book.

Gel plate printing has firmly secured its place in both my artistic practice and my teaching because, really, the possibilities never stop unfolding. Although this book won't cover every technique out there, it will focus deeply on the approaches I use most often in my practice and the classroom. By narrowing the scope, I can guide you step by step through the methods that I've found most effective, helping you build skills, refine your process, and develop a creative style that's uniquely yours.

MY JOURNEY WITH GEL PRINTING

My background in printmaking goes back years. I studied it in both my undergrad and graduate programs and have taught various types of printmaking since 2000. Printmaking wasn't new to me. So, when I first picked up a gel plate, I thought, "Oh, this will be easy enough. I'll mess around with it a bit and then teach it to my students." Yeah, no. I couldn't have been more wrong.

Unlike traditional printmaking, for which I had a structured process and an understanding of materials, the gel plate had a mind of its own. It didn't follow the rules I knew. There was no wetting the

paper, no need for high-quality printmaking paper, no press. It defied what I thought I understood about printmaking, and honestly, my lack of initial understanding of it bruised my ego a little.

I saw the potential, but I was feeling stuck. It was at that point I turned to social media. I started posting videos about my struggles, venting my frustrations into the digital world. To my surprise, these videos resonated with people. I wasn't alone. Others were having the same issues. Some generous creators shared their experience, and with a few minor adjustments, everything started to click.

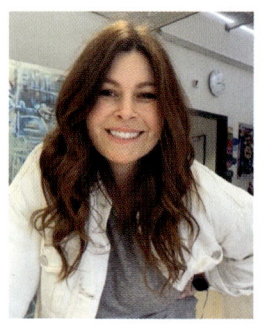

I finally pulled off a successful gel print. It was from a laser print of a truck stop restaurant in Florida. It wasn't flawless, but after all that trial and error, it felt like a win to me, so I shared how I got it to work on my social media. Those early videos of my struggles and minor successes went viral. I began to tackle the process better, then my follow-up videos gained even more traction. People were curious about how gel plate printing worked, and their curiosity fueled my drive to keep experimenting. Looking back, I think part of the appeal was that I wasn't just trying to recreate the original photo perfectly. Instead, I let go of perfectionism and embraced a more painterly, expressive approach. I didn't want my prints to feel like an advanced paint-by-number. I wanted them to be transformed into something beyond a simple reproduction.

Gel plate printing turned out to be more than just a crafty project to teach my printmaking students. It became a tool I could integrate into my own artwork. My style is all about layering, so gel plate printing felt like a natural extension of my work in other mediums, especially oil painting and collage.

Conceptually, my art is driven by cultural narratives, a sense of place, and the emotions tied to memory and history. Those themes along with the interplay of color, texture, and juxtaposition became the thread connecting my gel prints to the rest of my work. To show how my style has evolved, I've included examples of my own prints, from my early experiments to the more complex, layered pieces I create today. What started as creative exploration turned into an unexpected way to bring together my love of photography, painting, and printmaking.

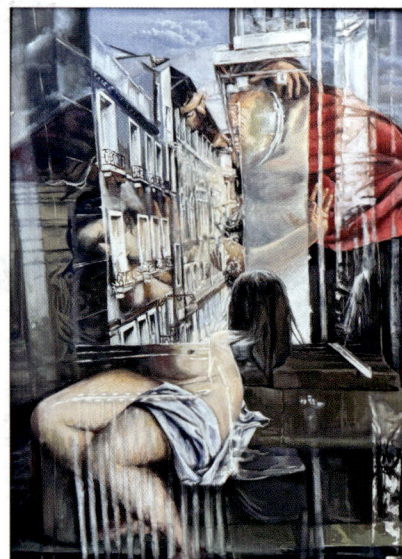

Jessica Russo Scherr, *Siena and her Elders*, 50 × 70 cm, oil on Masonite.

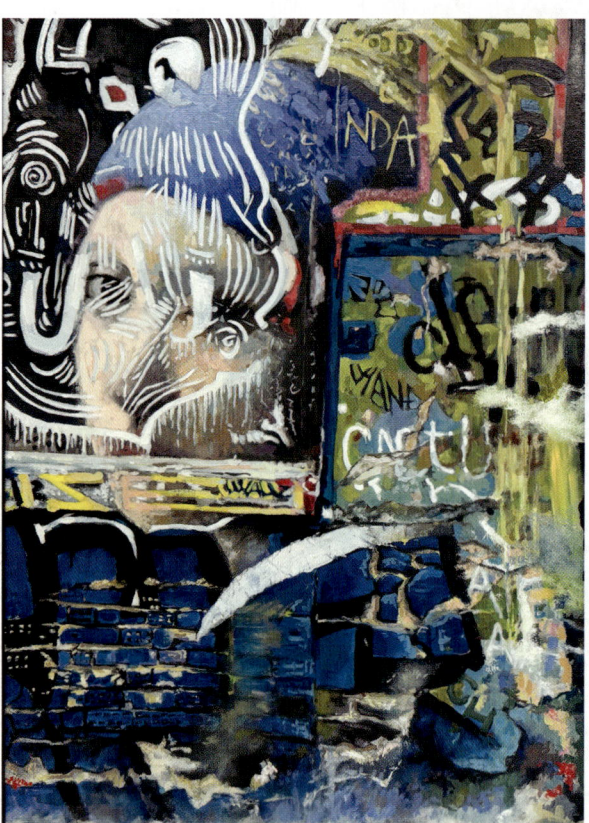

Jessica Russo Scherr, *Girl with Graffiti*, 50 × 70 cm, oil on canvas.

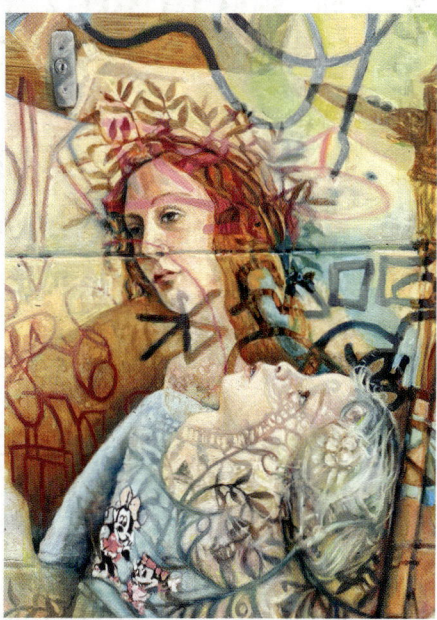

Left: Jessica Russo Scherr, *Pallas, Camilla, Florencia, Maia*, 50 × 70 cm, oil on canvas.

Below: Jessica Russo Scherr, *Tree of Life*, 145 × 135 cm, collage.

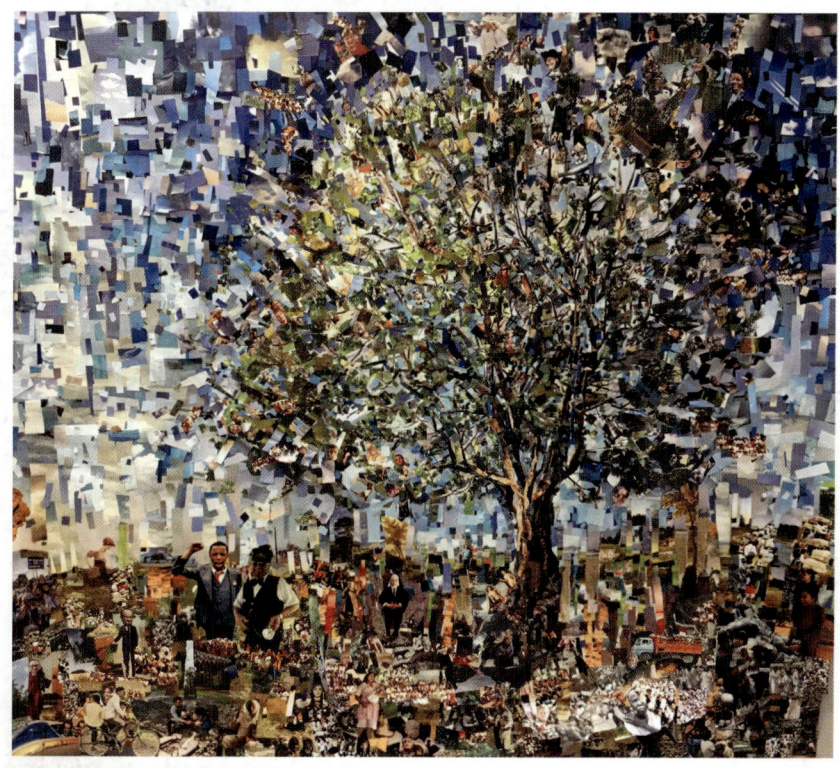

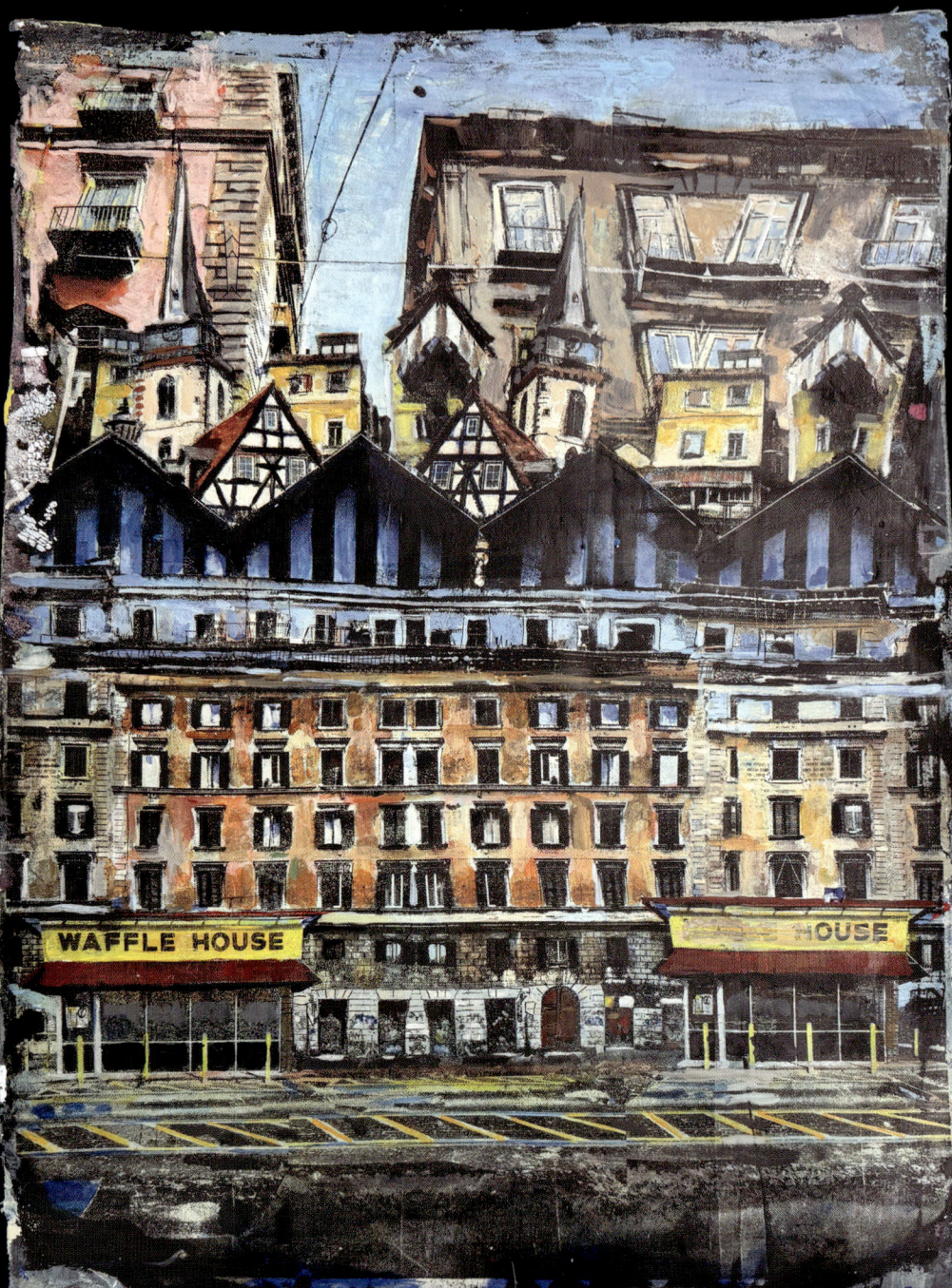

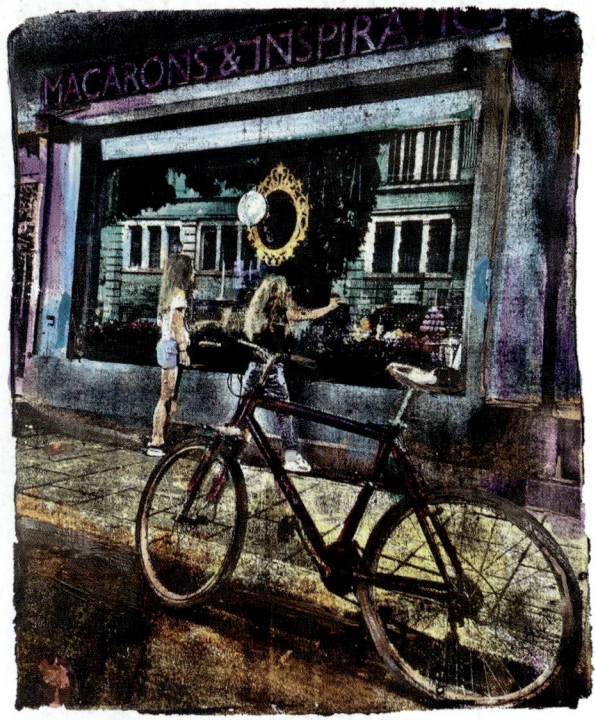

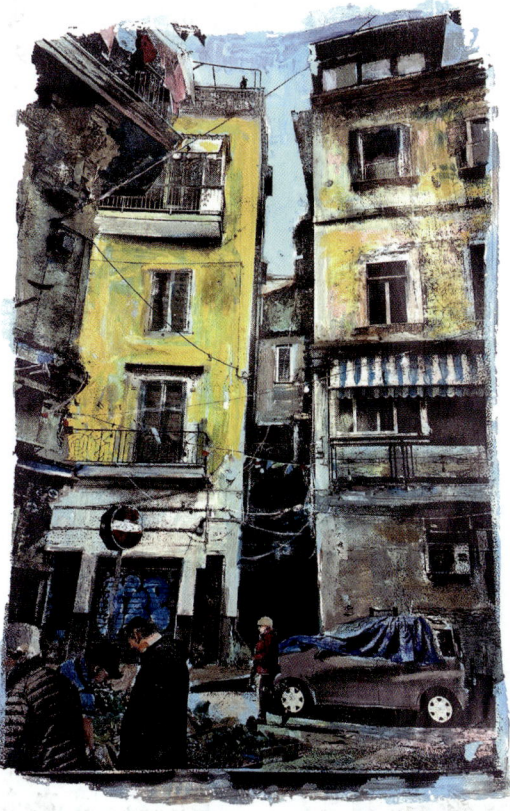

Above: *Macarons & Inspiration*, one of my early gel prints created from a photo of my children in Strasbourg, France.

Opposite: *Layers of Home,* created on my 18 x 24-inch gel plate, which allowed me to layer and connect visual narratives from the United States, Germany, and Italy into a single composition.

Life in Layers, created after time spent in the historic center of Naples, Italy. Getting a 16 x 20-inch gel plate expanded what was possible in both scale and depth. You can see how the clarity of my transfers improved.

WHY THIS BOOK?

In this book, I share the techniques I've refined over countless hours in my studio, breaking down what might seem like complex processes into approachable steps. I want to share the techniques that have helped me, not just so you can replicate them, but so you can develop your own approach—whether you're a seasoned printmaker or just beginning to explore artistic expression.

I believe in the power of experimentation and the joy that comes from those "aha!" moments in the studio. That's why I'm thrilled to be writing this book, not just as a step-by-step guide, but as a way to help you truly understand the process. By clearing up common misconceptions and breaking down techniques into approachable steps, I hope you'll experience the same breakthroughs I did. This book is an invitation to join me in exploring the endless possibilities of gel plate printmaking, where photography, paint, and print come together in unexpected and beautiful ways.

I hope this book empowers you to find your creative voice with the gel plate. And if you want to see more of my work, you can find me at **www.bluelavaart.com** or on social media **@bluelavaart**. Happy printing!

ABOUT THE AUTHOR

Making art is among some of my earliest memories. I can't recall a time when art wasn't central to my identity, so it didn't come as a surprise to anyone that I attended art school. I received my Bachelor of Fine Arts from Hartford Art School, University of Hartford, and went on to do several post-grad art programs, including Montclair State University, William Paterson University, and Boston University, where I refined my skills in both art making and art education.

For me, being a professional artist has always gone hand in hand with teaching art. While building my own artistic practice and exhibiting my work, I also began my teaching career in the New Jersey Public Schools, most notably at West Morris

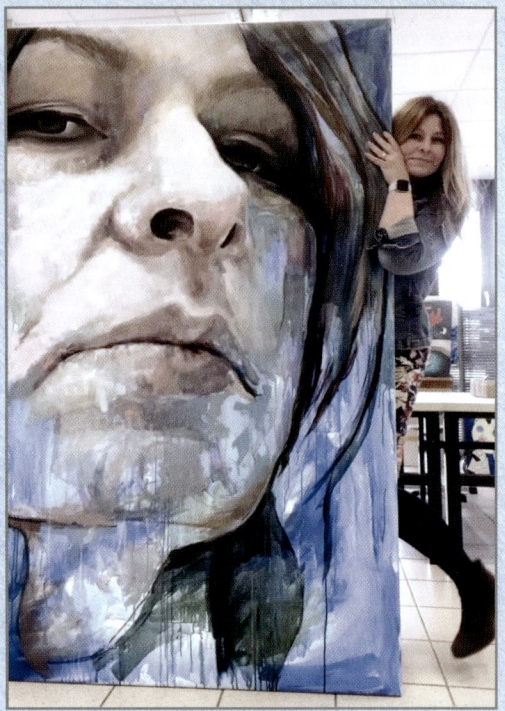

Jessica Russo Scherr, artist and art teacher

Mendham High School. The skilled, creative, and genuinely amazing art teachers I worked alongside, as well as the students I taught, many of whom I still keep in touch with after over 20 years, helped shape the foundation of my art education philosophy. Additionally, this experience introduced me to the International Baccalaureate program (IB) The IB is a well-known worldwide education program that focuses on critical thinking, cultural awareness, and well-rounded learning through a challenging, inquiry-driven curriculum. I often reflect on how fortunate I was to be at that school during that time. However, deep down, I knew that I needed more.

That was when I received a Fulbright Scholarship, which took me out of the American public school system and into a new world. My Danish boyfriend, Andrew (now my husband), and I packed up and moved to the Slovak Republic to start the next chapter of our lives. I taught at Škola umeleckého priemyslu Josefa Vydru (School of Applied Arts) in Bratislava. It was the most deeply impactful experience of my life, personally and professionally. There I learned to teach outside my comfort zone and confronted my own limited perspective on life and education. I also fell in love with the ease of travel that living in Central Europe granted us. Taking evening bike rides across the Danube into Austria to picnic in the evening shadow of castle ruins overlooking vineyards, wheat fields, and wind turbines with Andrew became a common way of life, and I couldn't imagine giving it up.

That yearlong adventure led us to Florence, Italy, teaching art in my first international school. Teaching diverse students from around the world was undoubtedly my calling. Living in such a beautiful and historically significant place influenced who I am at my core. Andrew and I were married in Palazzo Vecchio in Cosimo de Medici's bedroom (where all town hall weddings are held). Soon after, we welcomed our two children, Siena and Maia. We lived idyllically for a number of years in Florence, building friendships and experiences that influence us to this day. Although the art and the architecture drew us there, the food, wine, and gelato kept us.

Even so, I jumped at the chance to teach at a prominent and leading international school in Germany. Although we would miss Italy, I would be teaching in an art studio with seven faucets, an increase of six faucets! Who could pass up such an upgrade? At Frankfurt International School, I continue to teach the International Baccalaureate program alongside my incredible colleagues and nurture students to build their creative thinking skills and art-making techniques from middle school through high school.

My travels with family and friends continue to shape and inspire my work. Whether it's staying in a dodgy apartment in Reims, France, with my best friend Sarah and her family; visiting loved ones back in the U.S.; returning to Italy, a country deeply tied to my heritage and personal history; or exploring new places both near and far, I'm constantly reminded of the privilege I've had to live, work, and travel across different cultures. These experiences, combined with my identity as a woman, wife, mother, and immigrant, are woven into every piece of art I create.

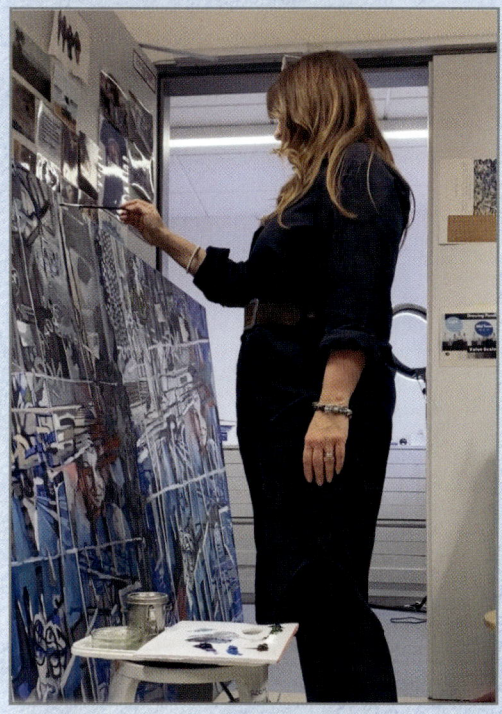

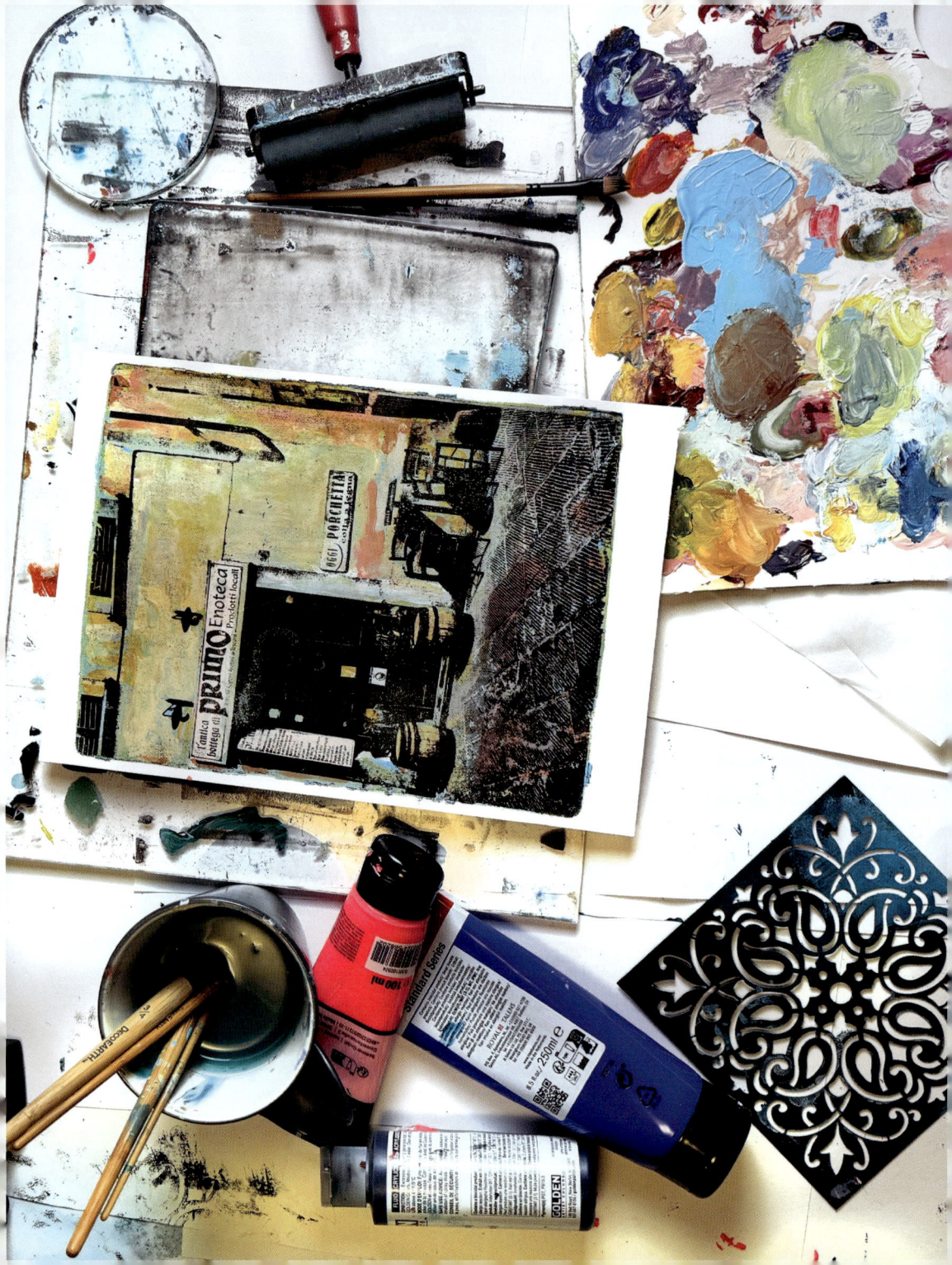

2
TOOLS & TERMS OF THE TRADE

Feeling overwhelmed by all the "essential" supplies for gel printing? Stepping into the world of gel printing can feel like walking into an art supply store where everything seems essential. Social media doesn't help. There's always someone showing off their latest "must-have" tool or "game-changing" material. You're not alone! I've been there. After a lot of experimentation, I've discovered that success in gel printing isn't about having every tool available. It's about thoroughly understanding how to use a few key tools well.

JUST THE BASICS

In this chapter, I'll walk you through the essentials: the tools that actually matter, the nice-to-haves, and the ones you can skip entirely. Although there's no single "right" way to gel print, a few key choices, such as the right paper or a reliable gel plate, can make all the difference. That said, I'm not here to hand out rigid rules. Experimentation is part of the fun, and what works for me might not be the magic solution for you.

I'll share my tried-and-true favorites (and why I swear by them), but the most important takeaway is finding the tools that fit your style. So let's dive in, and, hopefully, I can help you avoid some of the mistakes I learned the hard way.

IMAGES TO TRANSFER

Choosing and editing your images is an essential part of getting your supplies ready. Whether you're working with laser prints or magazine pages, image selection plays a critical role in the success of your print. There's so much to consider that it warrants a deeper discussion in Chapter 7, "Getting Your Photos Print-Ready" and Chapter 10, "Magazine Transfers."

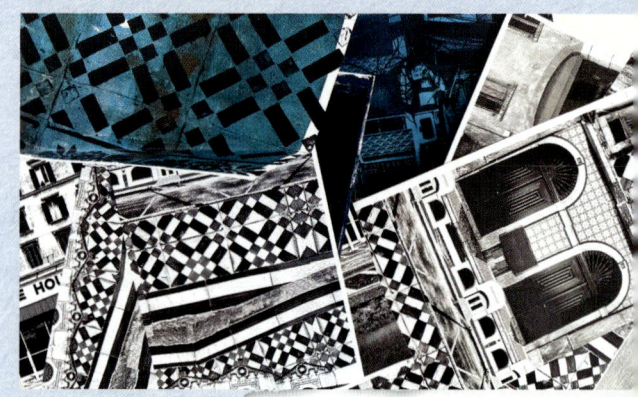

CHOOSING A GEL PLATE

Leading off my list of must-have supplies is a gel plate. I exclusively use gel plates from Gelli Arts®, including round plates, 8 × 10, 9 × 12, and larger sizes like 16 × 20 and 18 × 24. Why Gelli Arts®? Let me tell you a quick story. My first gel prints were on another brand's plate, and the experience was challenging. I struggled so much that one plate actually tore when I tried to peel off a dried print. It was beyond frustrating. After some advice from seasoned gel printers, I switched to Gelli Arts®, and from my first pull, I've been a loyal fan. That said, many artists make their own gel plates, which can be a great budget-friendly option. If you're up for the process, homemade plates work well and give you control over size and texture. Others have found that silicone baking mats can give you a similar type of experience. If you want durability, consistency, and a plate that lasts, however, Gelli Arts® is my go-to choice.

How many plates do you need? Multiple gel plates are nice to have. Gel printing takes time, and often, you are literally watching paint dry. If your budget allows it, get a few plates so you can use your art-making time more efficiently.

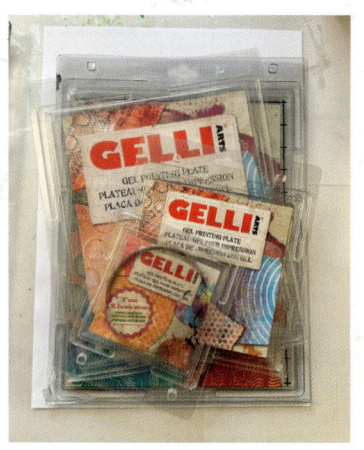

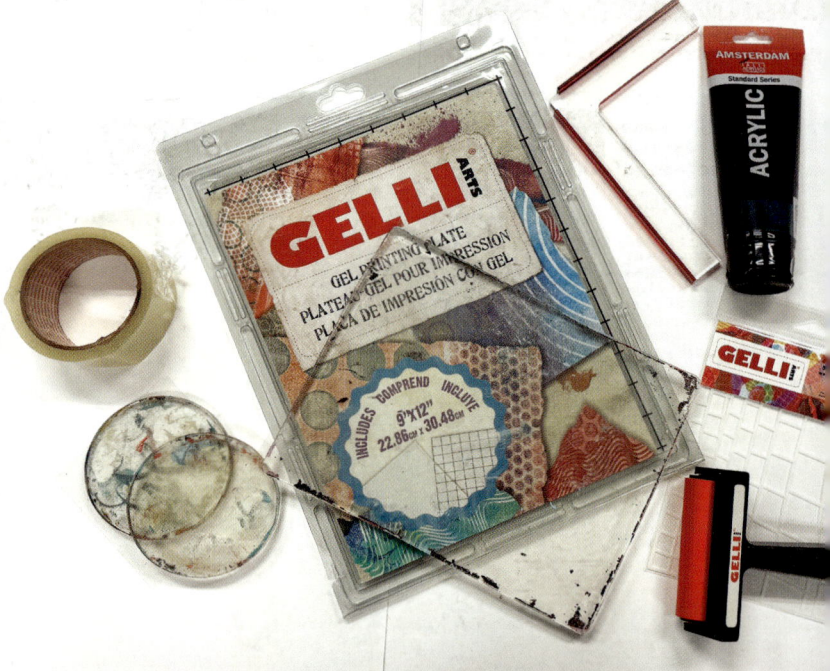

CARING FOR YOUR GEL PLATE

My biggest hurdle in caring for my gel plate is keeping my hair from getting stuck on it. Perhaps I should consider wearing a hairnet. Beyond the hair issue, gel plates are surprisingly durable but need proper care to maintain their performance.

When you first unbox your plate, it might be coated in a layer of mineral oil. This can cause paint to pool, but it's an easy fix. Start by gently washing your plate with soapy water and repeatedly using it to "season" the surface, like breaking in a cast-iron skillet. This simple prep ensures the plate is primed for even paint application.

With regular use, your plate may start to look cloudy or matte. This is completely normal and does not affect your prints. If you notice that the paint isn't lifting properly, however, a little conditioning can help. Massage a small amount of mineral oil into the surface. Think of it like moisturizing your skin. It prevents drying and extends the life of your plate.

Between prints your gel plate may need cleaning. I prefer baby wipes for quick touch-ups. If dried paint builds up, rolling a fresh layer of paint over it, laying paper on top of it, letting it dry, and lifting it off often removes the residue. Hand sanitizer also works well, breaking down stubborn layers without damaging the plate. If the paint still refuses to budge, painter's tape or packing tape can pull up any remaining bits.

STORING YOUR GEL PLATE

Storage is just as important as cleaning. Always keep your plate on a smooth, flat surface, such as acetate sheets or plexiglass. Any debris (hair), air bubbles, or dried paint trapped underneath will imprint onto the plate's surface, affecting your prints. Gelli Arts® recommends storing plates with paper on each side, which helps prevent unwanted textures from forming. Also, heat can warp a plate, so keep it away from direct sunlight or hot surfaces. If you use a hair dryer to speed up the drying process, use it on the cool air setting only.

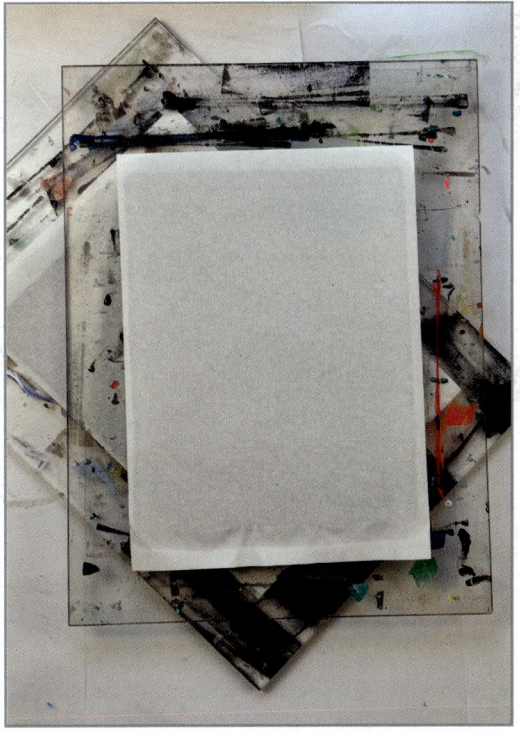

PAPER

A good substrate helps ensure smooth pulls and prevents tears both in your artwork and your patience! Your choice of paper will depend on the number of layers and techniques you're using. Experimenting with various types of paper will help you understand which works best for your specific projects. Factors like paint thickness, humidity, and drying time all play a role in choosing the perfect paper to print on. Test different papers to find what works best for your specific process. Remember, the right substrate is as important as the tools you use. It sets the foundation for every print.

PAPER FOR THIN LAYERS

Lightweight papers are your best friend if you're working with quick, single layers of wet paint or using your gel plate like a stamp. For example, 80-gsm printer paper or similar will do the trick. Tissue paper, wet-strength tissue, or even teabag paper are delicate but work beautifully. They're perfect for collage work, adding lovely translucent effects to your projects. Remember to keep a light touch when pulling these prints. Your gel plate is stronger than it looks.

PAPER FOR THICKER LAYERS

When your gel plate is loaded up with multiple layers, or you're experimenting with reverse painting techniques, durability is key. I generally use 200-gsm to 250-gsm papers. When in doubt, I reach for 200-gsm Bristol board. It's the Goldilocks of gel printing substrates: not too heavy, not too light, and just the right amount of smooth. Bristol board is a stiff, uncoated, machine-finished smooth paper often used for illustration and design. Its sturdy surface can handle the tug of pulling prints off a gel plate without ripping, even with thicker paint layers.

Surprisingly, printmaking papers, which are typically soft and absorbent, are not ideal for gel prints. When I first started printing, I thought that dampened beautiful, deckle-edged printmaking paper would work perfectly, as it did for other printmaking techniques. Instead, I found it stuck tightly to the gel plate and often tore when I tried to lift the print.

WHY IS IT CALLED BRISTOL BOARD?

You might think Bristol board has British origins, and you'd be right. However, it did not get its name fully from the city of Bristol where the paper was first milled. It's actually named after Frederick Hervey, the Fourth Earl of Bristol, a prolific art collector. That is also why the b in Bristol is usually capitalized. Who knew a paper could have such a fancy backstory? You can learn more about it at CAMEO: Conservation & Art Material Encyclopedia Online.

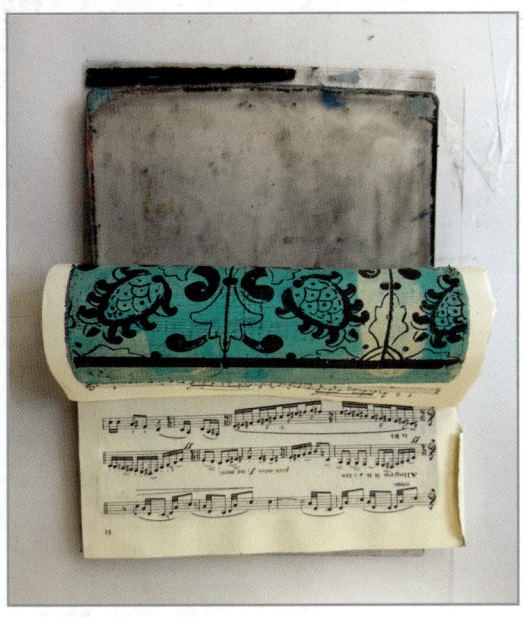

Similarly, avoid overly textured or soft papers like cold-pressed watercolor paper. Glossy and photographic papers should never be used on your plate as they tend to stick to the gel plate and can even damage it.

Looking for a more sustainable and budget-friendly approach to printing? Try printing on music paper, junk mail, recycled books, out-of-print textbooks, and other papers that have the same smoothness and strength as Bristol paper but without the added expense. My classroom is filled with out-of-print textbooks that find a second life in collages, as scrap paper, and as the foundation for many prints.

PAINT AND MEDIUM

Finding the right paint for gel plate printing takes some trial and error. If the paint is too thick, it won't spread evenly, creating unwanted textures and making it harder to lift off the plate. If it's too thin, it can bead up or pool, leading to uneven coverage.

For image transfers, my go-to is Amsterdam Standard Series. It's affordable, versatile, and has just the right consistency for a range of techniques. When layering or working with reverse painting, I turn to Liquitex Basics and Golden Fluid Acrylics for their smooth texture and strong pigmentation. These paints spread evenly over the plate, making it easier to achieve vibrant, consistent results.

While craft paints might seem like a budget-friendly option, they often lack the rich pigments and reliable viscosity needed for multilayered prints or detailed transfers. That said, they're great for quick, single-layer pulls and experimenting with new techniques.

If you're on a budget, it's better to invest in a few high-quality mid-range paints rather than filling your cart with the cheapest options. You'll see the difference in your prints.

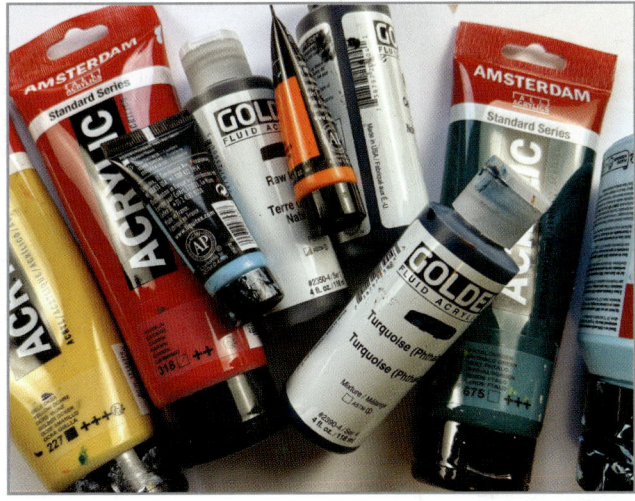

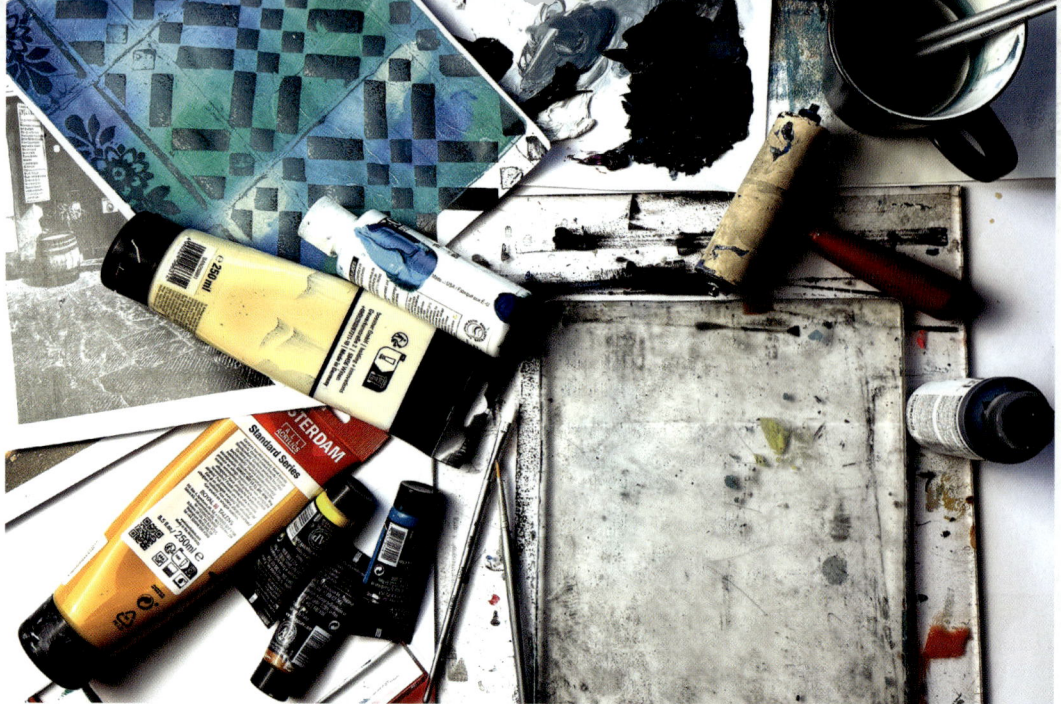

You also don't need to buy every color under the sun when you're first starting out. Instead, build a flexible palette with a few essential colors that mix well together. A great starter set includes:

- **Black Oxide:** Essential for image transfers
- **Titanium White:** A must for tints and highlights
- **Cadmium Red and Alizarin Crimson:** Warm and cool reds for mixing
- **Cadmium Yellow and Yellow Ochre:** Bright and earthy yellows
- **Phthalo Blue and Ultramarine Blue:** A cool and warm blue for versatility
- **Payne's Gray:** A deep, moody alternative to black
- **Burnt Sienna and Burnt Umber:** Rich earth tones for neutralizing colors

If your budget allows, add a few extra colors that spark your creativity, like Buff Titanium, which is a softer, natural off-white, and powerful pigments like Viridian Green and Quinacridone Magenta, which expand mixing possibilities. But with just these basics, you can mix a huge range of shades without breaking the bank.

There is a long list of other nice-to-have paints. You can experiment with other types of paints and inks, including water-soluble printmaking inks, alcohol inks, spray paints, powdered pigments, and fabric paints. Washable and permanent markers also work, though they behave differently. Permanent markers dry quickly, so you need to work fast. In contrast, washable markers stay wet longer, giving you more time to manipulate the pigment on the plate, although it may pool. Be aware that the gel plate absorbs dyes and ink. Although this can cause permanent staining, the stains won't affect the plate's performance.

One of my must-have supplies is gel medium. Although you can create beautiful prints without it, *gel medium* expands the possibilities by preventing paint from pooling, enhancing transparency, and making layering more dynamic. I prefer satin gel medium; it strikes a balance between glossy, which can be too shiny, and matte, which sometimes creates a slightly hazy finish. Applying a thin layer with a brayer (see below) can also improve paint adhesion, especially when working with thinner layers.

Another helpful addition is a *paint retarder* or *extender*, which slows the drying time of acrylics on the gel plate. I typically don't use it for image transfers, because I want my layers to dry quickly, but it can be useful when working directly on the plate and manipulating the paint. If you enjoy building up layers or smoothly blending colors, this might be a nice addition to your toolkit; otherwise, skip it.

A BRAYER, NOT A "ROLLY THING"

A good *brayer*, a hand roller for applying paint, is essential for achieving an even, thin layer of paint to your gel plate. I prefer softer brayers because they allow for smooth blending and better control over the paint. I also prefer using correct terminology. As I tell my sixth through twelfth graders, it's not a "rolly thing," it's a brayer.

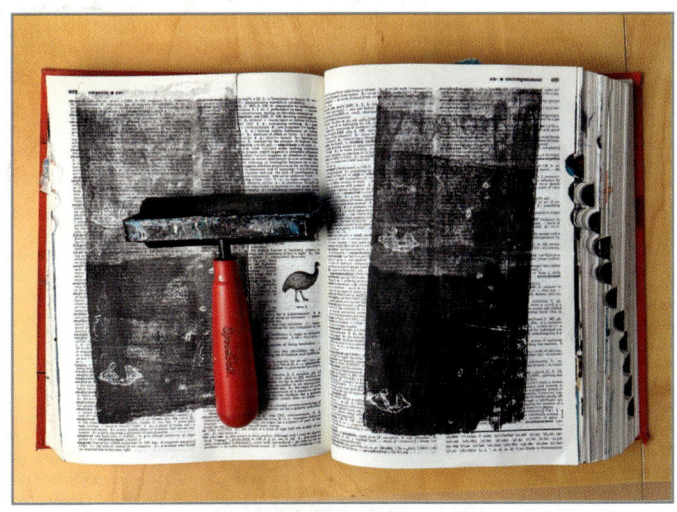

One of the biggest challenges with brayers (besides breaking the "rolly thing" habit), however, is keeping them clean. Acrylic paint has a way of clinging to the surface, making it difficult to scrub off once dried. The best way to prevent buildup is to roll off excess paint immediately onto scrap paper. Over time, these roll-off sheets take on a life of their own, often becoming beautiful backgrounds or collage elements. I keep an old dictionary nearby to roll off extra paint. It's my go-to scrap paper. It's a great way to repurpose, keeps my workspace a bit tidier, *and* the painted pages make amazing collage material. Total junk journaling gold.

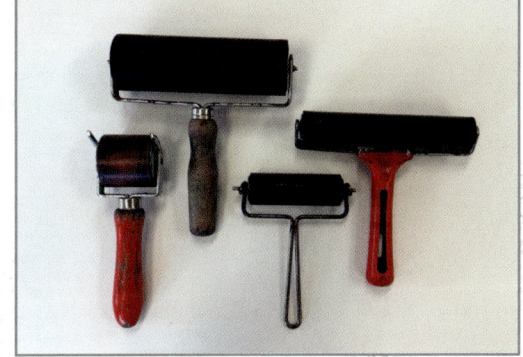

If paint starts to build up on your brayer, an orange-based cleaner diluted in warm water can help break it down. Letting your brayers soak for a bit will also make the task more manageable, saving you from an unnecessary arm workout.

BRUSHES

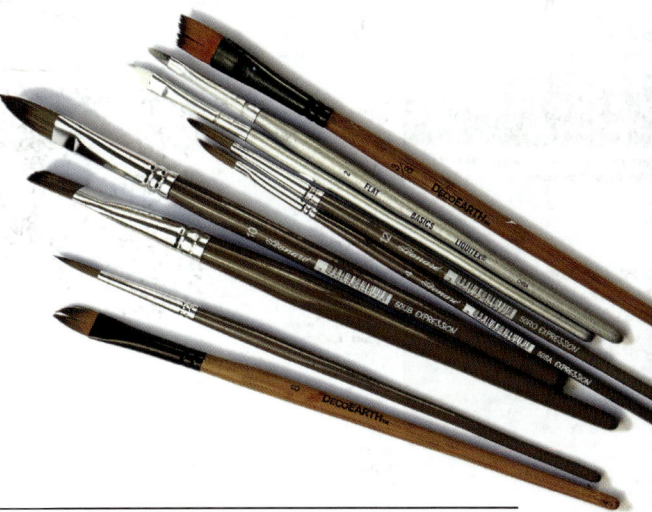

Of course, if you are doing more elaborate prints with some reverse painting, you will need a few brushes. They don't need to be fancy, but do choose brushes that are sturdy enough to avoid losing bristles on your gel plate. I prefer synthetic smooth brushes and usually have a few rounds, flats, a chisel, and a filbert.

NICE TO HAVES AND ALTERNATIVES

A few extra supplies can definitely make your art making easier and more fun. One of my favorite "nice-to-haves" is a *baren*, a hand tool that helps you apply even pressure when transferring an image from the gel plate to paper. It's originally from Japanese printmaking and is traditionally made from bamboo and wood with a felt base. Don't worry if you don't have one; a wooden spoon or even just your hands work perfectly fine. Just make sure to press the paper evenly onto the plate.

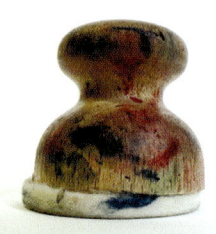

I suffer from the affliction where I cannot align my paper evenly on my plate. If this sounds like you, then *alignment tools* are worth considering. These help you line up your paper and gel plate perfectly, which is super handy when you're working with multiple layers. This technique, called *registration*, keeps your prints centered and the layers stacked just right. It's like making a blueprint for your artwork and takes the guesswork out of the process. You can buy *corner angles* that make aligning your prints even easier.

There are other handy tools to play with too, like *palette knives* for mixing paint and store-bought *stencils* for quick patterns. But honestly, you don't have to spend much to get creative. Everyday household items, like bubble wrap, cardboard, combs, and even hot glue on cardboard tubes can make great textures. Plus, it's a fantastic way to give new life to things that would normally end up in the trash.

At the end of the day, you don't need all the bells and whistles, but having a few of these tools can definitely expand your creative possibilities and make gel printing even more enjoyable.

WHAT TO BUY?

The best way to determine which supplies you truly need is to experiment with the basics or what you already have. Test different paints, papers, and tools to see how they interact, noticing how each layer builds upon the last. Pay close attention to textures, transparency, and color blending. As you create, you'll naturally discover gaps in your toolkit. When you find yourself needing something specific to achieve a certain effect, that's when it belongs on your shopping list.

Most importantly, embrace the process. Some of my best prints have come from happy accidents of unexpected textures, surprising color shifts, and repurposing prints I initially thought were failures. The beauty of gel printing lies in its unpredictability, so give yourself the freedom to play. Your next great print might be just one experiment away.

BUILDING YOUR GEL PLATE VOCABULARY

Before we go deeper into gel plate printmaking, let's get on the same page with some key terminology. Understanding these words is essential, not just because I'll be tossing them around throughout this book, but also because they'll help you better grasp the process. You've already learned about brayers and registration, let's build on that. Knowing the lingo makes you sound way more professional when you casually drop words like *gel medium* or *hickey* into a conversation. (Yes, we'll get to that one.)

WHY CALL IT A GEL PLATE?

Why do we call it a gel plate when it's clearly not a plate? Some people insist on calling it a "gel pad," but in printmaking, a *plate* is simply the surface used to create an image. A plate is the matrix that holds the design in various printmaking processes. It can be made of metal, wood, linoleum, rubber, glass, paper, stone, or even a stretched textile screen. Whether you're etching on metal, carving into linoleum, or spreading paint on a squishy gel slab, they're all plates in the printmaking world. So, yes, I'm sticking with *gel plate*, and now you know why.

MY CUSTOM TERMINOLOGY

Some of the terms I use are a mix of traditional printmaking jargon, adaptions of printmaking terminology to fit gel plate printing, and phrases I've coined along the way. Whether or not they're "official" terms doesn't matter. I'm making them official for this book.

Hickey might be my favorite printmaking term, mainly because it's hilarious to explain to middle school students. In printmaking, a hickey is an unwanted spot surrounded by a white ring, usually caused by debris or a chunk of dried paint on the plate. It doesn't transfer the paint, leaving a blemish on your print. Just like in real life, a hickey is usually unwanted... unless you're going for that kind of vibe.

Here are a few that I'll be using throughout:

- **Pull:** Lifting the paper off the gel plate. In printmaking, *hand-pulled* simply means each print is produced one at a time, by hand, without any mechanized processes.
- **Transfer layer:** Applying a laser-printed image onto the gel plate to transfer it
- **Wet pull:** Lifting wet paint off the gel plate with paper, using the plate like a stamp.

Transfer layer

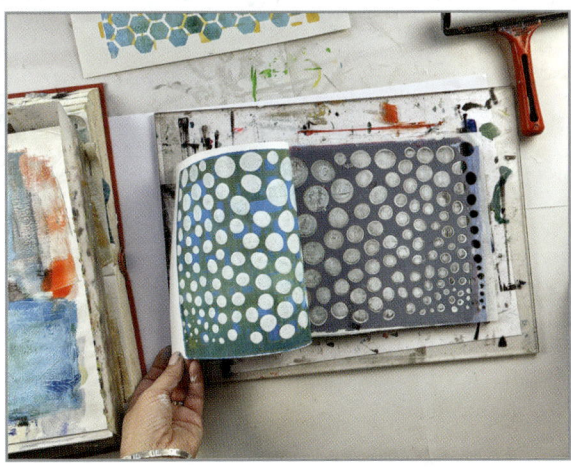

Wet pull

- **Dry lift:** Removing dry layers of paint using a pickup layer.
- **Pickup layer:** The final, full layer of acrylic paint that adheres to all the dried layers underneath. You lay a piece of paper on top of the full layer of acrylic, let everything dry, and then, thanks to the pickup layer, the paint releases from the plate and sticks to your paper.
- **Plate tone:** The texture that occurs when the paint does not fully lift off of the gel plate and attach to the paper. It is that little bit of texture that adds to the beauty of gel prints. The term comes from intaglio printmaking; there it describes areas where the plate hasn't been fully wiped and the ink leaves a bit of a tone on the final print.

- **Reverse painting:** Quite literally painting on the reverse side of your image. When you do an image transfer, it becomes the top layer of your final print. This means all the other layers will appear underneath on your final print, which means you need to paint them in reverse order, which is definitely different from traditional acrylic painting.
- **Additive painting:** Applying paint on top of a pulled print. You may do this to fix any imperfections, add more detail, adjust colors, or simply embellish your final print.

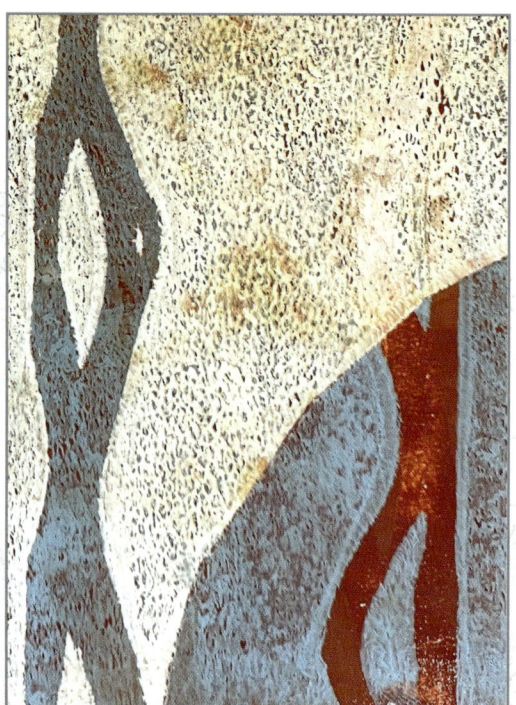

Plate tone

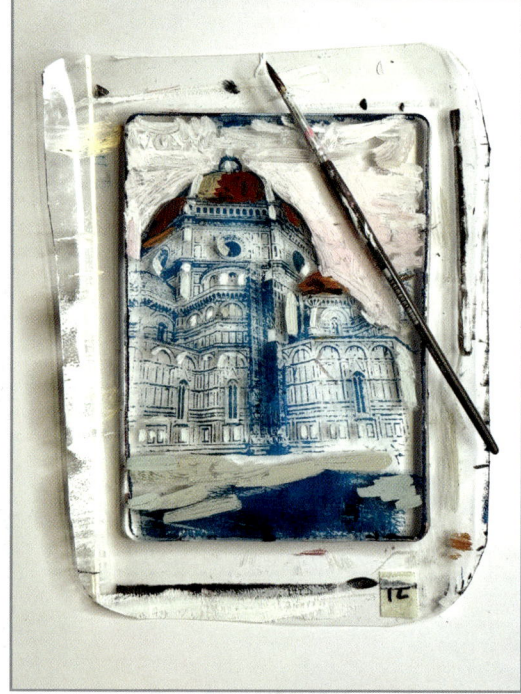

Reverse painting

MAKING YOUR PRINT OFFICIAL

An original print is a unique fine artwork generally produced in a limited number of impressions, collectively known as an *edition*. Each hand-pulled print is usually given an edition number, typically written as a fraction. For example, 12/50 means the print is number 12 out of a total of 50.

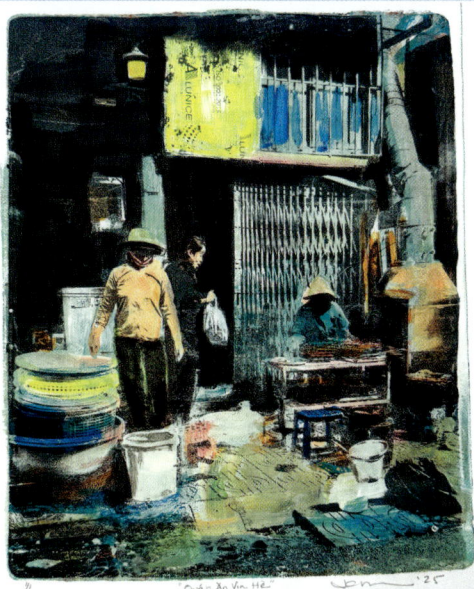

An artist may also produce a limited number of artist's proofs, often marked A/P, like A/P 1/10. These are identical to the standard edition but reserved for the artist's personal collection or special uses.

Because you are most likely creating individual monotypes, you can mark them 1/1 (one of one) or A/P (artist's proof). Using a pencil, sign them on the right-hand side with the year underneath your print, and place the edition number on the left.

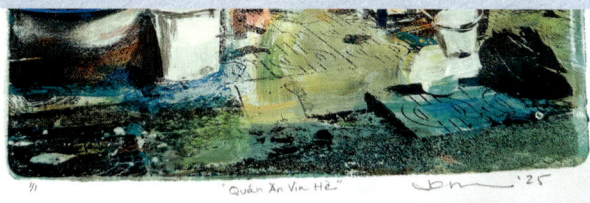

WHY VOCABULARY MATTERS

Getting familiar with these terms won't just help you follow along more quickly, it'll also give you the confidence to experiment and troubleshoot like a pro. Plus, you'll sound impressive when you casually drop "Looks like the brayer gave my print a little hickey during the pickup layer!" Trust me, it's a great conversation starter.

Now that we're speaking the same language, let's get back to the fun part: creating prints that make people wonder, "How on earth did you do that?"

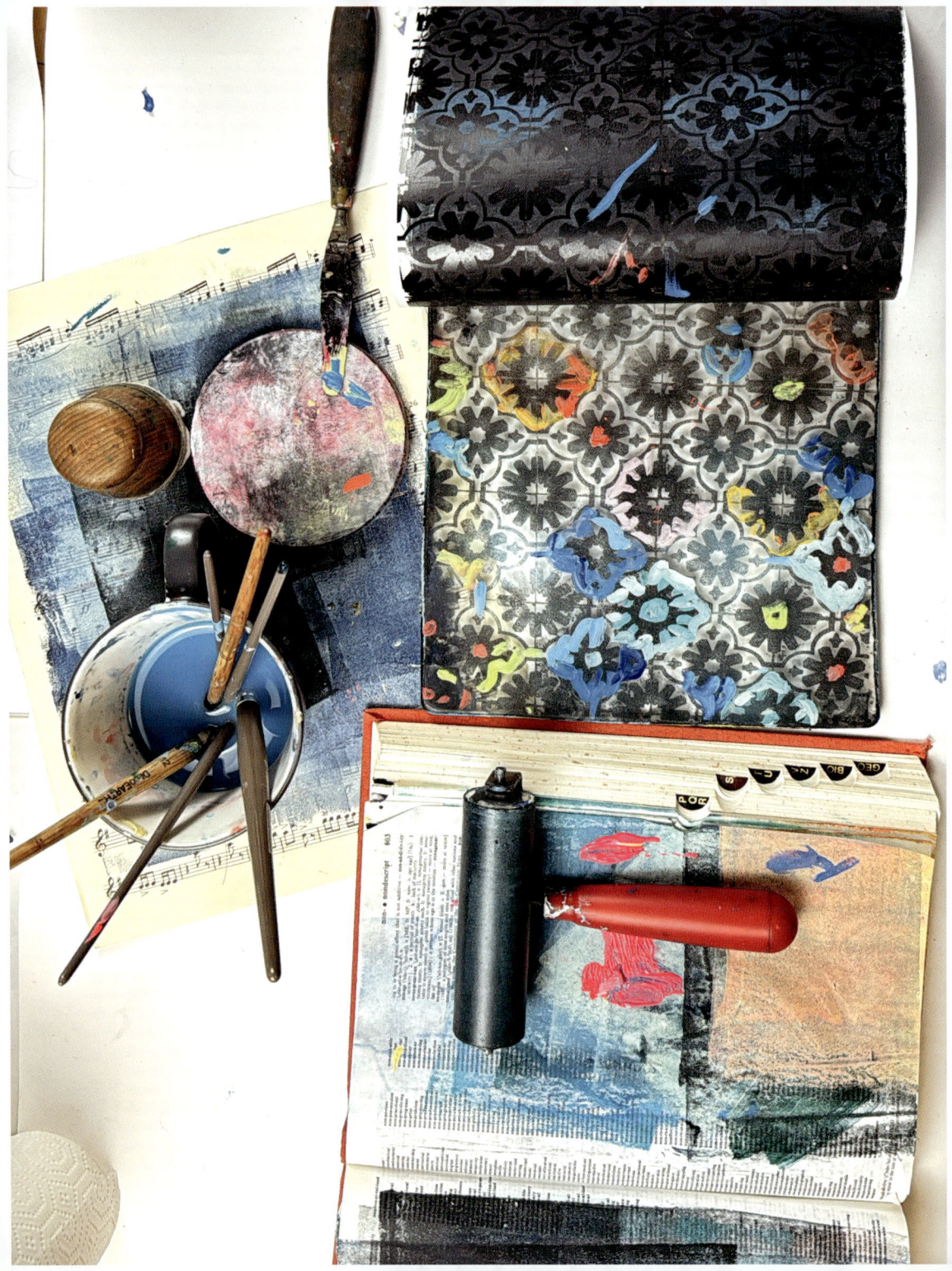

3
WHAT IS IT & HOW IT WORKS

WHAT IS PRINTMAKING?

Printmaking is an art process that involves transferring images from a block, plate, screen, or gel plate onto another surface, most commonly paper. For instance, in relief printing a raised surface is inked and pressed onto paper; woodcut, wood engraving, and lino block printing are all examples of this. Intaglio printing, which includes etching and engraving, involves incising lines into a plate that holds the ink. Lithography relies on the immiscibility of oil and water to create prints, while screen printing pushes ink through a stencil on a mesh screen. Gel printing falls under the category of monotypes. Unlike other printmaking methods, monotypes produce a single, unique impression, making each piece one of a kind. This chapter explores the history of gel printing and delves into the techniques that make it a captivating form of artistic expression.

THE HISTORY OF GEL PLATE TRANSFERS

Gel plate printing has its origins in the *hectograph*, a 19th-century duplication method that used a gelatin-based surface to transfer violet aniline dyes. Invented in the 1860s, the hectograph provided an inexpensive way to reproduce handwritten documents and became widely used in classrooms for making worksheets and illustrations. It even played a role in early tattooing as one of the first stencil transfer techniques. Before carbon paper and mimeograph machines became widespread, the hectograph was a popular choice for duplication. Its name comes from the Greek word *hekaton*, meaning 100, reflecting the optimistic goal of producing up to 100 copies from a single gelatin-based transfer. Its core principle is creating an image with aniline dye on paper and pressing paper onto the gelatin. It is remarkably similar to modern gel plate printmaking. Although today's gel plates are designed for artistic expression rather than mass duplication, they continue the tradition of using gelatin as a printing matrix, seamlessly connecting historical techniques with contemporary creativity.

Gel plate printing makes printmaking easier and more accessible. No expensive presses, fancy studios, or harsh chemicals required. You can do it just about anywhere, whether in a home studio, a classroom, or a shared creative space. Blending elements of printmaking, painting, and mixed media, gel printing offers flexibility that appeals to a wide range of artists. Many have incorporated it into textiles, book arts, collage, and even ceramics and sculpture, expanding its creative potential. As more people experiment with gel printing, its applications continue to grow. What started as a simple method for making copies has become a widely used and adaptable artistic technique.

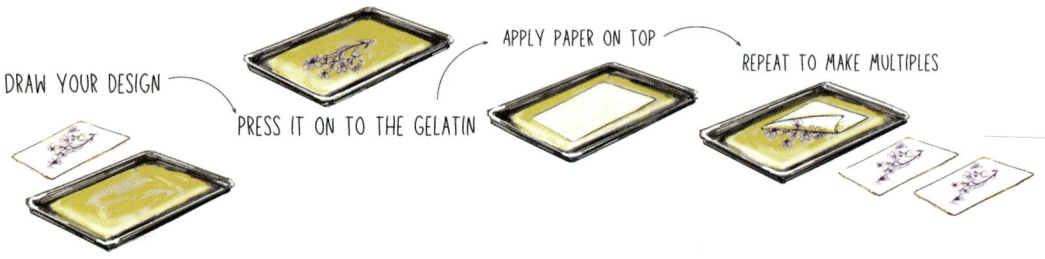

DRAW YOUR DESIGN

PRESS IT ON TO THE GELATIN

APPLY PAPER ON TOP

REPEAT TO MAKE MULTIPLES

The hectograph process can produce several prints using one image on a sheet of gelatin.

MONOTYPE VS. MONOPRINT: WHAT'S THE DIFFERENCE?

Let's clear up a common confusion right away: The terms *monotype* and *monoprint* are not interchangeable.

A *monotype* is a one-of-a-kind print. It is a single, unrepeatable moment captured on paper. It's usually created by painting or drawing directly on the gel plate or by using a unique image transfer. Because no template or repeatable pattern is used, each print is entirely individual. I tend to create monotypes because even if I reuse the same photograph, I approach it differently every time, making each print a stand-alone piece.

A *monoprint*, on the other hand, is part of a series where each print shares a common underlying image but may have variations in color, texture, or other design elements. For example, if I used the same photograph multiple times but changed the paint colors or added different textures, the results would be considered monoprints. It's like making siblings instead of identical twins.

THE SCIENCE OF TRANSFERS

At first glance, gel plate printing might seem like magic. Images appear effortlessly, textures layer seamlessly, and no two prints are identical. But there's a logical process behind it all. Understanding how gel plates work can help you take control of your prints, troubleshoot issues, and improve your image transfers. Instead of relying on trial and error, knowing the science behind the process will help you make more intentional creative choices.

Gel plate printing is all about the interaction between acrylic paint, the gel plate, and the paper. Each component plays a role in how colors transfer, how details emerge, and how layers build on one another. The gel plate itself is a soft, non-porous surface that holds paint in a way that allows for layering, texturing, and manipulation. Unlike paper or canvas, which absorbs paint immediately, the gel plate suspends the paint temporarily, keeping it wet long enough to work with it. This happens because of the chemical properties of acrylic paint and the plate's unique material. Acrylic paint contains water, pigments, and polymers that act as binding agents, while the gel plate contains mineral oil, which repels water. This resistance prevents the paint from fully bonding with the plate, making it easier to lift and transfer onto paper when the time is right.

When paper is pressed onto a painted gel plate, a series of reactions take place. The paper absorbs moisture from the paint, which weakens the bond between the paint and the plate. At the same time, the fibers in the paper grab onto the pigments and polymers, pulling them away from the plate's surface. As the paint dries, it naturally detaches, making lifting a clean, detailed print easier. The key to a successful print is finding the right balance between paint thickness, drying time, and the absorbency of the paper. The details will become muddy and blurred if too much paint is applied. If there is too little paint, the image may not transfer entirely or may appear faint.

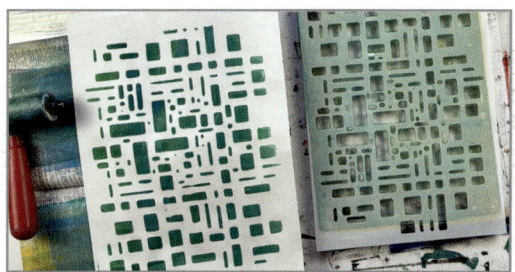

The green paint lifted from the negative spaces of the stencil is still wet on the paper and under the stencil on the gel plate.

WET PULL PRINT (STAMP-LIKE TECHNIQUE)

A *wet print* is when you treat the gel plate like a stamp, applying paint and immediately pressing paper onto the surface to lift the print. This is great for fast, spontaneous prints with bold textures or stencils. The results are often fresh, immediate, and gestural. You can still layer prints, but the layering is done on the paper rather than on the plate.

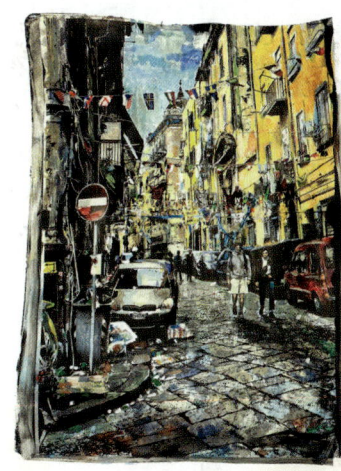

MULTILAYERED PRINTS (DRY LAYERING + PICKUP LAYER)

For *multilayered prints*, instead of lifting the print immediately, you let colors and textures dry in stages on the plate. Once the layers are complete, you roll a final wet pickup layer (a thin coat of paint) over everything. This layer reactivates and lifts the dry layers underneath, transferring the entire composition onto the paper in one go. The paper sits on the gel plate until all layers of paint are dry. The paint bonds with the paper and can be peeled off of the gel plate.

I made this print using a transfer layer, several layers of reverse painting, and a final pickup layer.

USING RESISTS

Before moving into image transfers, you need to understand how resists work. A *resist* is a technique that blocks paint from sticking to certain areas of the gel plate, creating intentional gaps in the print. You can use resists to build layers, add texture, or create high-contrast designs.

Since oil and acrylic don't mix, you can use oil pastels to block paint from sticking to certain areas. To try this, start by drawing a design with oil pastels on a sheet of paper. You can see my simple design in Figure A. Once your design is finished, roll a thin, even layer of acrylic paint onto the gel plate. I laid out blue paint in Figure B. Place your drawing face down onto the plate and press gently. In Figure C, you'll see that only the blue circles remain on the plate and that the paint soaks into the printer paper where there's no pastel. Once that first layer dries, roll a second, contrasting color over the plate; I chose light blue in Figure D. Press a clean sheet of Bristol board onto the plate and let it dry. I used Bristol to cover the plate, pressing down to make sure the paper makes full contact with the wet paint (Figure E). When it is dry, you can pull the Bristol off of the plate. All of the paint including the resist marks from the oil pastel are now on your print. You can see how the blue circles stayed intact in Figure F.

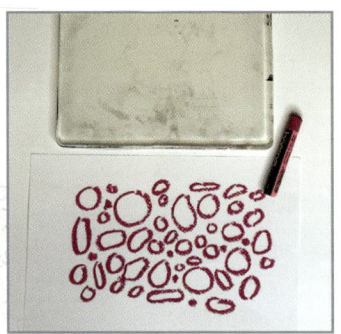
Figure A

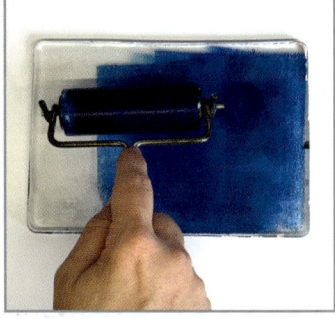
Figure B

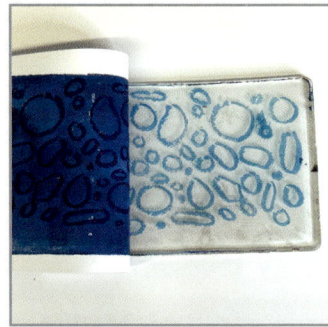
Figure C

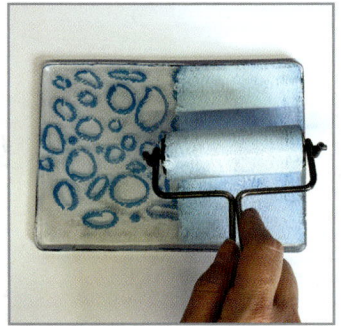
Figure D

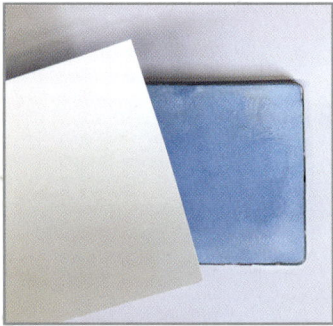
Figure E

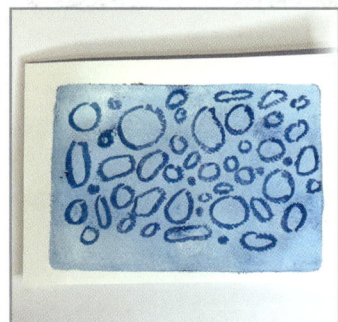
Figure F

IMAGE TRANSFER RESISTS

Through a resist-based process, you can use laser-printed images and magazine pages to create image transfers on a gel plate. Like oil pastel resists, image transfers work by allowing acrylic paint to bond selectively to the surface. The key to this method is how toner or magazine ink interacts with the paint.

In a laser print, the toner sits on the paper's surface rather than soaking in, allowing it to act as a resist. When pressed into a layer of wet acrylic paint on a gel plate, the toner prevents the paint from fully adhering in those areas. When you lift the paper away, an impression of the image remains on the plate. Magazine images work similarly, but because they are printed using oil-based inks on glossy paper, their slick surface helps release the image when pressed into the paint, often producing more organic and unpredictable results.

In both cases, after the initial transfer dries on the gel plate, you can roll a thin layer of fresh acrylic paint over the surface to act as a pickup layer, then press a sheet of paper onto the plate. When you then pull, you will lift both the dried transfer and the new layer of paint, resulting in a print that combines photographic details with painterly textures. The success of this process depends on contrast. Dark toner or magazine ink holds the image; lighter areas allow the acrylic paint to absorb.

Gel plate image transfers require patience and practice, but once you get comfortable with the process, they open up endless creative possibilities. Experimenting with different images, adjusting paint thickness, and varying drying times will help refine your technique. You can take your prints even further by layering multiple methods, such as combining resist techniques with image transfers, to create intricate and dynamic effects. Success in gel plate printing comes from curiosity and problem-solving. Building an understanding of the process leads to more consistent and intentional results. The more you explore the medium, the more control you'll have in shaping your creative individual approach to gel printing.

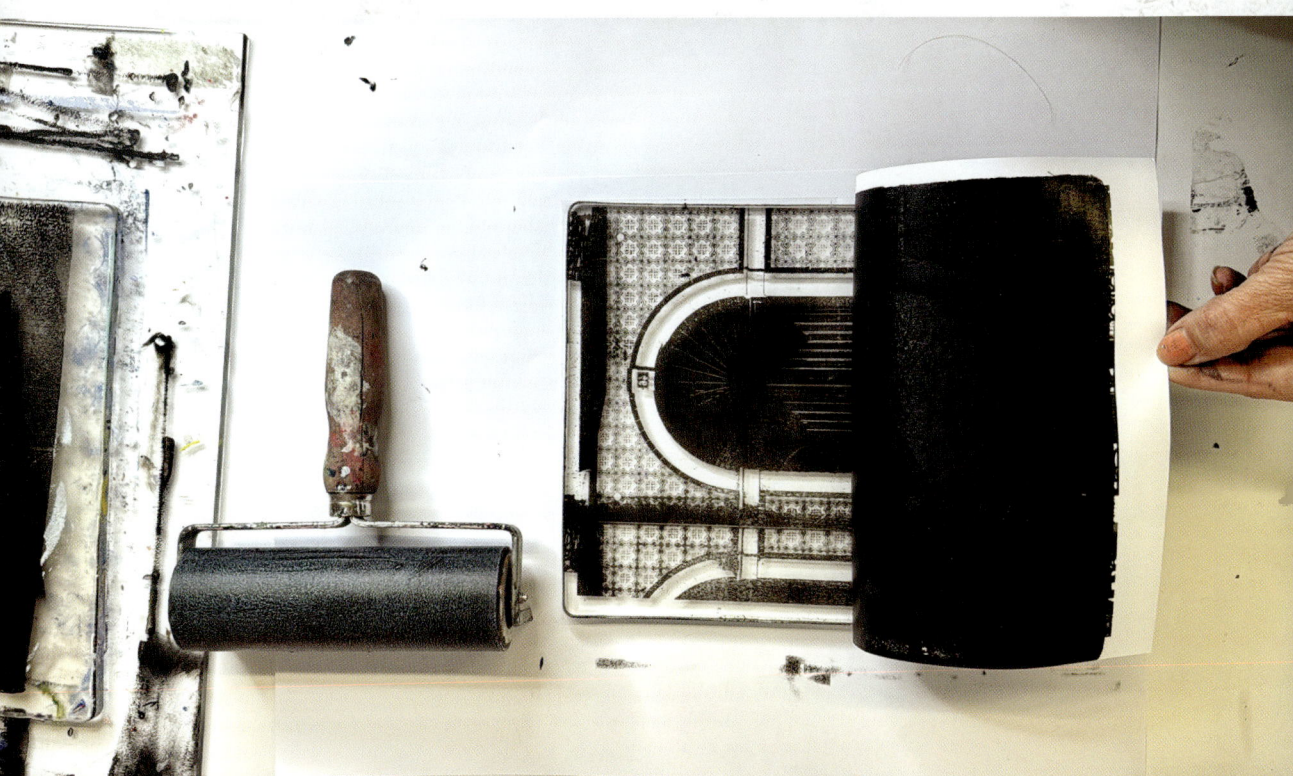

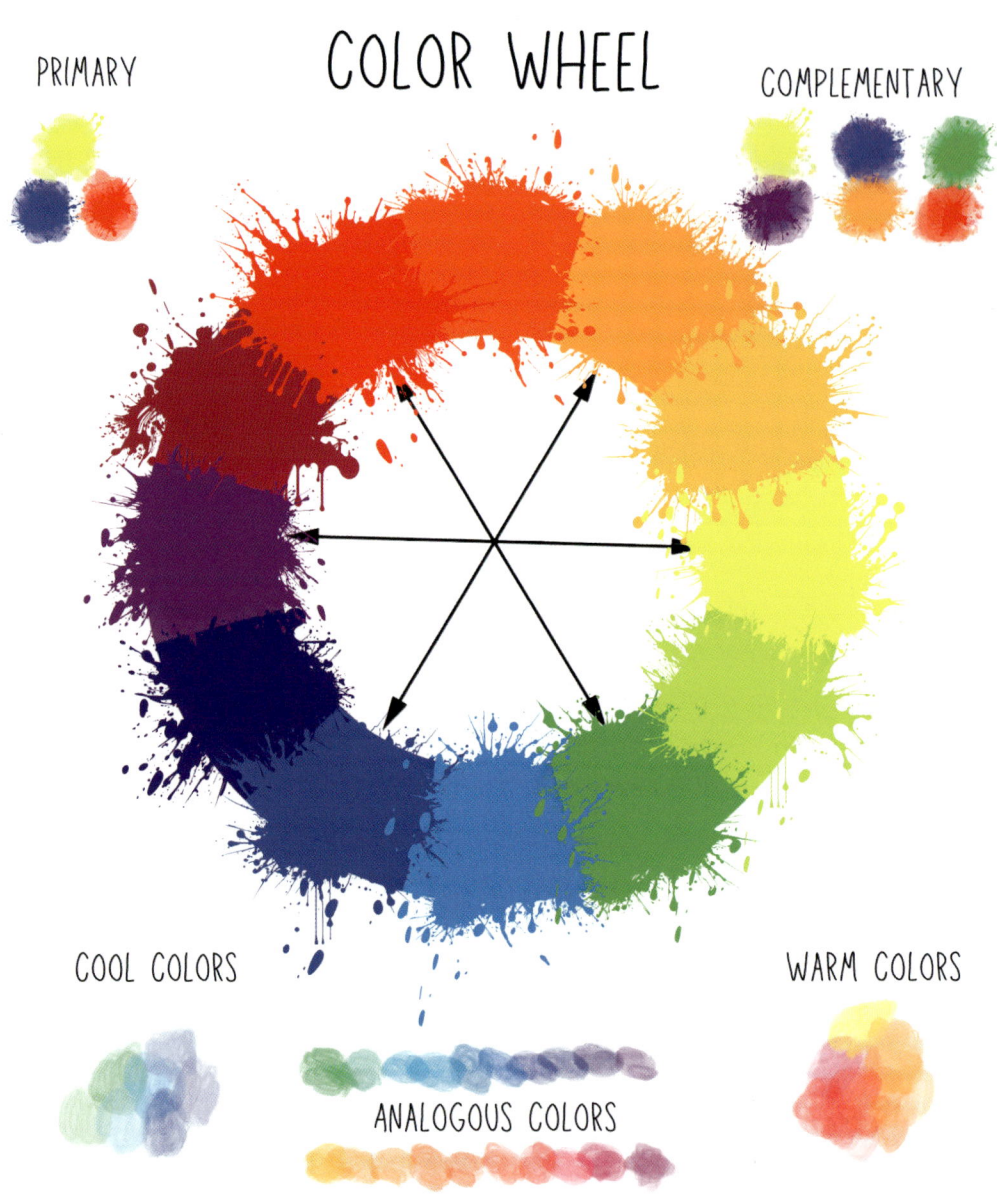

4
MAKING COLORS WORK FOR YOU

Color is one of the most powerful tools in an artist's process. It sets the mood, creates contrast, and adds depth to a composition. If you're unsure where to start, color theory can help—not as a rulebook, but as a guide. That said, paint companies shouldn't dictate your palette, you should. Straight-from-the-tube colors often feel artificial or flat, but custom-mixed colors bring depth, nuance, and personality to your work. Learning to mix your own colors gives you complete creative control.

Let's break down the essentials so you can make more intentional and impactful color choices in your gel prints.

THE COLOR WHEEL

The color wheel is a handy tool that organizes colors in a way that shows how they relate to each other. It starts with the *primary colors* (red, blue, and yellow), then moves to *secondary colors* (green, orange, and purple), and includes all the in-between shades created by mixing them. As an artist, the color wheel helps you figure out which colors work well together.

Complementary colors, opposite each other on the wheel, create bold contrasts, while *analogous colors*, next to each other, give a more subtle, blended look. By understanding how colors interact, you can use the color wheel to make intentional choices that shape the mood and feel of your work.

The color wheel is based on color theory, which

provides a framework for understanding how colors relate to one another and how they can be combined to create harmony or contrast. It's important to remember that color theory operates in an idealized way. For example, the traditional color wheel shows how primary colors (red, blue, and yellow) mix to form secondary colors (green, orange, and purple), but in reality, paint colors don't always behave as expected—hence it's a theory, not a strict rule.

Paints are made from synthetic and natural substances that don't always mix as purely or predictably as theoretical models suggest. Factors like the pigment's chemical properties, texture, and how the paint interacts with light can affect the resulting color. For example, the color wheel says that red and blue mix together to make purple; however, the way a red pigment reacts with a blue pigment might create a different hue than you'd expect based on the color wheel.

Additionally, there are different types of color wheels depending on the medium. The CMYK color model, for instance, is used for printing and is based on cyan, magenta, yellow, and black ink (often referred to as printer's colors). This system is quite different from the traditional color wheel used in painting, because of the way it deals with light and pigments. So, while the color wheel is an excellent guide for understanding how colors relate in theory, in practice, your results may vary.

CMYK PALETTE

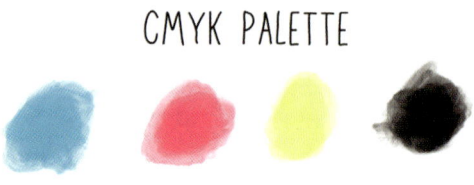

UNDERSTANDING COLOR VARIATIONS

Hue, value, and saturation are the three main components that define a color. *Hue* is the name of the color, such as red or blue. *Value* refers to how light or dark a color appears without changing its hue. *Saturation* measures the intensity of a color, from bold and vibrant to soft and muted.

Saturation plays a critical role in color perception. A fully saturated red is bright and dominant, while a desaturated red shifts toward a neutral, earthy tone. Lowering saturation eventually removes all color, leaving a grayscale version of the image. When working with image transfers in gel printing, Black Oxide paint already creates a strong contrast, so adjusting saturation, rather than relying on pure black and white, can help fine-tune the visual impact.

VALUE SCALE

SATURATION

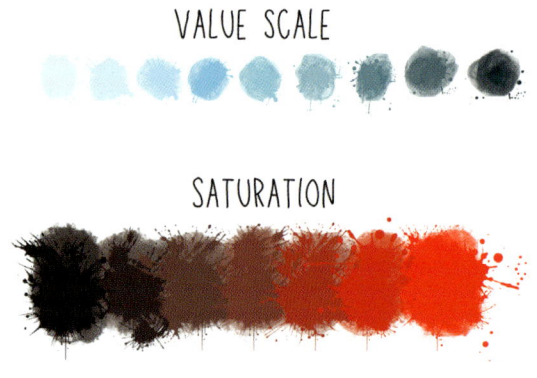

TINTS, TONES, AND SHADES: CONTROLLING COLOR DEPTH

Tints, tones, and shades allow you to better control color relationships in your prints. A *tint* is created by adding white to a base color, making it lighter. For example, adding white to red results in pink, while mixing white with blue creates a pale sky blue. Tints are especially useful for highlights and layering, because they add lightness without overpowering a composition. Rather than always using bright Titanium White, a softer alternative like Titanium Buff Light can create more natural, subtle tints with reduced contrast.

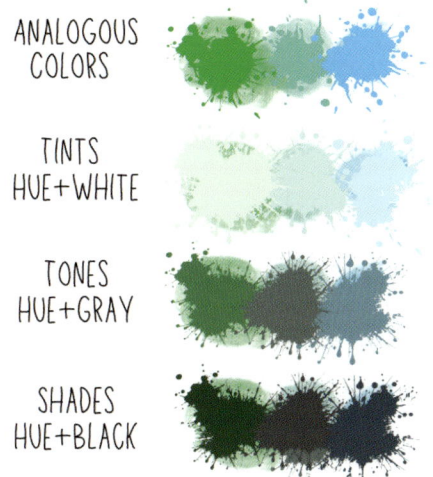

ANALOGOUS COLORS

TINTS
HUE+WHITE

TONES
HUE+GRAY

SHADES
HUE+BLACK

A *tone* is created by adding gray, which mutes the color's intensity without making it significantly lighter or darker. Mixing in gray is useful for balancing high-contrast colors, adding dimension, or creating more natural, desaturated variations. If bright yellow is toned down with gray, it becomes more of an ochre. A vivid blue softened with gray turns into a muted slate blue. Tones work well when you want to add complexity without making the composition feel too bold or overpowering. A mix

of Payne's Gray, Burnt Umber, and Titanium White can create a more interesting gray that won't leave you flat.

A *shade* results from adding black to a color, making it deeper and more intense. Unlike tints, which create an airy effect, or tones, which soften the color, shades add richness and depth. A small amount of black will slightly darken a color; a heavier application will push it toward a moody, dramatic tone. Adding black to red creates burgundy, and blue mixed with black results in navy. Instead of using pure black, which can make colors appear flat, a mix of Payne's Gray or Ultramarine Blue, and Burnt Umber creates more complex darks that retain vibrancy. Some pigments, like Phthalo Blue or Quinacridone Magenta, are powerful and can easily overpower a mix. When using these, start with the less intense color first and gradually add the stronger one in small amounts.

Mixing colors strategically can also create more dynamic near-neutrals than simple grays. Instead of black and white, complementary colors produce rich, nuanced grays. Ultramarine Blue and Burnt Sienna create a cool-toned gray, while Viridian and Alizarin Crimson form a warm-toned gray that shifts depending on the proportions of each color and the amount of white mixed in.

AVOID MUDDY PRINTS

Muddy prints often result from accidental mixing of complementary colors. If your prints look dull, try sticking to two to three colors that sit next to each other on the color wheel. Although blending complementary colors can create beautiful muted tones and help desaturate a color, it's usually best to control when and how this happens to avoid a lifeless result.

In my prints, I prefer to focus on tints and tones, allowing for a softer color contrast rather than sticking to a strict color formula. Take this print of mine, for example, where I used tints and tones of analogous colors to create a more subtle mood. I encourage you to experiment with gradual adjustments and observe how tints, tones, and shades can influence the overall feeling of your work. When used thoughtfully, these variations can turn a flat composition into one that feels rich with depth and atmosphere.

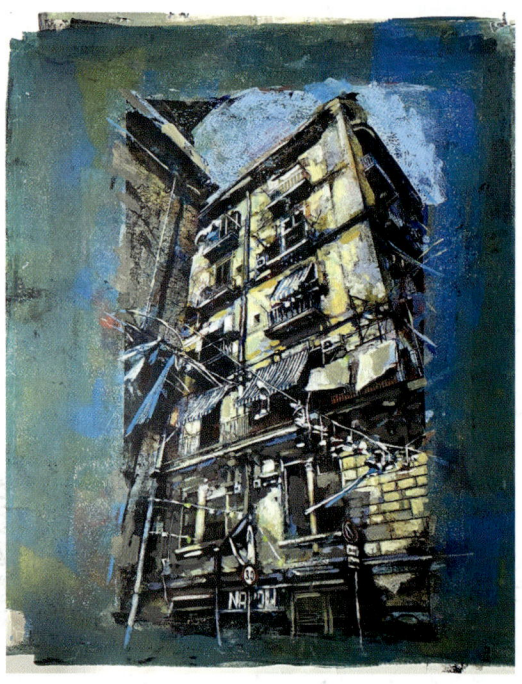

ANALOGOUS COLOR PALETTE
TINTS, TONES & SHADES

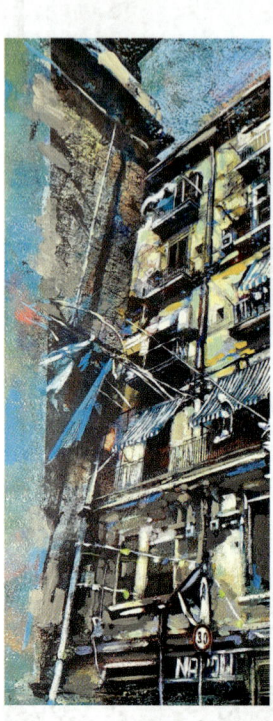

MY SPLIT COMPLEMENTS

Complementary colors are pairs of colors that sit directly opposite each other on the color wheel. These color pairs, such as red and green, blue and orange, or yellow and purple, are powerful because they create a striking contrast when placed next to each other. The vivid difference between these colors makes them stand out and enhances their vibrancy. When I paint, I either consciously or subconsciously lean toward a split-complementary color scheme. A *split-complementary color scheme* is a variation of the complementary color scheme that provides strong visual contrast while

SPLIT-COMPLEMENTARY

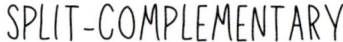
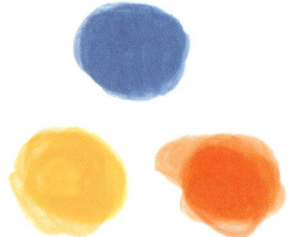

maintaining harmony. Instead of using two directly opposite colors on the color wheel, this scheme involves selecting a base color and pairing it with the two colors adjacent to its direct complement. For example, if red is the base color, you would use blue-green and yellow-green instead of pairing it with its direct complement of green. This approach softens the contrast found in traditional complementary pairs while still creating a visually interesting pairing. Here you can see how I took a traditional complementary scheme with blues and oranges and leaned into more of a split-complementary color scheme.

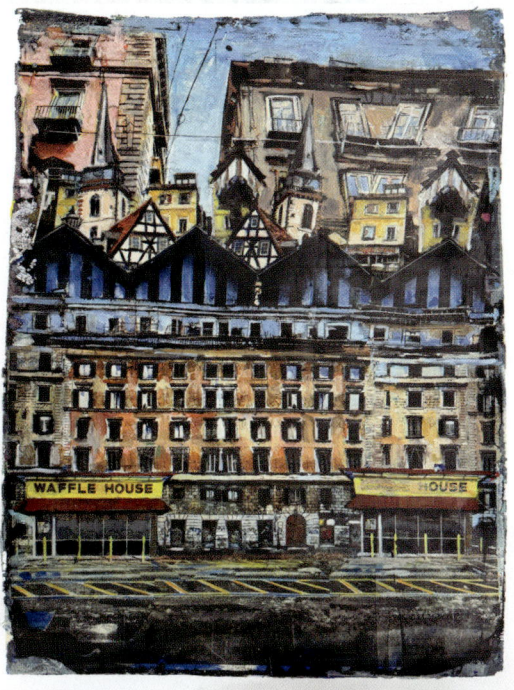

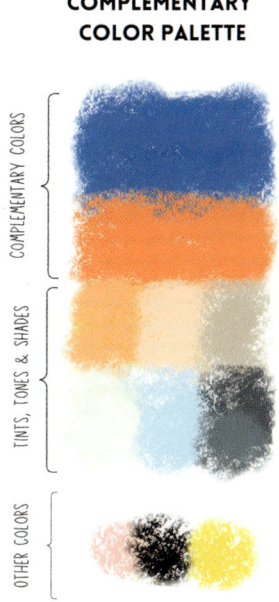

COMPLEMENTARY COLOR PALETTE

COMPLEMENTARY COLORS

TINTS, TONES & SHADES

OTHER COLORS

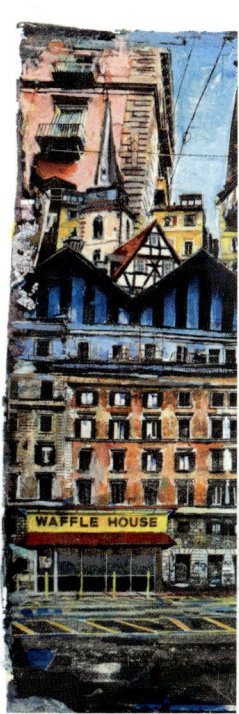

THEORY INTO PRACTICE

Color theory provides a foundation for making thoughtful choices, but the best way to learn is through experimentation. Some of the most interesting results in gel printing come from unexpected discoveries, whether it's a new way to layer transparent colors or an unusual mix that creates the perfect near-neutral. The more you mix, adjust, and layer, the more intuitive your understanding of color will become.

Technical knowledge gives you the freedom to push boundaries and create more expressive work. Keep these principles in mind, but don't be afraid to break the rules when necessary. Playing with tints, tones, and shades, adjusting saturation levels, and fine-tuning color relationships will help you develop a stronger, more intentional approach to color in your prints.

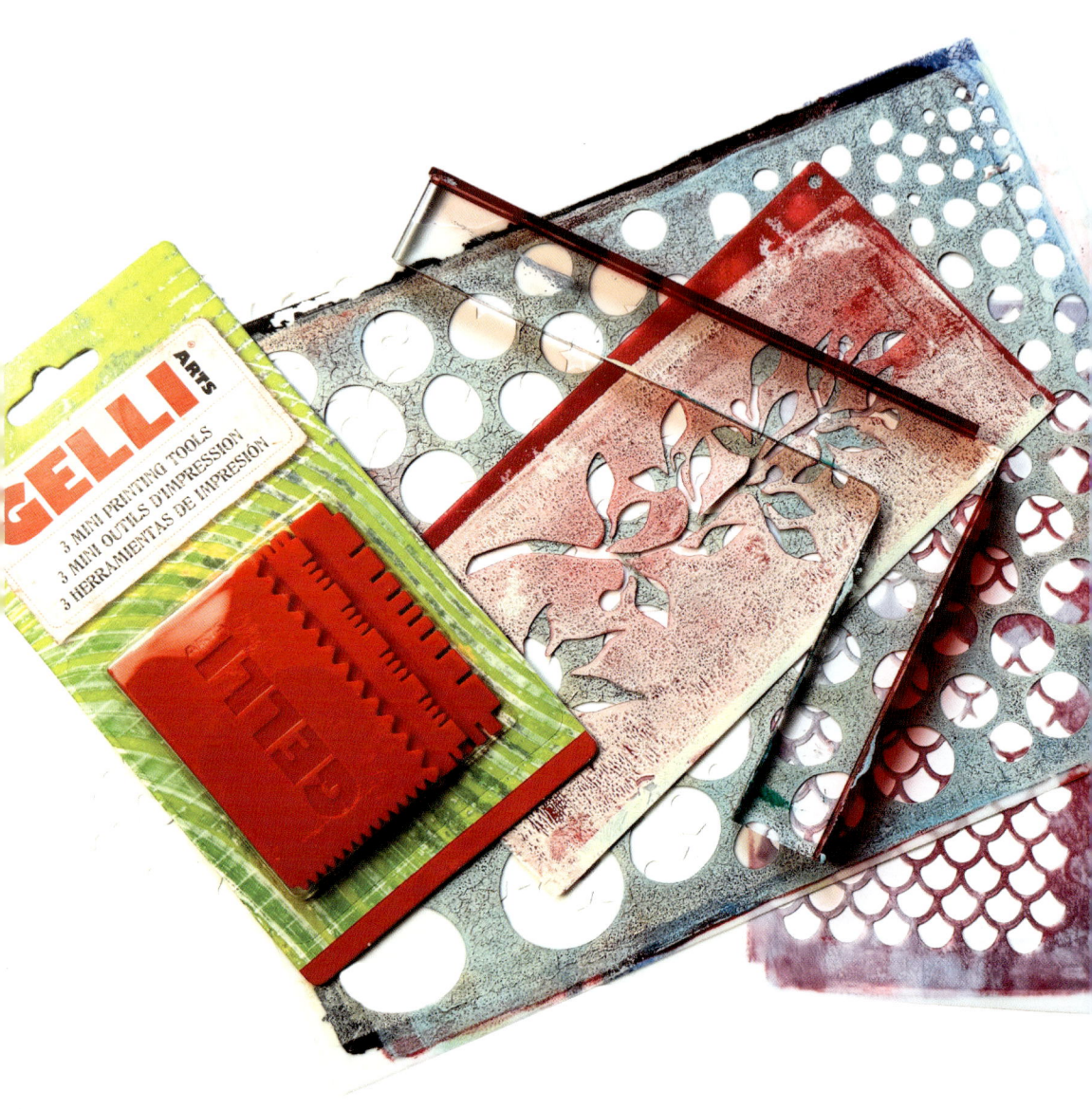

5
LAYER UPON TEXTURED LAYER

Layering is where craft transforms into art. Although I don't always draw a hard line between the two, understanding layers transforms gel plate prints from simple monotypes into something that feels like a fully realized painting. When you build multiple layers thoughtfully, you create depth, richness, and intrigue that makes viewers pause and ask, "How did you do that?" The answer is simple: It's all in the layers.

In this chapter, we'll dig into the core methods of layering: transparency and opacity stencils, and masks, and textures. Each technique offers distinct ways to build complexity in your gel prints. But keep in mind that color theory plays a crucial role, too. Understanding how colors interact across layers will help you make intentional choices that will enhance the final impact of your work. Let's break down these techniques so you can create captivating and complex prints.

SEEING THROUGH IT

Transparency and opacity are key to controlling how your layers interact. *Transparency* refers to how much of the layer beneath shows through your paint, while *opacity* refers to how much it blocks the surface underneath. Transparent paints let light and your previous layers shine through. They're perfect for adding depth, blending colors, or creating subtle layered effects. They enrich your work without completely hiding what's underneath. On the other hand, opaque paints completely cover the surface, offering bold, solid coverage when you need vibrant colors that really pop or you need to conceal earlier layers. Acrylic paints come with their own natural levels of transparency or opacity, so check your paint labels to see if they have an indication of their transparency. Some brands include handy indicators as you can see with the Golden paint label.

If you find a color that is too opaque, simply mix it with a gel medium. This spaces out the pigment particles in the acrylic binder, letting more light pass through. It gives you a more translucent paint for even more layering and blending options. Transparency and opacity exist on a scale, and you can play around with them to create different effects in your prints. It may take some practice (and even a few happy accidents), but once you understand how to balance these qualities, you'll have much more control over the final look of your prints.

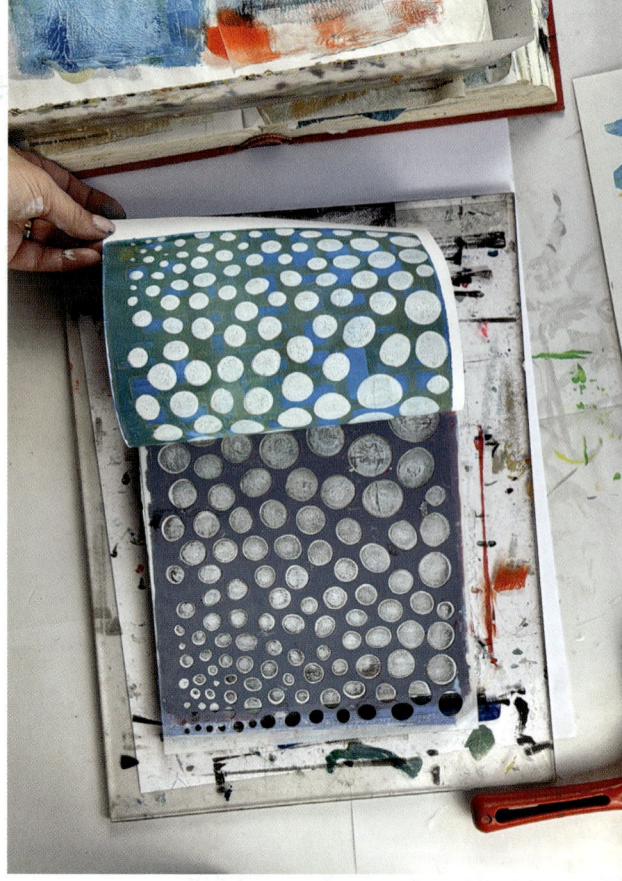

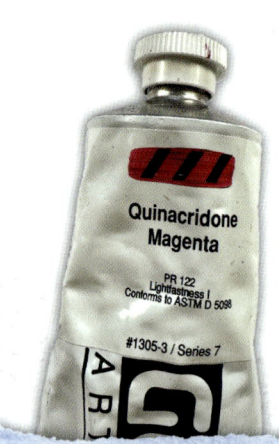

KEEP THOSE LAYERS IN LINE: REGISTRATION TIPS

We've all been there. The "oops, it's all crooked" moment. Want to avoid that? Here's a simple trick: Set up a registration system using basic tape hinges or an alignment guide. You don't need fancy tools. Just mark a few reference points on scrap paper under your gel plate. This will help guide your layers and make sure they land exactly where you want them to. Think of it as a roadmap for your prints. Trust me, your future self will thank you when those layers line up just right!

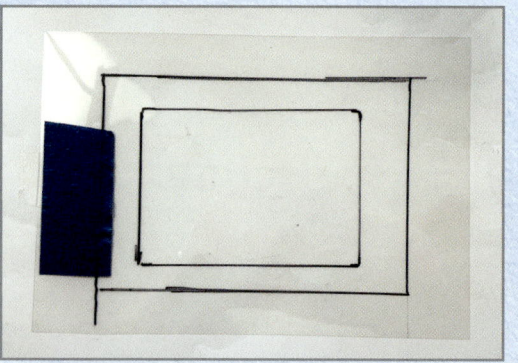

I drew an outline of my gel plate and my paper with a permanent marker on a sheet of acetate to help align the paper and keep the gel plate center.

STENCILS AND MASKS

In printmaking, stencils and masks control where paint is applied but work oppositely, allowing you to play with positive and negative shapes on your gel plate. *Stencils* have open spaces where paint passes through, adding positive space by applying color in specific shapes. *Masks* are solid shapes that block paint, creating negative space by preserving the blank area beneath. Depending on how you use it, a stencil can be used as a mask. You don't need to stress about whether you're using a stencil or a mask. Some materials happily play both roles, and that's perfectly fine (see figure below)!

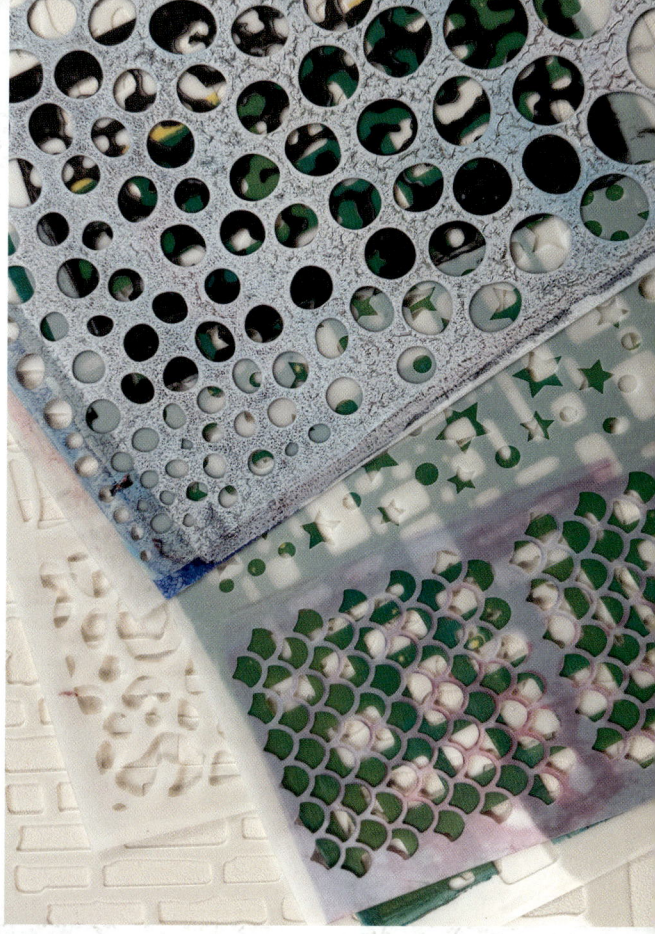

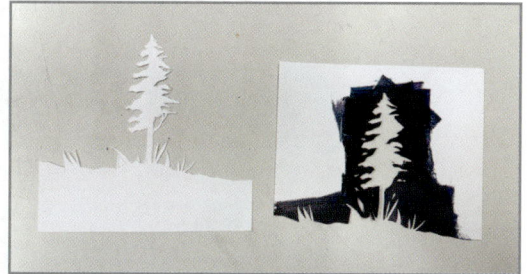

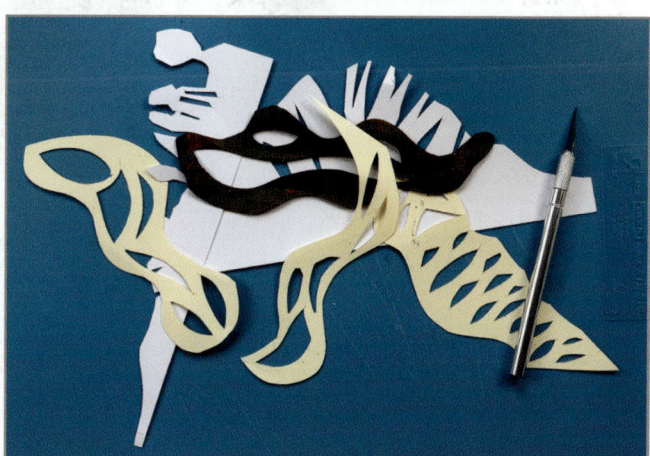

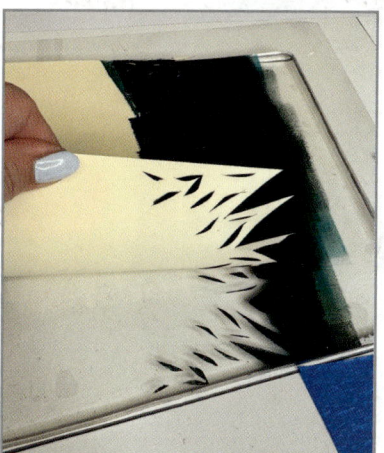

Want to know the best part? You don't need to spend a fortune on fancy commercial stencils and masks. That plastic binder insert gathering dust in your drawer? Perfect stencil material. The file folder you were about to recycle? Instant mask. Once you start looking at everyday objects through a printer's eyes, your whole house becomes an art supply store.

USING BOTANICALS AS NATURAL MASKS

You can use botanicals on the gel plate much like masks, creating beautiful, layered silhouettes as you build your print. Start by placing your leaves or flowers directly onto the plate after rolling out your first layer of paint. When you pull your print, the botanicals block the paint underneath, leaving behind their shapes. For a more dimensional effect, rearrange the leaves between layers and use progressively lighter colors as you work. This method builds depth and subtle shifts in tone.

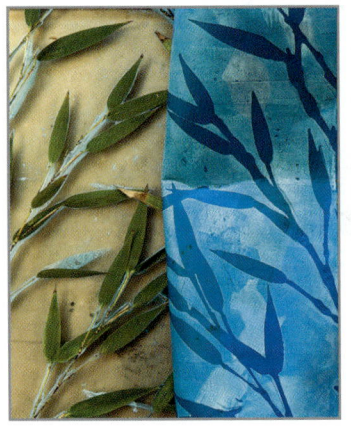 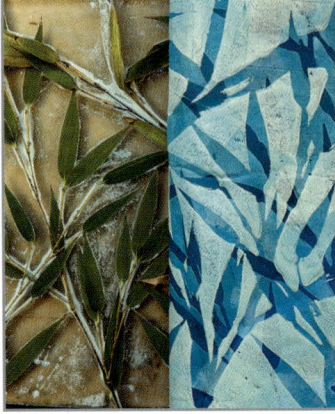 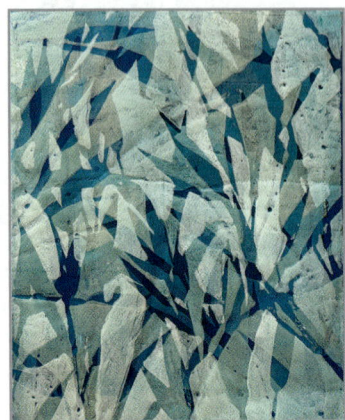

TROUBLESHOOTING YOUR STENCILS

Not every material works seamlessly with gel plates, but a few adjustments can help you avoid common issues. Most importantly remember the two rules that matter most: The material must be flat enough to lay smoothly on your gel plate and avoid sharp edges.

If the material is too glossy, it might be hard to peel off the plate. I found this out the hard way. I made a stencil from the front cover of a pad of drawing paper. When I laid it on the plate, the slightly glossy card stock gripped so hard that removing it was challenging. If your stencils start to stick to your gel plate you can lightly dust both sides with cornstarch. Just be aware that this may add subtle texture to your print.

If your stencil material is too flimsy and curls or wrinkles during printing, try ironing plastic materials between parchment paper on low heat or pressing them under heavy books overnight to flatten them.

Paint bleeding under the stencil's edges is a common frustration, often caused by excess paint or an uneven stencil surface. To fix this, make sure the stencil lies completely flat and use a minimal amount of paint. Rolling off extra paint from your brayer before applying can help, as can using thicker paint or a sponge for more control. Additionally, try applying paint from the stencil outward to keep it from seeping underneath. Layering multiple thin coats rather than applying too much paint at once will also improve precision and keep your prints crisp.

TREASURE HUNT: HOUSEHOLD ITEMS FOR PRINTING

Look around your house. You're probably surrounded by potential printing tools:

For stencils, try plastic produce containers (those rigid ones that hold cherry tomatoes), old file folders or manila envelopes, plastic placemats and table runners, scrap Bristol board from failed prints, or plastic binder dividers.

For Masks, try botanicals (fresh, dried, plastic), paper doilies, string or yarn, or lace trim.

STEP-BY-STEP: SIMPLE STENCIL TRANSFER

You can either lay your stencil first on your gel plate and sponge or brayer paint on top of it, or you can add paint to the plate before laying your stencil on it. I rolled out a light Cerulean Blue first, then added the stencil on top.

Let the paint dry, then roll a color over the entire plate. I chose a semi-transparent metallic gold, which would allow the blue to peek through the gold layer.

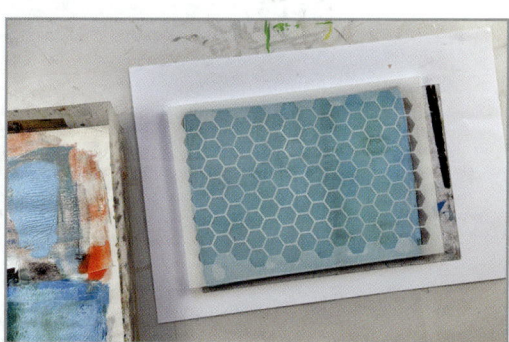

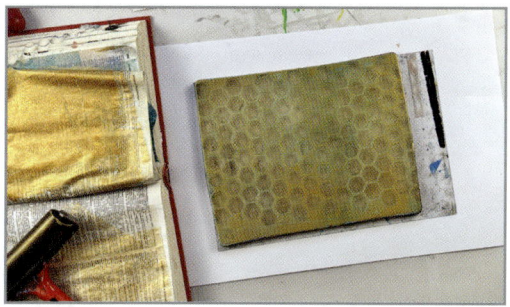

Use tissue paper or scrap paper to lift the paint from the negative spaces. I recycled printer paper that had some Yellow Ochre paint from a previous print—a scrap worth saving in my collage drawer for future work. Carefully lift the stencil to reveal the design.

Cover the plate with a piece of paper and let it dry. Because it's only two layers, it shouldn't take more than five minutes (although humidity and paper thickness can affect drying time).

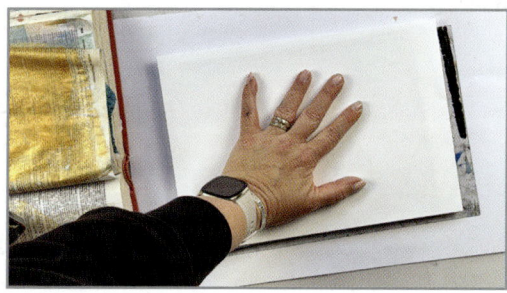

Pull your print, and get ready to be amazed.

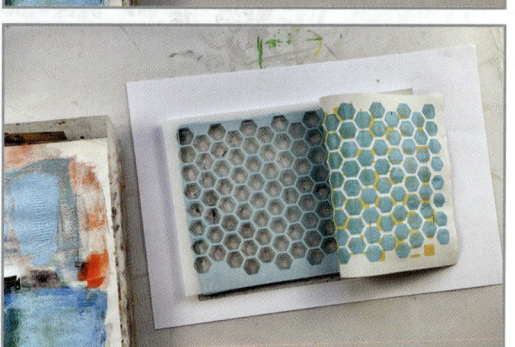

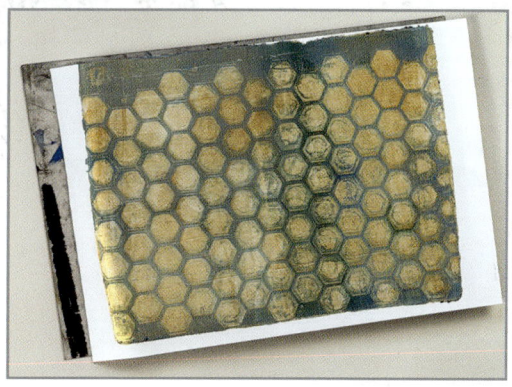

TURNING TRASH INTO TEXTURE TREASURE

Your recycle bin is about to become your best friend. Recycled materials are cheap, sustainable, and give you endless opportunities to experiment. Plastic inserts from candy boxes, torn cardboard from online orders (we've all been there), bubble wrap, and more can be pressed into wet acrylic paint on the gel plate to create amazing textures.

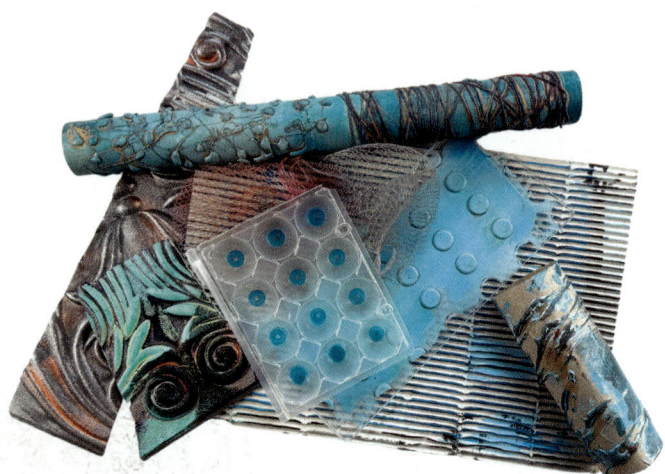

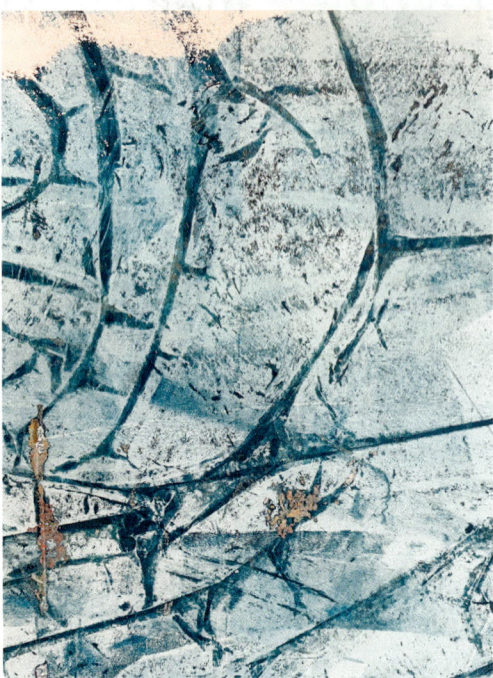

DIY TEXTURE ROLLERS

If you're the DIY type or just love a good hack, try making your own texture rollers. Grab a cardboard tube and wrap it with rubber bands, foam shapes, string, hot glue, foam sheets, oven-baked clay stamps, or bubble wrap. You'll have a custom roller that adds a whole new level of texture to your prints. I have made loads of these.

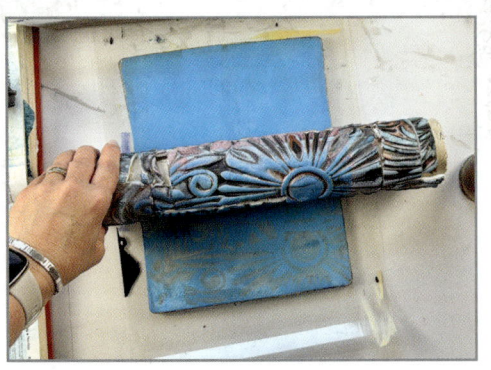

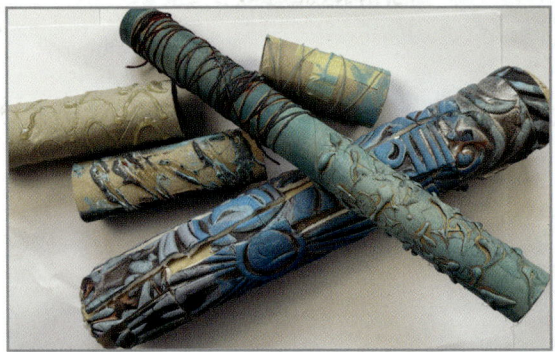

STEP-BY-STEP: SIMPLE TEXTURE

Let's create some layers with texture.

Find an item with interesting texture that will cover your gel plate. I chose a plastic table runner and unrolled a length slightly larger than my gel plate.

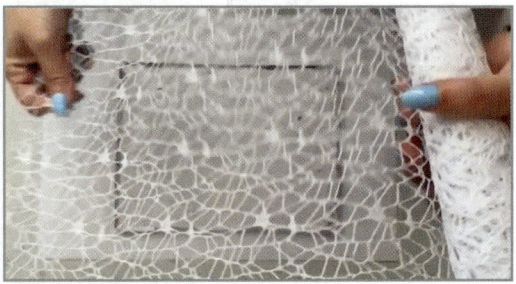

Roll a layer of paint on your gel plate. I chose the same metallic gold as I used for the stencil example. Next, lay your texture material on top of the wet paint. Depending on the texture you are using, you can press it down, roll it, or stamp it.

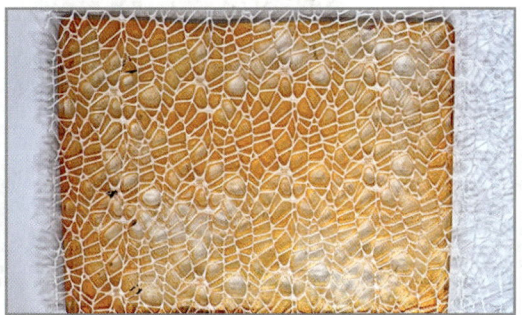

I chose to press down this texture onto my plate and remove the excess paint with scrap paper. You can see the webbed-like texture that is left on the plate.

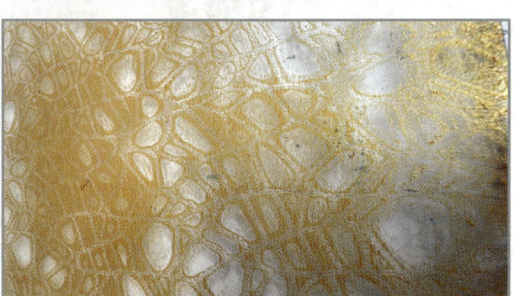

Let the paint dry, then roll a color over the entire plate. I used the same light blue as for the stencil but added a bit of Yellow Ochre to the color. Cover the plate with a piece of paper, and let it dry (again, it should only take about five minutes, depending on humidity and paper thickness). Start to pull up your paper to see if it is ready. If it is sticking, still wet, or tearing, lay it back down and wait a bit longer.

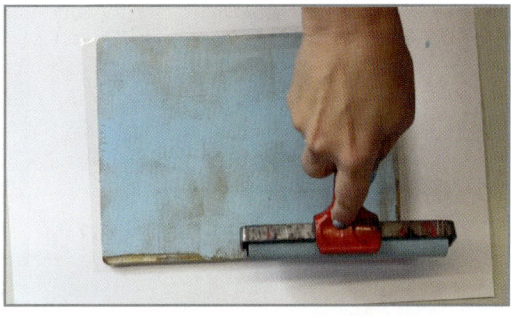

Pull your print. It's that easy, but the results are anything but basic!

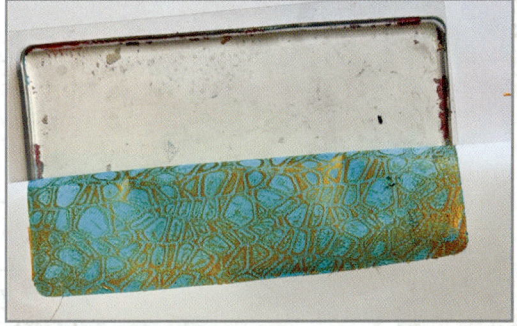

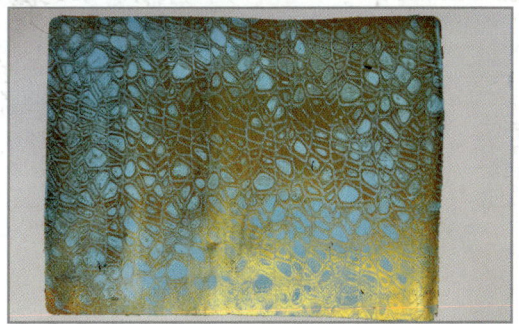

MORE TEXTURE, MORE CREATIVITY: SGRAFFITO

Sgraffito sounds fancy, right? It's just an Italian term for scratching into wet paint, and it's one of the easiest ways to add hand-drawn details to your prints.

This technique has its roots in historical mural painting, pottery, and architecture. Sgraffito involves layering contrasting colors or materials, then scratching through the top layer to reveal what's underneath. Dating back to the Renaissance, it's often used to create intricate patterns and imagery in frescoes and ceramics.

For gel plate printmaking, sgraffito introduces another layer of texture and detail. To try it, simply apply layers of paint to your gel plate and then scratch through the surface with the end of a paintbrush, a cotton swab, a paper edge, or even your fingernail (no judgment). The scratched designs will be printed as part of the final monotype, adding depth and visual interest. For the best results, remember to add a slightly thicker layer of paint to your plate. Also, consider mixing in a slow-drying medium with your acrylic paint. A paint retarder, often made from glycol, is a great way to extend the drying time of your acrylics, giving you even more time to create.

By adding layers of texture, stencils, and carefully balanced transparency, you can transform a simple print into something truly dynamic. With these techniques, you'll be well on your way to creating prints that not only impress but inspire. So let your imagination run wild, layer by layer!

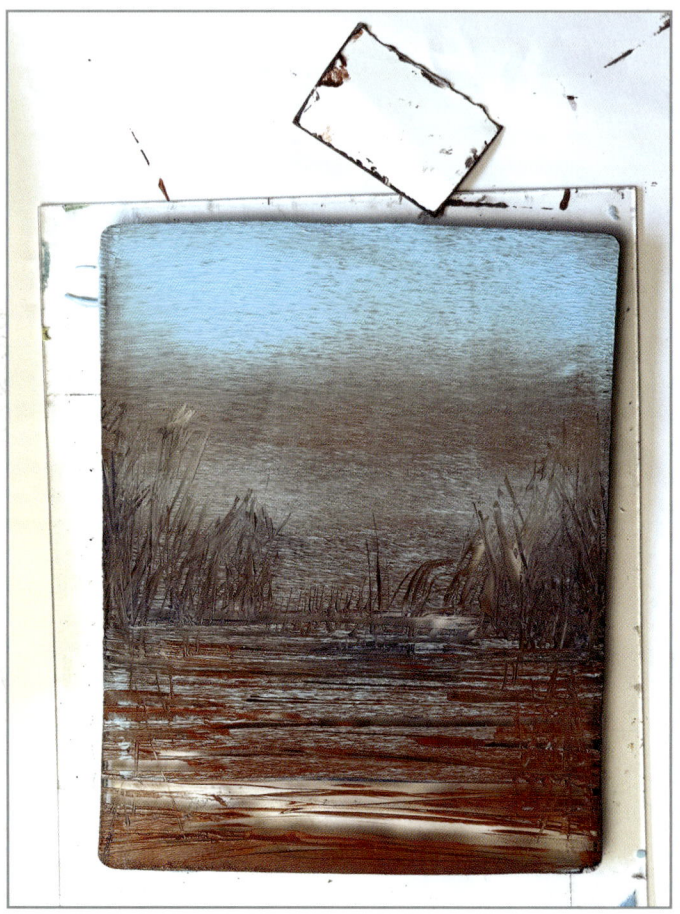

I scratched in angular lines with a piece of Bristol board to make this look more like a moody landscape.

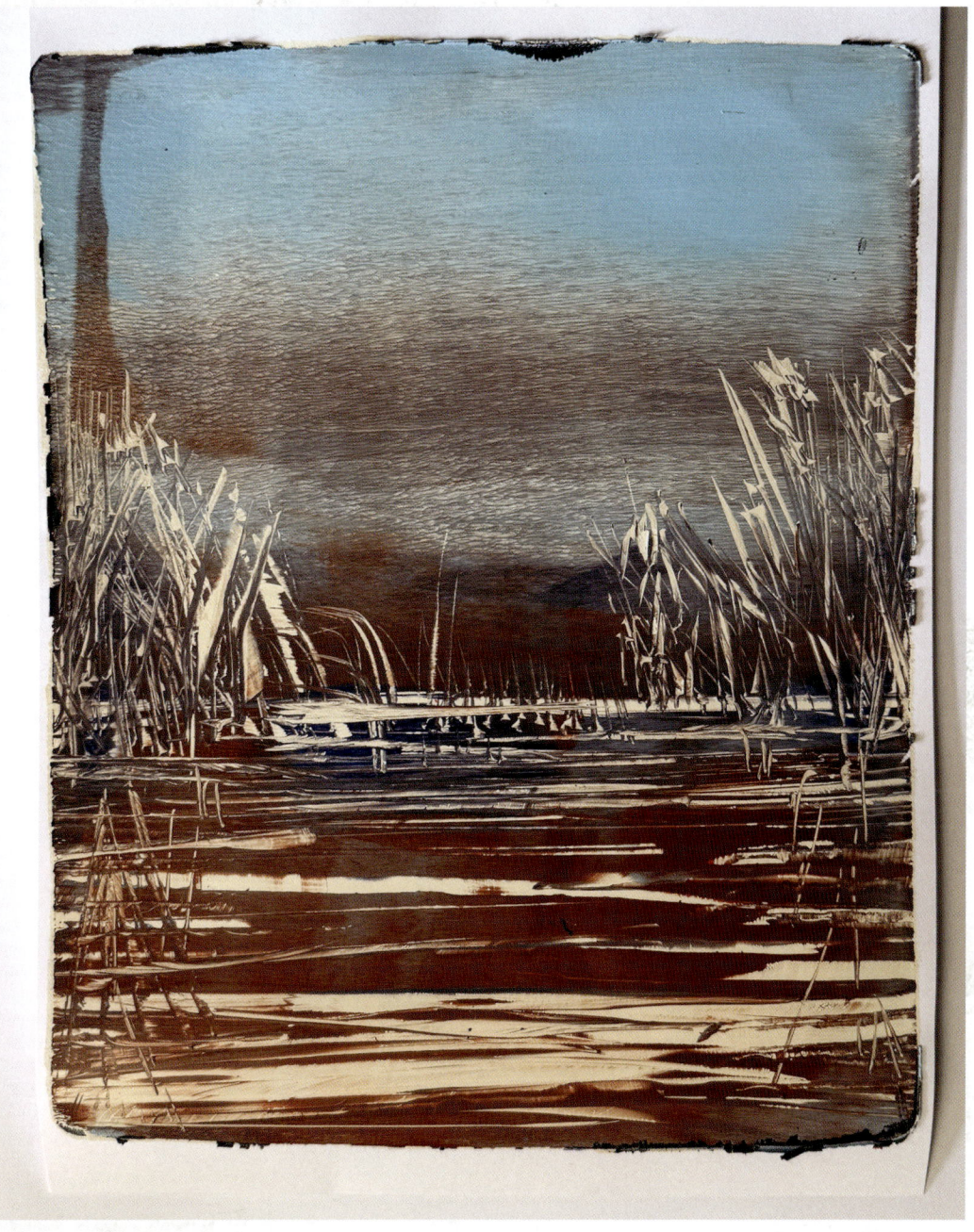

I used Buff Titanium White as the pickup layer. You can see how the warmer tone of the pickup layer peeks through all of the scratches in the paint.

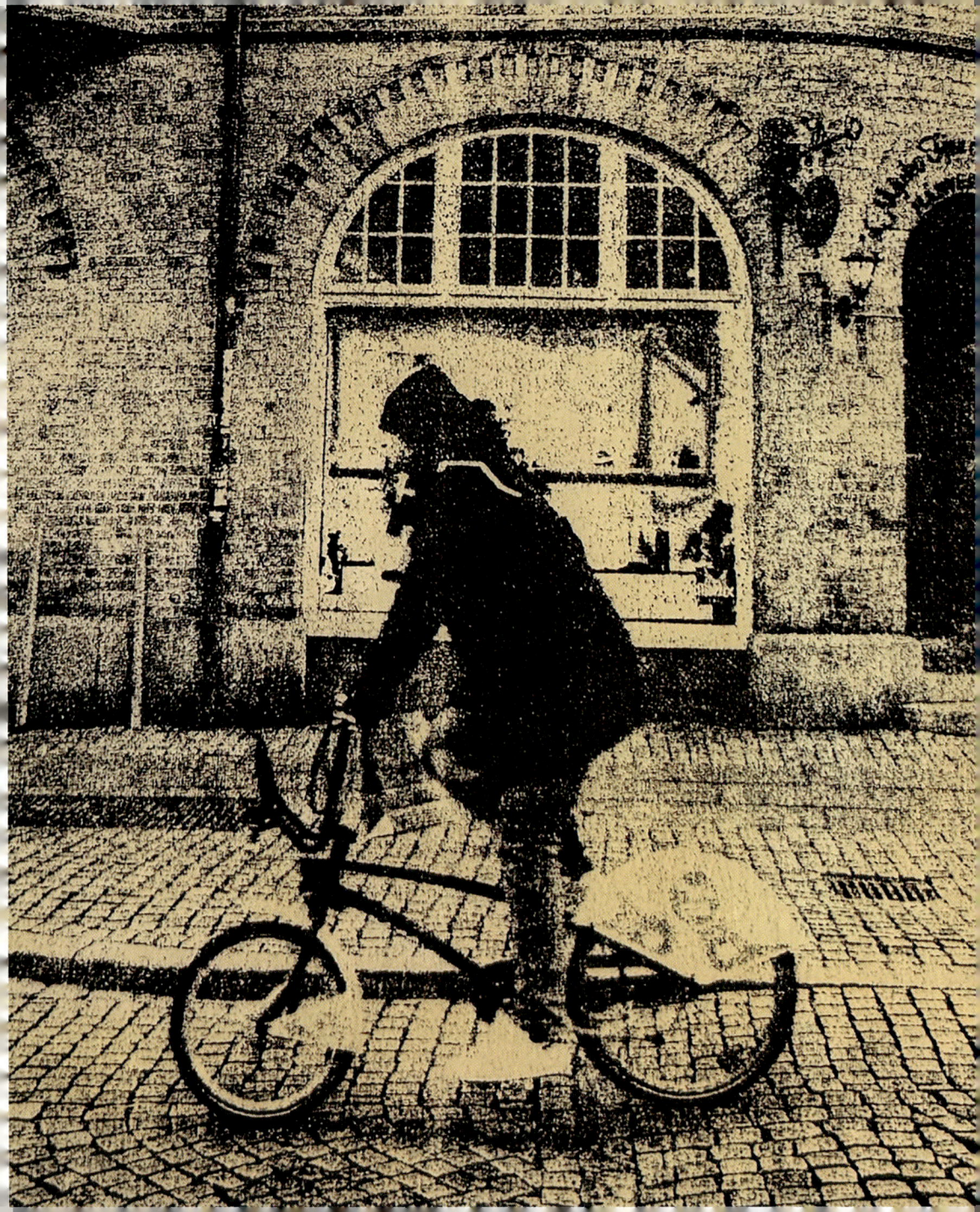

6
THE PERFECT TRANSFER

Getting the perfect image transfer on a gel plate can feel like chasing a unicorn: elusive and almost mythical at times. You can easily begin to wonder if it's even possible. The truth is, the tiniest details can tip the scales between success and frustration. In this chapter, I'll help you tackle these variables head-on. From selecting the right photo to mastering the transfer process, I'll walk you through each step so you can create perfect transfers and maybe start believing in unicorns too.

CHOOSE YOUR PHOTO

The right photo can make or break your image transfer, so start strong. Choose a photo with bold, graphic qualities, one that would still make sense if it were stripped down to the basics. For the smoothest results, use a high-resolution, high-contrast, halftone image, printed with a laser printer on 100-gsm regular printer paper. Trust me, the sharper and cleaner the starting point, the better your final print will look.

I chose a photo I took in Malmö, Sweden, and then edited it to brighten the window behind the man. The adjustment increased the contrast, allowing him to stand out more clearly from the background. While the image contains a fair amount of midtones, they're primarily concentrated in the bricks. Even if some of the midtones don't transfer perfectly, the image will still be recognizable as a man on a bike in front of a building. The blend of symmetry and asymmetry in this photo adds an extra layer of visual interest. (Chapter 7, Getting Your Photos Print Ready," digs deeper into photo editing, printers, and paper choice.)

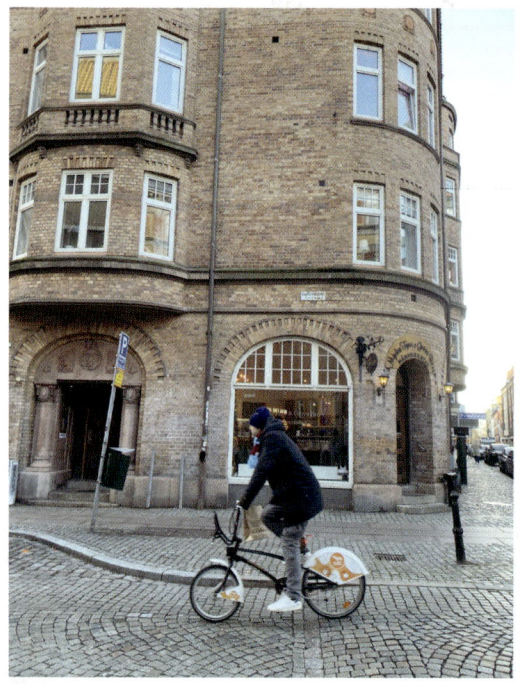 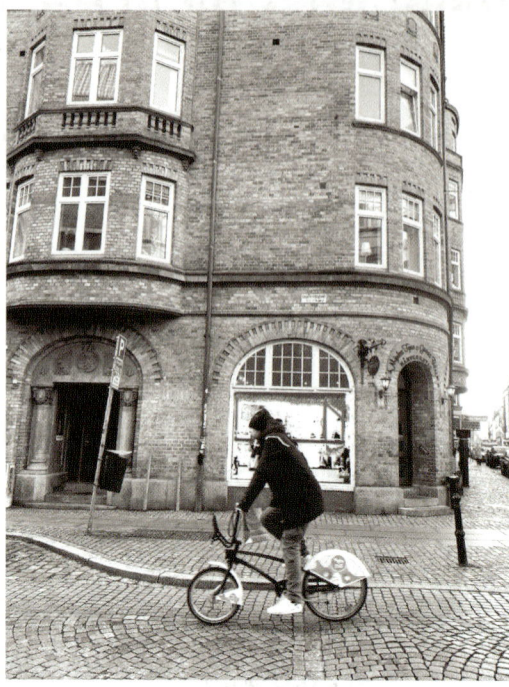

The photo on the left is my original unedited photograph. I turned the one on the right into black and white, increased the contrast, and converted it to halftone. Plus, I lightened the main arched window to make the dark silhouette of the bicyclist pop.

A close-up of the bicyclist's face shows how the image is made up of halftone dots. While halftone photos aren't essential for good transfers, the concentrated toner in these dots often results in clearer details and helps midtones transfer more effectively. Halftones work by breaking an image into dots of various sizes to reproduce tones of gray or color.

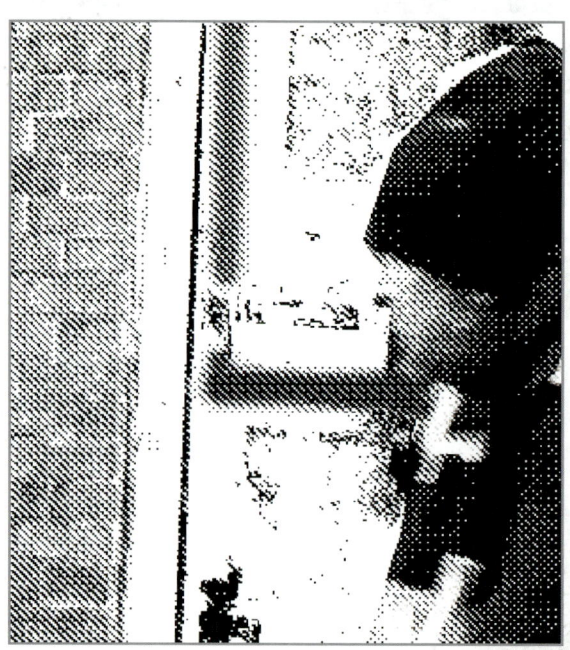

DON'T ROLL UNTIL YOU ARE READY

Timing is key to a flawless transfer, so having all your supplies organized and within easy reach is essential before you begin. Here's what you'll need:

- **Paint:** I highly recommend Amsterdam Black Oxide. It strikes the perfect balance between opacity and smoothness without being too thick. Its consistency makes it predictable and easy to work with, which is important for the clarity of your image transfers.
- **Tools:** You'll need a clean gel plate (or at least one that's reasonably clean), a brayer to roll out the paint, a palette or spare plate for rolling and controlling the paint, and a scrap piece of paper for cleaning your brayer.

- **Photo:** Keep your image nearby so you can apply it to the gel plate as soon as the plate is ready.
- **Final paper:** This is the paper that you will use as the substrate for your final print. I usually choose Bristol board for this.

Having these items ready to go will save you valuable time during the process and allow you to work quickly without the paint starting to dry on you.

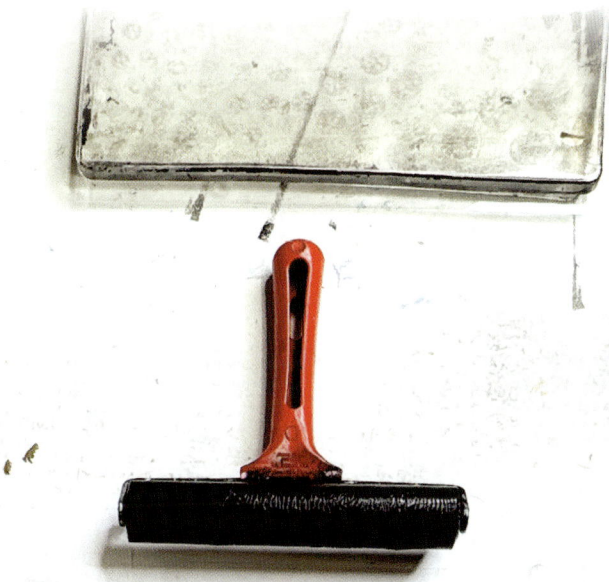

A LITTLE SEASONING ADDS FLAVOR

Although brand-new gel plates can work, slightly seasoned plates often yield better results. Cleanliness is important, but your plate doesn't need to be spotless. A well-loved gel plate, with its subtle imperfections, can enhance the process and create a more nuanced transfer.

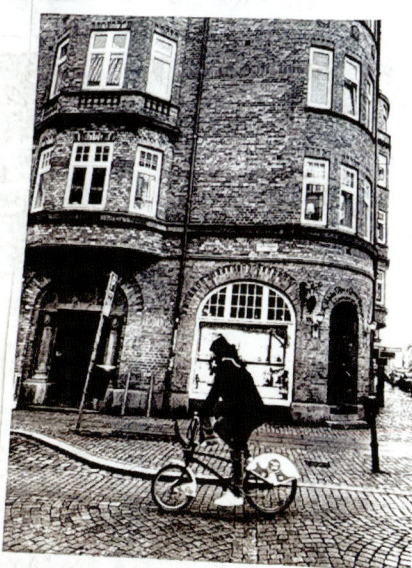

PEA GLOBS AND PAINT LAYERS

How much paint will you need? For an 8 × 10-inch gel plate, about three pea-size globs of paint should suffice. This measurement feels both universally relatable and practical. It mimics the small squeeze we typically use to get paint out of a tube, which naturally forms a pea shape. In my classroom, I often use toothpaste on a toothbrush as a unit of measurement, although there's always that one middle schooler who insists they use a massive amount of toothpaste and gleefully squeezes a giant blob of paint onto their plate. I trust you'll be more restrained. Adjust the pea size up or down depending on the size of your gel plate.

I prefer to squeeze out the paint onto a palette next to my gel plate. This approach enables me to control how much paint is applied and ensures the brayer picks up an even layer before it touches the gel plate. Roll the paint onto the gel plate evenly, then roll off any excess paint onto a scrap piece of

paper. Keep this scrap paper; you can repurpose it later for collage work.

The balance of paint is critical. Too much paint, and the resist won't work because the acrylic paint won't soak into the raw parts of the printer paper. Too little paint, and it may all lift onto the printer paper or dry too quickly for the process to work.

To gauge if you've got the right amount of paint, look for a slight transparency. Lift the gel plate, and place your hand beneath it. If you can see the outline of your hand and a hint of your skin tone, you're good to go. If it's too opaque, roll off the excess paint from your brayer onto the scrap paper and then gently roll it back onto the gel plate. This step helps lift just enough paint off the plate for optimal results.

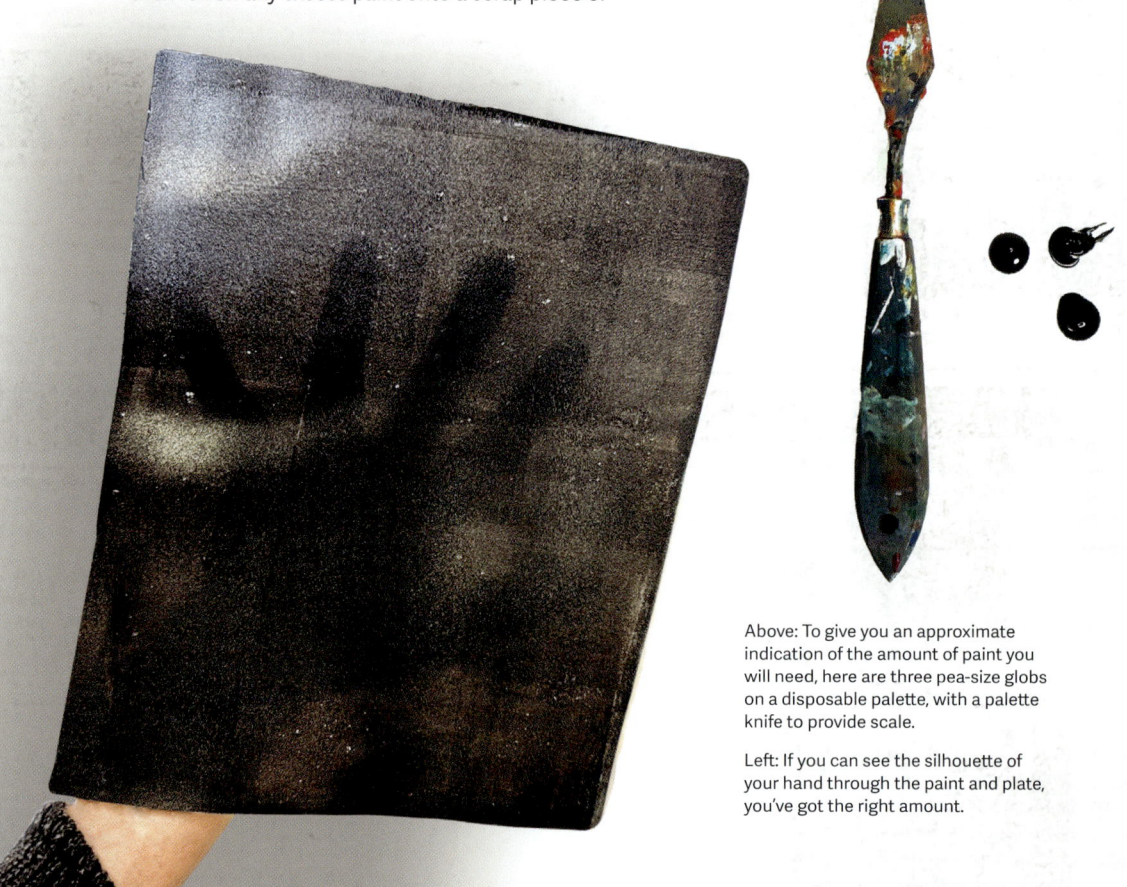

Above: To give you an approximate indication of the amount of paint you will need, here are three pea-size globs on a disposable palette, with a palette knife to provide scale.

Left: If you can see the silhouette of your hand through the paint and plate, you've got the right amount.

LAY IT DOWN

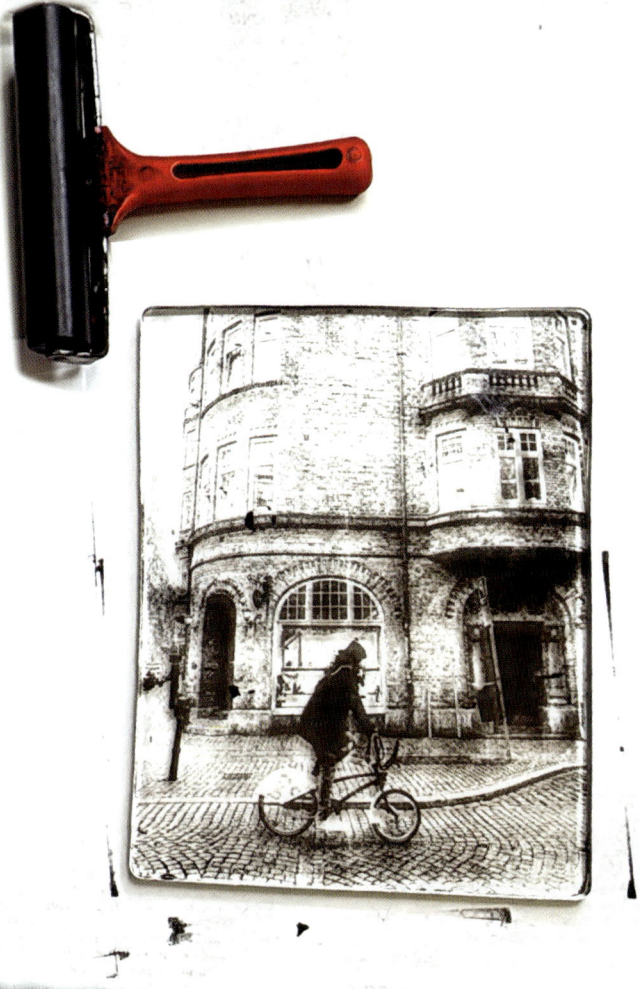

With your gel plate covered in a smooth layer of paint, it's time to position your photo. Gently place your laser-printed image face down on the plate, making sure it's lined up exactly as you want. Once the paper touches the paint, repositioning can smudge or distort the transfer.

Next, roll your brayer over the back of the paper with steady, even strokes. Avoid doubling back over areas you've already rolled to keep the transfer clean and uniform. You can use your hands to press evenly, but a brayer often provides a more consistent result.

After about 10 seconds, lift a corner for a sneak peek. If you see areas where the paint hasn't transferred, give them a bit more attention with the brayer or your fingers. Work quickly because when the paint starts to dry, all the paint will stick to the paper and lift off of the gel plate. This is your Goldilocks moment—not too short, not too long. Just right is key for a clean transfer.

Once you've successfully transferred the image, step back and let the black acrylic paint dry completely on the gel plate. This pause is crucial to avoid smudging and to ensure that the next steps, like adding pickup layers, go smoothly. Patience is your best friend.

BRAYER VS. BARE HANDS: WHICH TEAM ARE YOU ON?

To be completely honest, I rely on my hands more than a brayer when transferring photos to the gel plate. This method allows me to control the pressure with greater precision and focus on specific areas of the image. For instance, I can press more gently in delicate sections to avoid over-transferring fine details, while applying firmer pressure in other areas to ensure a strong and complete transfer.

That said, if you're new to this process, I recommend starting with a brayer to achieve consistent pressure across the entire image. Brayers are excellent for even coverage, especially if you're still learning how much force to apply. Nevertheless, if your brayer is significantly smaller than the paper you're using, you may find it easier to switch to hand pressure. Using your hands allows you to work more intuitively, addressing specific spots without worrying about the overlapping strokes that can sometimes happen with a small brayer.

With practice, you'll discover what works best for you—whether it's a brayer, your hands, or a combination of both. The key is to develop a sense of control and adaptability, tailoring your technique to the needs of each image.

THE SECRET SAUCE

Okay, it may not be completely secret, but still let me share a printmaking trick that's become my go-to technique for my image transfers. If you've noticed areas where paint pools or beads up, you're witnessing a common challenge caused by the mineral oil content in gel plates. This oil can sometimes repel acrylic paint, creating frustratingly uneven spots that can compromise your print's quality.

To overcome this artistic hurdle, carefully apply a thin, even layer of satin gel medium over the transfer. Think of this gel medium as a stabilizing barrier. It helps the paint adhere more effectively to the plate and minimizes the pesky effects of oil seepage. The key is to create a smooth, consistent layer that allows your following layer(s) of paint to attach more smoothly to the plate.

Allow the gel medium to dry completely before moving forward. This isn't a step to rush. Applying additional layers too quickly can disturb the delicate surface and introduce unwanted inconsistencies to show up in your final print. Give the gel medium the time it needs to set properly. Later in the book, I will completely break this rule. But that is in the future when you've had more practice. For now, stick with the rule of letting it dry fully.

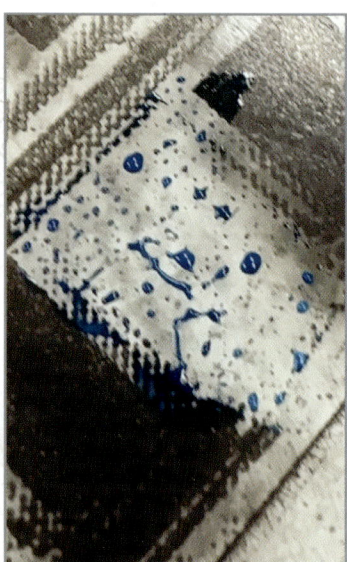

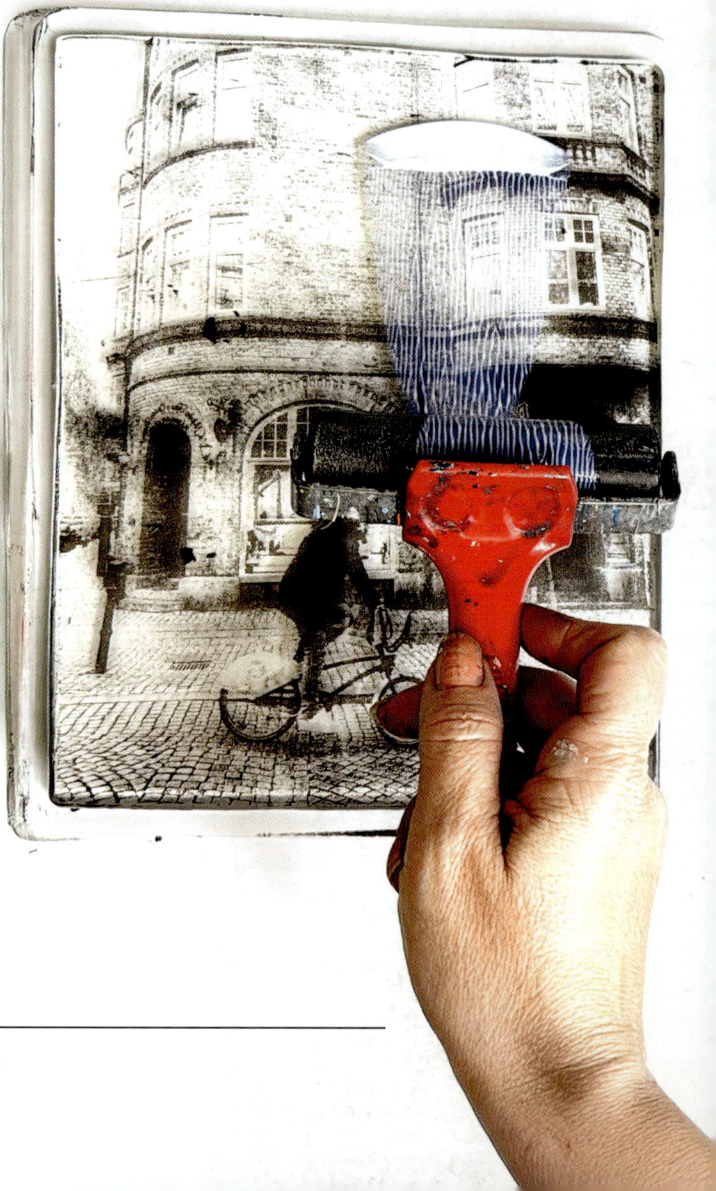

Above: You can see how the paint starts to pool while being repelled by the mineral oil. It creeps and gathers into the small puddles.

Right: A thin layer of gel medium applied with the brayer may look slightly opaque at first, but it will dry transparent.

PICK UP AND SEAL THE DEAL

At this stage, you could choose to reverse paint, gradually building up your image by starting with the finer details in the foreground and working your way to the larger areas in the final layers. I go into more detail about that technique in Chapter 8, Reverse Painting. For now, though, keep it simple by adding just one layer of color to the plate. This layer will also double as your pickup layer. The fresh coat of paint acts like glue, bonding the dried transfer to your paper. It's straightforward and effective, perfect for getting a clean print.

Once the black paint (and gel medium, if you used it) is completely dry, apply a slightly thicker layer of acrylic paint in your chosen color. Spread it evenly with a brayer, making sure there are no gaps or streaks. Uneven coverage can leave parts of your transfer behind or cause flaky spots later. Aim for full opaque coverage.

Time for the paper. Sturdy is the way to go. I recommend Bristol board or heavyweight printer paper, as they're durable enough to hold up during the transfer process and create a solid bond. Avoid overly absorbent papers. They'll drink up too much paint, weakening the transfer and leaving uneven results.

Align the paper to ensure it covers the entire surface. Use your hands or a baren to press firmly across the paper, ensuring full contact between the paper and the painted plate. Pay special attention to the edges and corners, as these areas are often the most prone to incomplete transfers.

I like to place a stack of heavy books or a weighted object on top of the paper. Use books that are bigger than your plate to ensure even pressure. The added weight helps ensure an even bond and allows the paint to adhere uniformly across the entire surface.

The order of how you stack your plate, paper, and books will influence your final print. Make sure you are placing the books on the paper side and not the gel plate side. Placing books on the gel plate side can cause the paper to buckle and wrinkle.

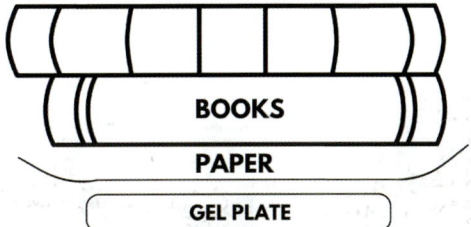

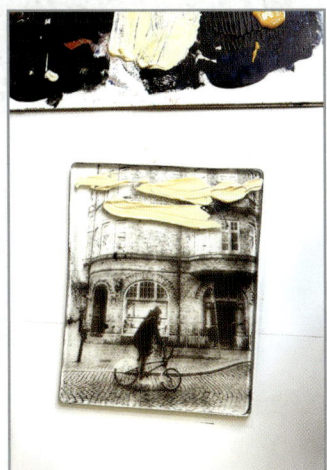 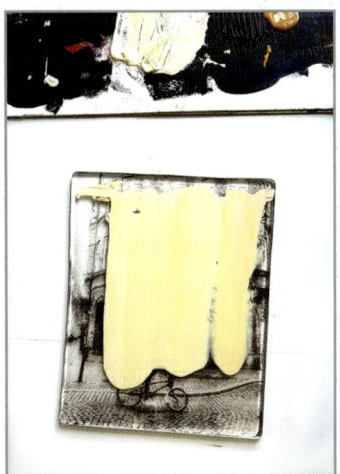 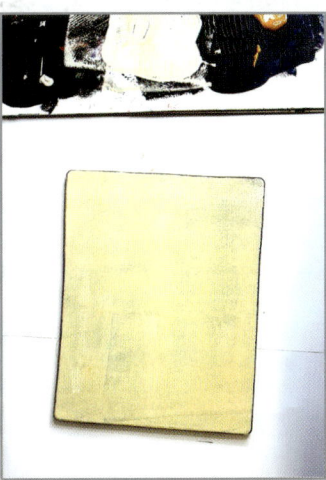

Here is the sequential process of covering your plate with the pickup layer. Sometimes I put the paint directly on the plate, as you see here, and then roll it on with a brayer. Look at how opaque this layer needs to be compared to the image transfer layer.

CAN YOU PULL IT OFF? THE GRAND REVEAL

The two most powerful warriors are patience and time.
— Leo Tolstoy, War and Peace

How long you'll need to wait before pulling your print depends on a mix of factors. First, there's the thickness of your paint. Heavier layers naturally need more time to dry. Next, consider your paper: Thicker or more absorbent types may require extra drying time. Don't forget your environment. High humidity can slow things down, but a dry room might speed it up. Finally, there's the wildcard I call the will of the printmaking gods. Even when everything seems perfect, your print might have a mind of its own. I have offered many a sacrificial brayer to the printmaking gods in hopes of better prints.

As a general rule, I let the books sit on the plate for at least 20 minutes. After that, I remove the books and allow the paper to dry naturally. Here's a pro tip: Gently run your hand over the back of the paper. The level of dampness will clue you in on whether it's ready or if it needs more time before you start to pull the paper off of the plate.

When it's dry, remove the paper with the same care as unwrapping a precious gift. Savor every moment of this. Start at one corner and peel slowly, paying close attention to any resistance. Try to roll the plate off of the paper rather than pull the paper off of the plate. If the paper clings in spots, use your fingertips to coax it free. If you discover areas that aren't fully dry, lay the paper back down, reapply the books, and give it more time. Rushing this step is the fastest way to compromise your results. That little bit of extra waiting can mean the difference between a good transfer and an exceptional one. Patience is your secret weapon here. Trust the process and resist the urge to hurry.

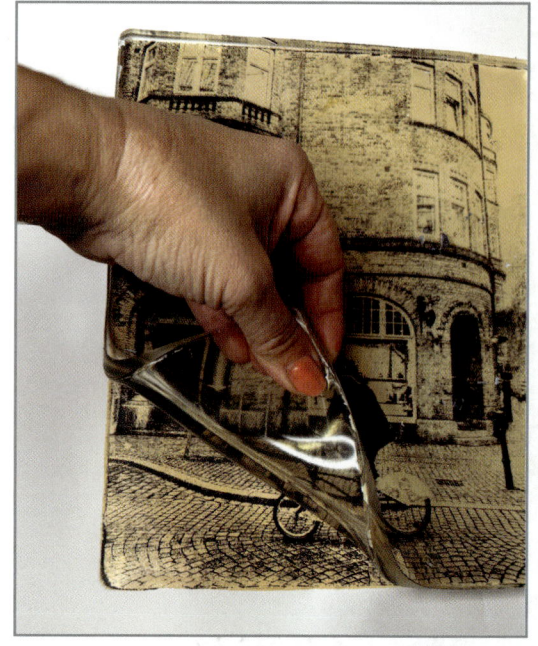

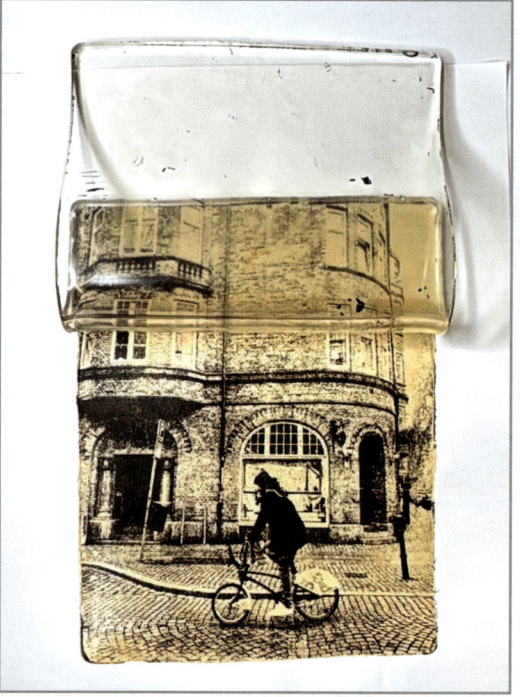

Roll the gel plate off of the paper slowly.

EMBRACE IMPERFECTION

I admit it. Calling this chapter "The Perfect Transfer" was a bit misleading. But now that you got this far in the chapter, there is no going back. The truth is perfection isn't the goal here. What really makes an image transfer special is its character. Those small inconsistencies, the unique textures from the paint, and even the quirks you didn't plan for—that's where the art happens. If we were after flawless reproductions, we could just photocopy the image onto colored paper and be done with it. But where's the fun in that?

If your image transfer isn't as perfect as you would like or perhaps it has too much "character" even after carefully following these steps, don't worry. Small adjustments can make a big difference. Tweak one variable at a time, like paint thickness, pressure, paper type, or timing, and observe how each change impacts the results. This method helps you pinpoint what works and makes your prints more predictable. And if all else fails, consider setting up a small altar to the printmaking gods. They might just smile upon your next attempt!

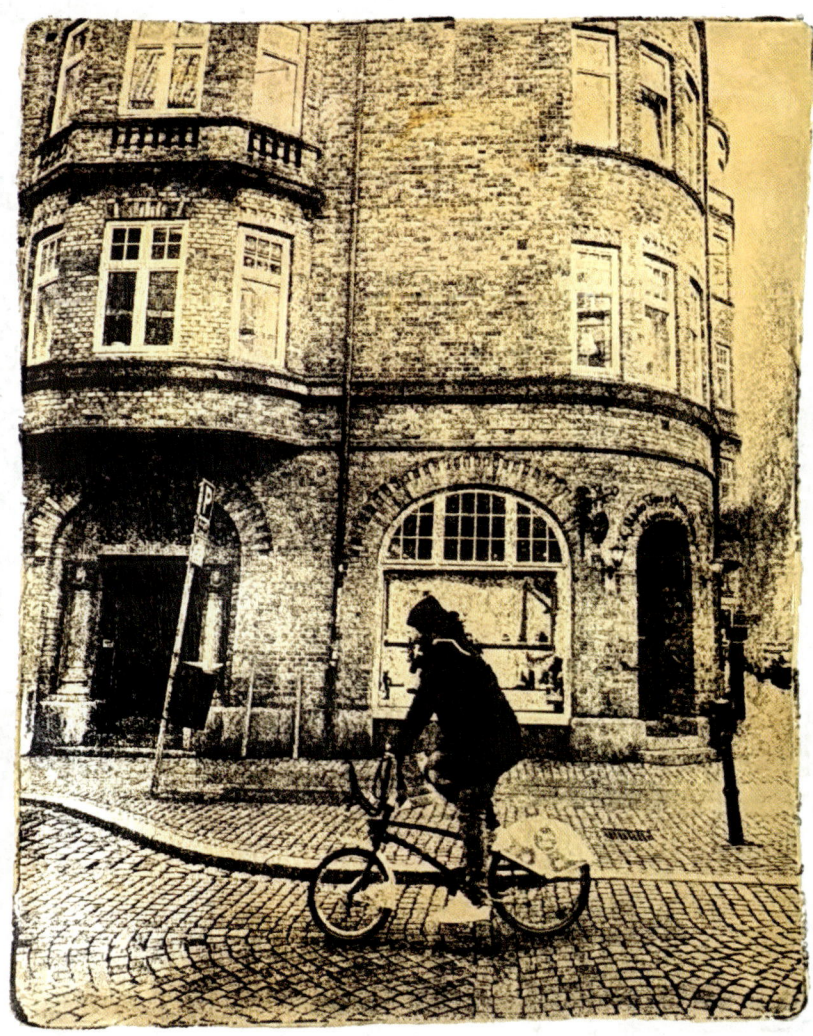

Here is the completed image transfer monotype using a gel plate.

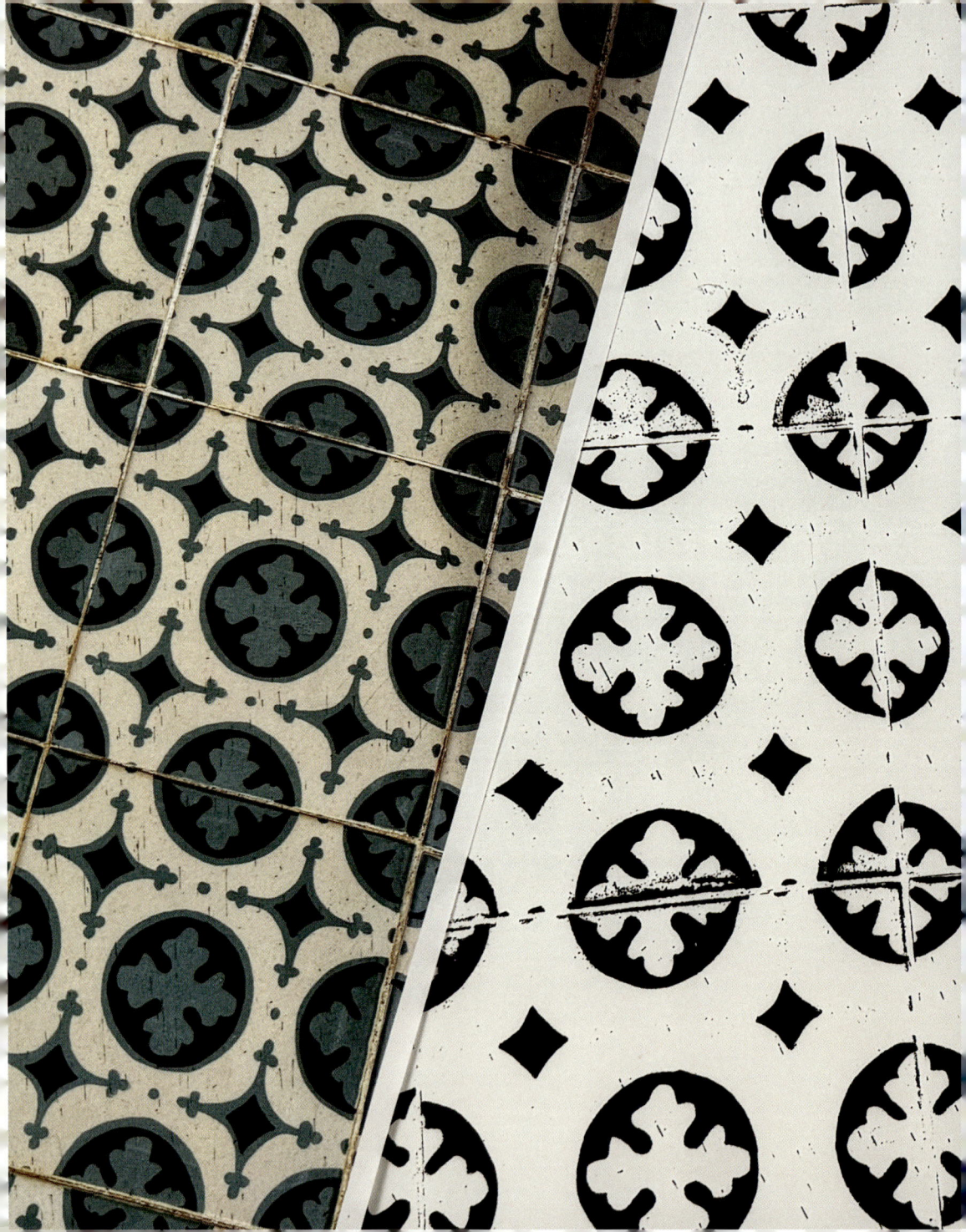

7
GETTING YOUR PHOTOS PRINT READY

If you're struggling to get a good image transfer, learning to edit your photographs isn't optional, it's essential. I'd argue that editing is just as important as the printing or transfer process itself. The subtle choices you make here, long before paint touches the gel plate, can be the difference between a detailed transfer and a frustrating one. In this chapter, I will walk you through a few editing methods and approaches. The tools you use might differ, but the goal is always the same: to prep your photo to make the best image transfers.

CHOOSING THE RIGHT PHOTO

You don't have to be a fortune teller to predict whether a photo will transfer well. Just be aware of the big three—resolution, subject, and contrast—when you choose your image.

HIGH RESOLUTION

Before anything else, start with a high-quality photo. If you're working with a low-resolution screenshot or something pulled from the internet, you're already at a disadvantage. To check whether your photo's resolution is high enough resolution, zoom in to 100%. If the photo still holds together without turning into pixels, you're in a good place. If not, it might be worth reshooting or choosing a different image.

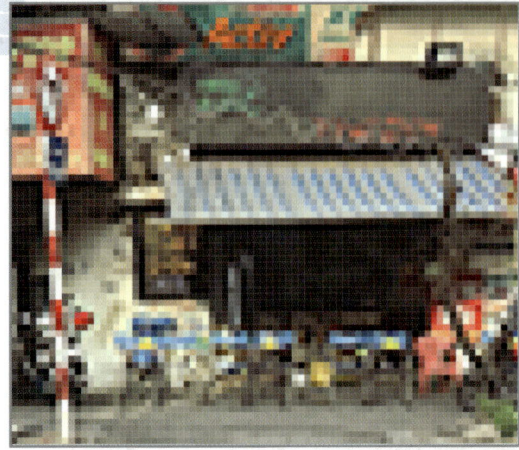

Figure 7-1 This is a good example of a pixelated image. It doesn't need to be this extreme though. Even small bits of blurriness or pixelation can influence your transfers.

SUBJECT MATTER

When you're just starting out, choose photos that are more forgiving, like the examples in Figures **7-2**, **7-3**, and **7-4**. Try using bold patterns. That way, if a photo doesn't transfer cleanly, it still feels intentional, like a distressed effect. If you jump straight into transferring a detailed portrait of your grandmother and her eye doesn't transfer, now you've got a real problem. You either have to fix it by hand-painting a new eye or consider adding a pirate patch. Either way, it's more pressure than it needs to be.

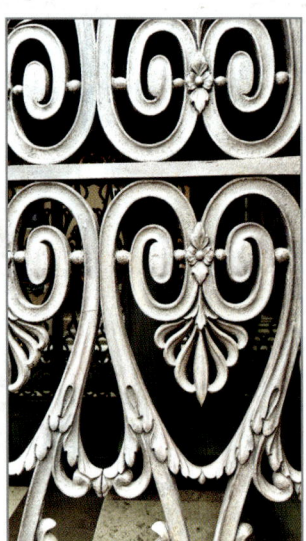 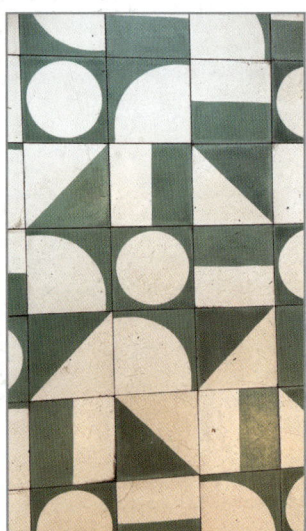 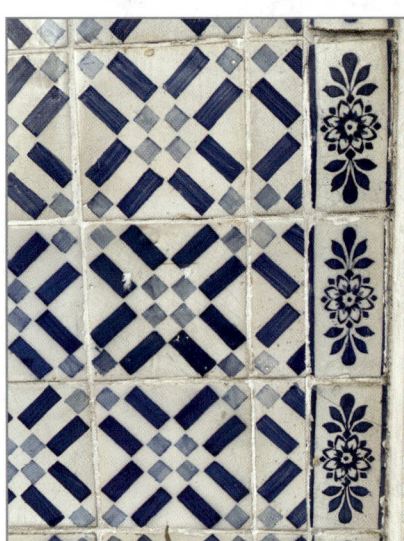

Figures 7-2 to 7-4

HIGH CONTRAST

Choose a photo that still reads clearly when pushed into high contrast. Some images lose important information in this process. Watch out for blown-out whites or deep chunk blacks eating up the details. Compare the example photo with a high-contrast version of it. The buildings still maintain their structure, but the photo is simplified enough that it can be transfered easier. If you're taking photos outside, try to avoid shooting in strong, direct sunlight. It can create harsh highlights and blown-out areas. Slightly overcast or cloudy days are ideal for capturing more balanced lighting, which helps your images translate into strong, high-contrast transfers.

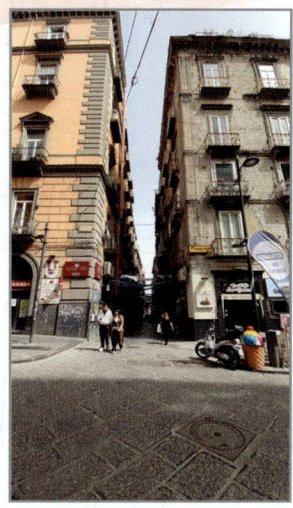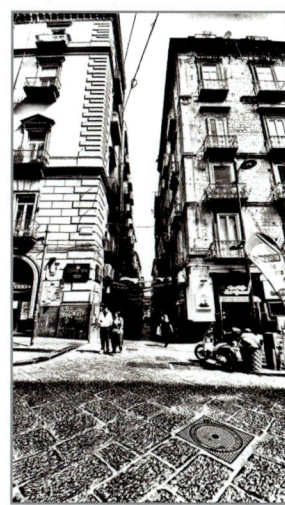

EDITING ISN'T ABOUT FANCY TOOLS

Most of the technical terms in the tools will be the same across apps. You can find plenty of editing apps out there, both paid and free. The tool you use isn't the point. What matters is knowing how to use what you have. Some of my best transfers started with quick edits on my phone. Others came from detailed work in Adobe Photoshop. There's no one right way. Each photo needs something different, and each image asks for its own approach. So, let's take a look at how I go about editing a couple of my photos. Remember, there's no universal formula here. Trust your eye, and adjust as needed.

EDITING ON A PHONE

Sometimes the tools built right into my phone are enough to transform a photograph into something ready for the gel plate. The key is understanding how to push the image so it holds together through the process. For this example, I worked with a photo I took in Siena, Italy, of the Cathedral of Santa Maria Assunta (**Figure 7-7**). When I took the photo, I had a feeling the structure and contrast of the architecture could translate well in an image transfer.

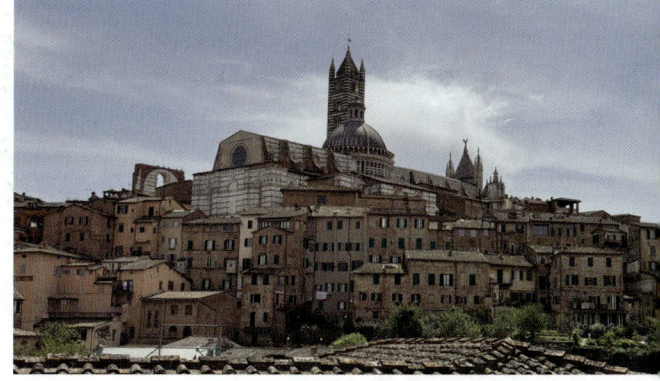

Figure 7-7

I started by scrolling through my photos to find the right shot. Once I settled on this photo, I cropped it to match the format of my gel plate (**Figure 7-8**).

Next, I converted the image to black and white. Most phones offer a few ways to do this. Sometimes I use a filter; other times I manually adjust the saturation. Desaturating the image removes the color evenly, but it doesn't allow much control over how the values shift. Using a black-and-white filter lets you get more specific and helps you determine how the red, blue, and green color channels translate into the grayscale spectrum. Sometimes, however, the filters are too heavy handed with the editing. Choose the option that will give you more drama, which is important for successful transfers (**Figure 7-9**).

After that, I began adjusting the individual settings. I moved between fine-tuning the brightness, black point, highlights, and exposure until the image felt right. I was after an image that retained its structure even when I pushed the contrast to its extremes. I wanted the darkest areas to remain grounded and the lightest ones to remain open (**Figures 7-10** to **7-13**).

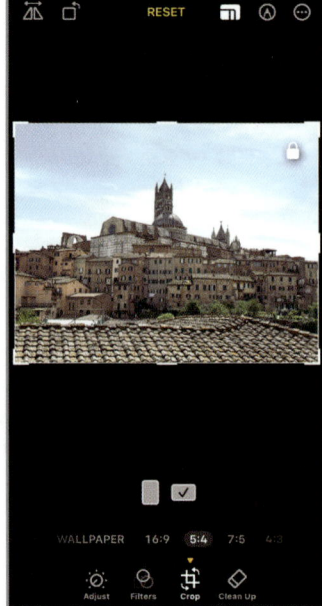

Figure 7-8

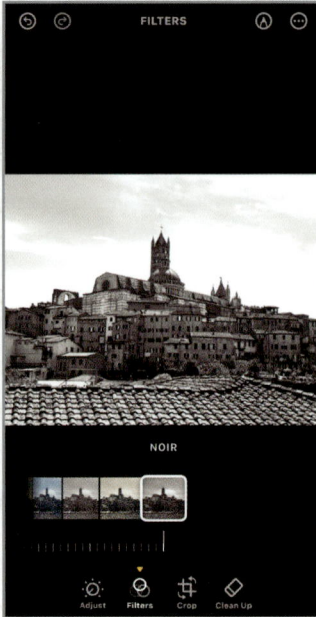

Figure 7-9

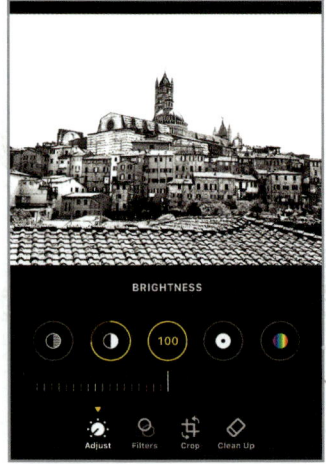

Figure 7-10: Adjusting brightness

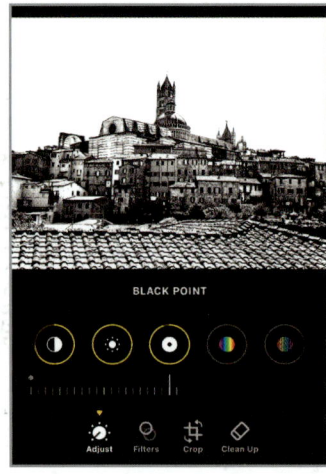

Figure 7-11: Adjusting black point

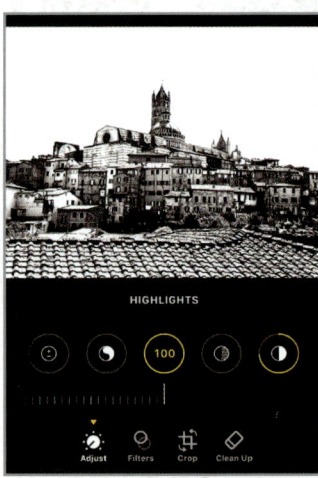

Figure 7-12: Adjusting highlights

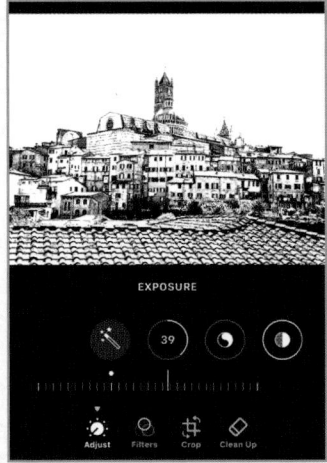

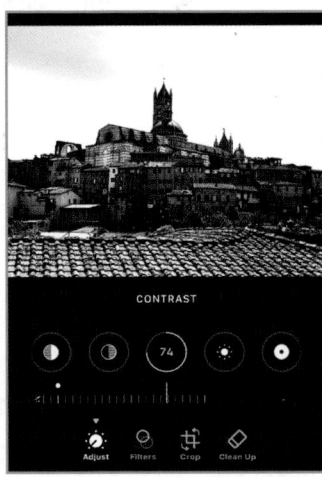

Left: If your photo looks like this, it may transfer poorly. The midtones are too muddy and won't transfer as middle grays but as blacks (if you are using black to transfer).

Figure 7-13: Adjusting exposure

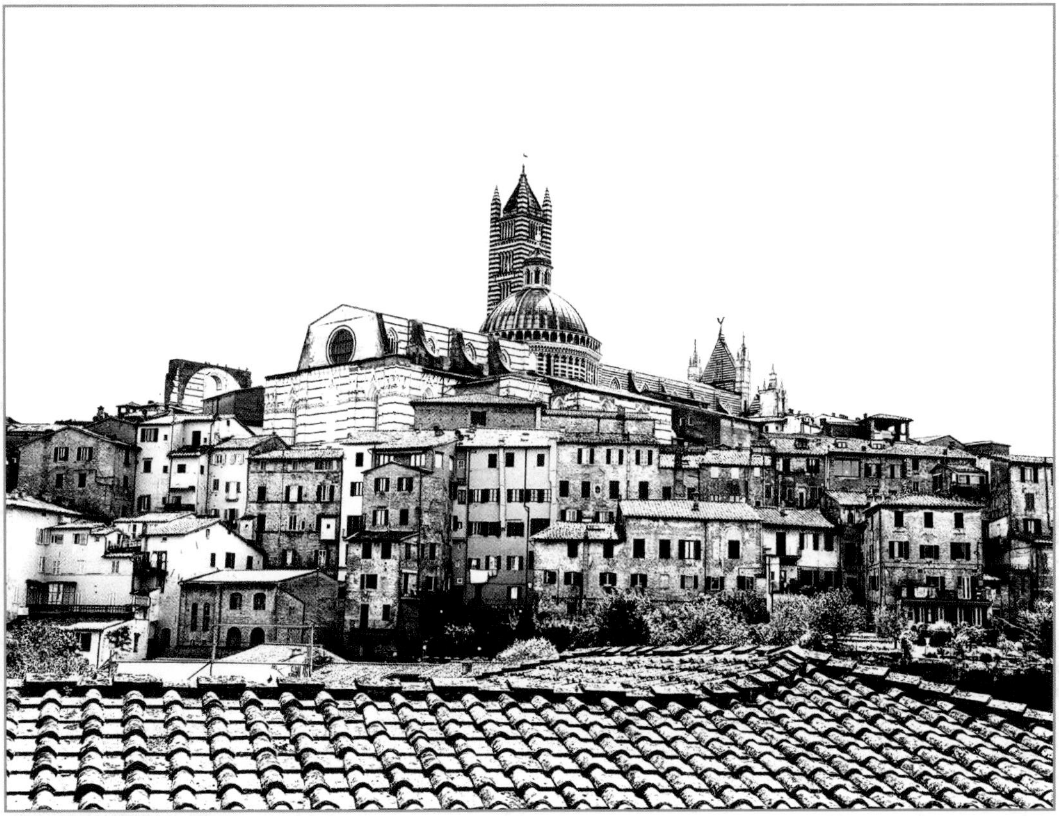

The final edited photo retains enough detail while still having rich blacks and bright whites. I look forward to making this the first image transfer that I do after finishing writing this book.

EDITING IN PHOTOSHOP

I started with a photograph of a tiled floor I took in Tam Cốc, Vietnam. I chose this photo because of its strong contrast and bold shapes. Even if parts of it failed to transfer during printing, the composition would still hold. To improve my chances of success, I decided to edit it in Adobe Photoshop.

The first step was adjusting the resolution and size. I changed the DPI to 300 and scaled the image without resampling, because resampling would stretch the pixels and compromise the integrity of the original photograph. I was aiming for a reorganization of the existing information—a reframing, not an artificial expansion.

I converted the image to grayscale in Photoshop, then used the Hue/Saturation adjustment, as I often do. This adjustment lets me remove color while keeping control over the values, so I can study the image without being distracted by hues. I was looking for the value structure and how light and dark played off one another, which I could adjust by using the Brightness and Contrast sliders.

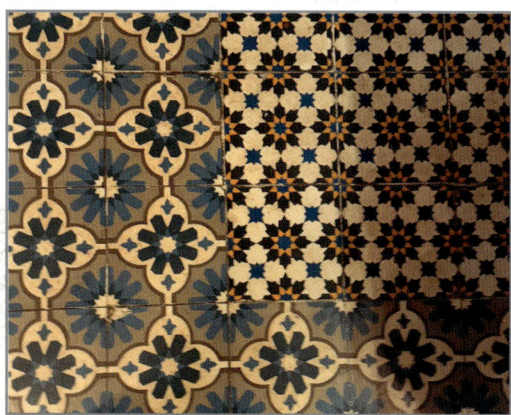

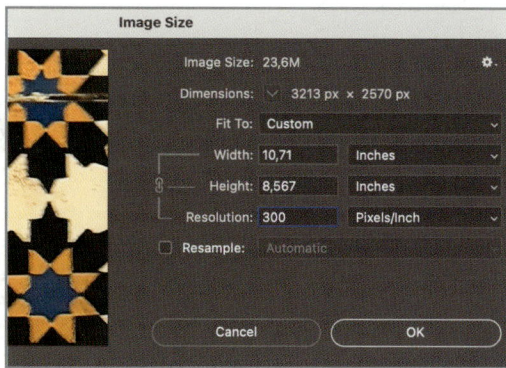

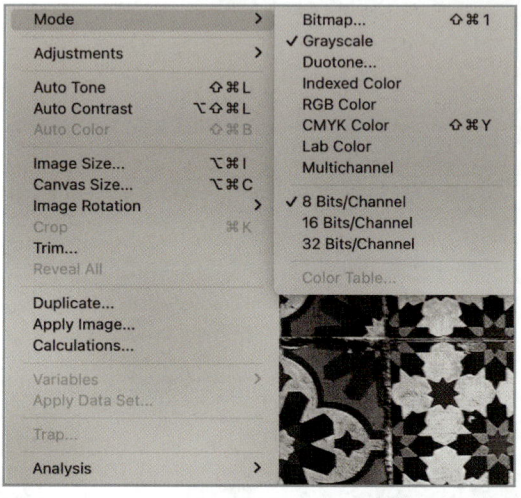

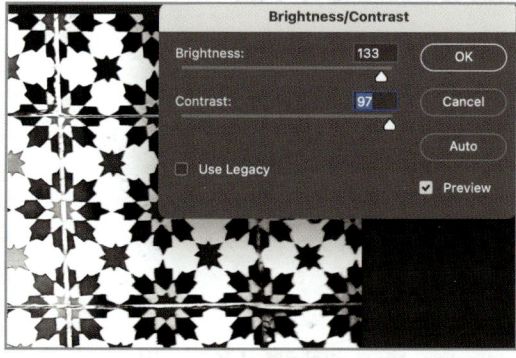

To further fine-tune the image, I used the Levels tool. Levels let me pull the darks deeper and push the lights brighter, adjusting the contrast until the image felt balanced and graphic. The Curves tool is also a good way to further tweak your photo. If I want to strip the image down to its bare essentials, just black and white with no midtones, I use Threshold.

It's a more extreme approach, but sometimes that starkness is exactly what the print needs.

The ultimate goal is to produce a print anchored by strong darks, with enough bright light areas to create contrast. A little more white space than black is ideal because you can always control lightness later during the painting phase.

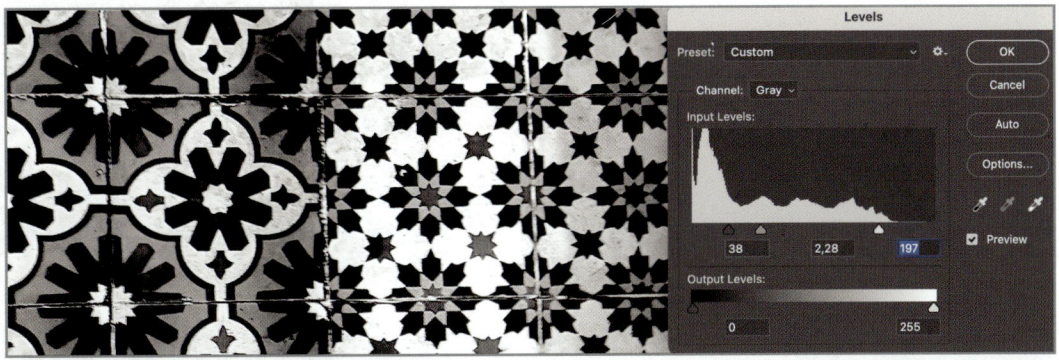

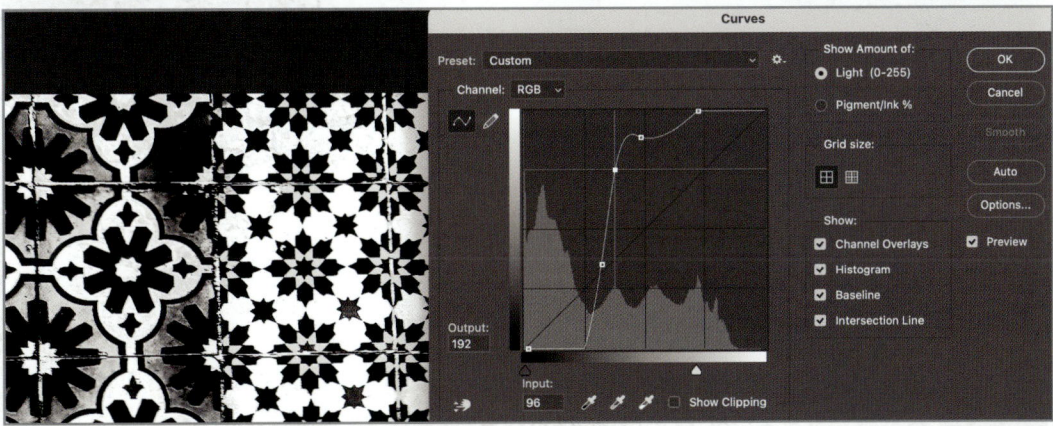

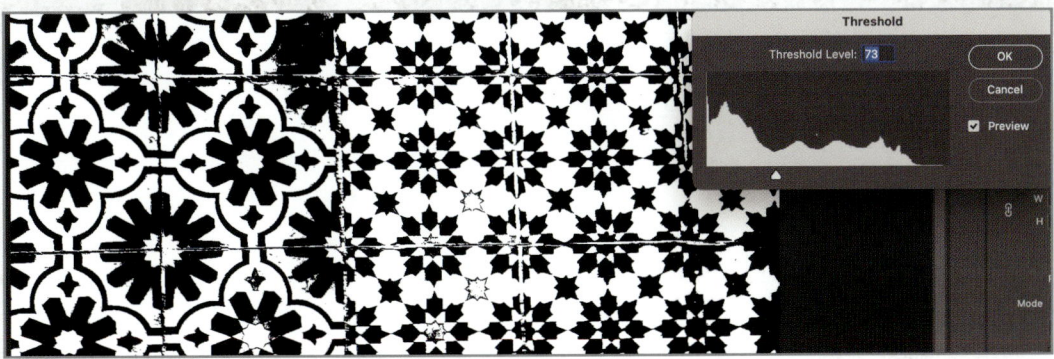

Halftones

Halftones simulate gradients using tiny dots of varying size and spacing. This classic printing technique translates continuous tones, like soft shadows or subtle highlights, into patterns the eye perceives as smooth shading.

For image transfers, halftones do more than just mimic value shifts. They actually lay down more toner, which strengthens the image's ability to transfer cleanly. The pattern itself can make a huge difference: The tiny spaces between the dots allow the acrylic paint to soak up into the printer paper. This often leads to cleaner, more consistent transfers, especially in areas that would otherwise go muddy.

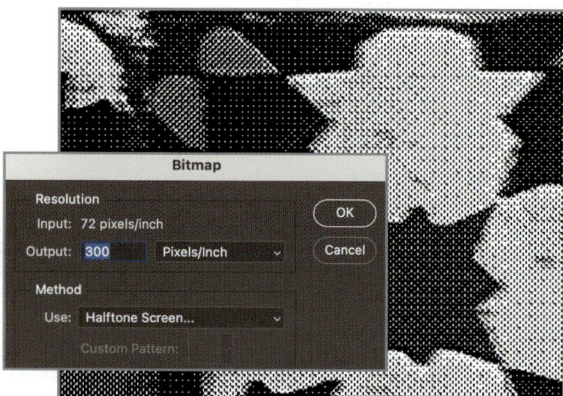

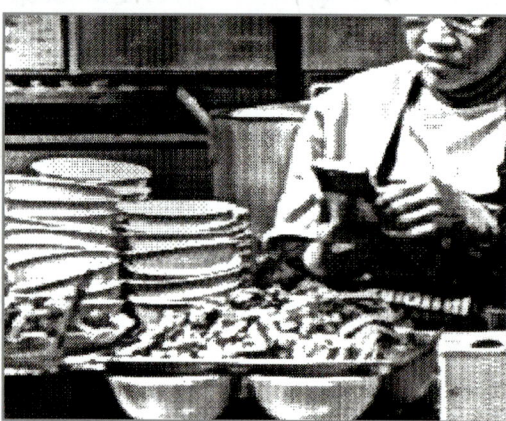

As you can see in this zoomed in detail of one of my photos, the tiny dots help fill in information that would be easily lost if I made this photo high contrast only.

So, When Should You Use Halftones?

I reach for Halftone Screen when I'm working with images that have a lot of detail or sit heavy in the midtone range. These middle grays are notoriously tricky in the transfer process. They often turn into dense black masses. The Halftone Screen method solves that by breaking those grays into distinct, transferable marks. It is a lot more effective. You're not losing the information; you're just translating it into something the process understands better. It preserves nuance without sacrificing clarity.

For example, I started with a photo that I took in Naples, Italy. Next, I transformed it into black and white, and I used the Halftone Screens method in Photoshop to maintain a level of detail in the midtones. What I was after wasn't just a duplicate of the original photo but rather a new artwork inspired by it. The final print is its own thing, and that's what makes the process so rewarding.

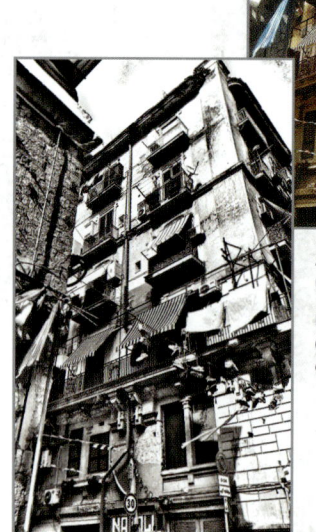

Above: The original photo, unedited.

Left: The edited photo (CMYK, Halftone Screen, edited in Photoshop).

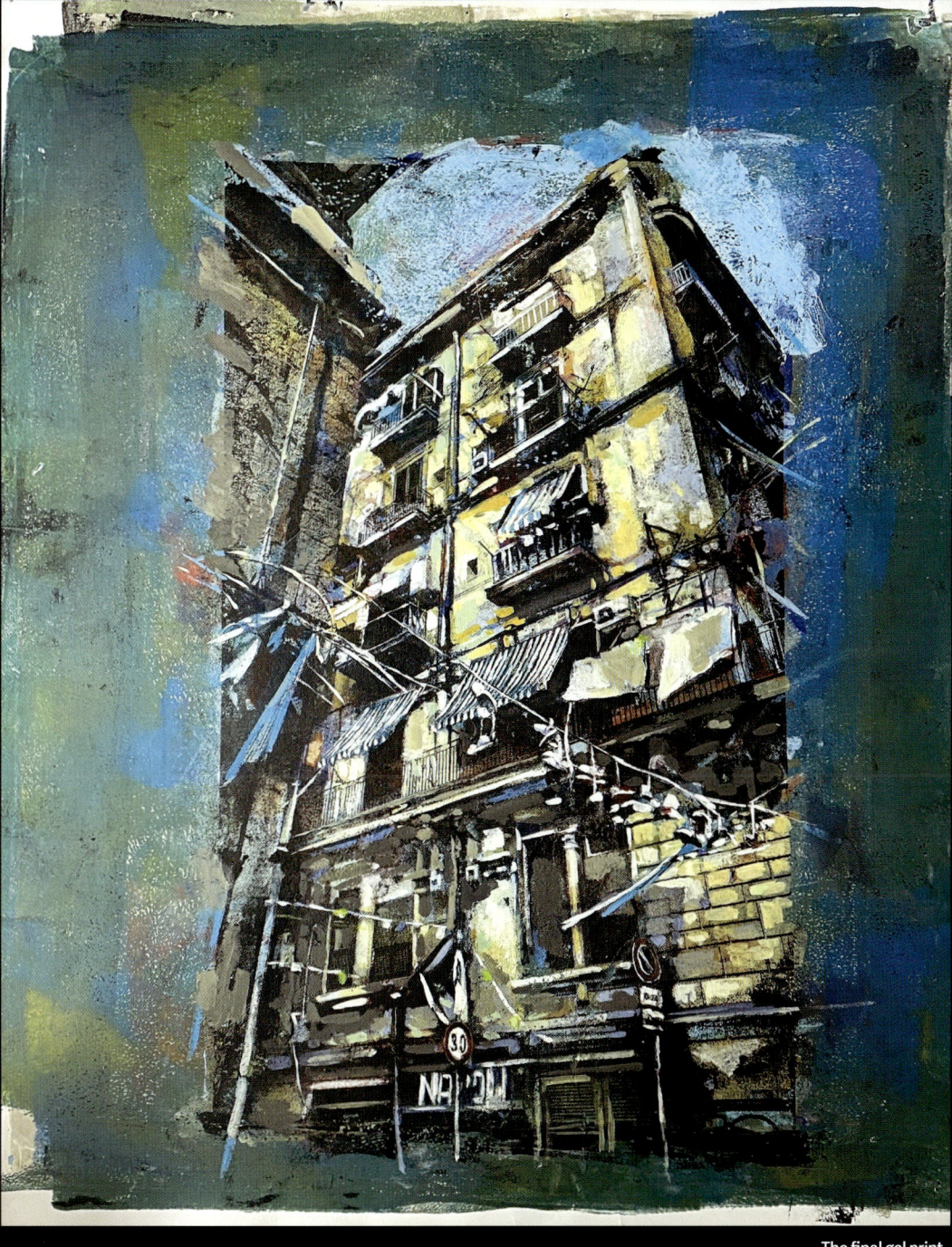

The final gel print.

PRINTERS

Why use a laser printer specifically? Their toner isn't just a pigment. It's a powder made of fine plastic particles. These tiny bits of polymer are what make laser prints behave so differently from inkjet prints. When a laser printer lays down toner, it uses heat to fuse those tiny plastic particles onto the paper. That heat-bonded toner becomes a physical layer on the surface, not something absorbed into the paper like the ink from an inkjet printer. When you later press that printed image face down onto a gel plate covered with acrylic paint, the toner acts as a resist.

CHOOSING THE RIGHT PAPER

Use uncoated bond or standard printer paper. Glossy or coated papers resist toner, rarely work well for transfers, and could potentially damage your gel plate. Likewise, avoid heavily textured or recycled papers, which often lead to uneven toner coverage. Weights of 80–160 gsm are ideal for image transfers. Such paper is light enough to release toner but strong enough to handle the process. You *can* go up to 200 gsm for a heavier feel, but it may take more pressure and longer drying time. Even small changes in paper type can affect your transfer. Try a few and see what suits your process.

Although my photos are in black and white, I print them out in CMYK color. CMYK printing uses four toner cartridges: cyan (C), magenta (M), yellow (Y), and black (K). When you print an image in color, the printer carefully combines these powders to reproduce the tones and shades in your photo. Even black areas in a color print are a mix of all four colors, not just black toner. I like to print my photos in color because this method lays down more toner, creating a stronger area to create that resist. Black-and-white printing, by contrast, uses only the black (K) toner cartridge, which lays down solid black toner without mixing in any other colors.

No matter what printer you use, check its settings to ensure that enough toner is being laid down. Make sure you are not printing in economy or toner-saving mode. These settings help conserve toner but will sabotage the quality of your transfer. You want maximum toner coverage in the darker areas. Some printers offer settings for high-density or transparency modes that push more toner onto the paper, giving you a richer print. If you are still not getting dense enough toner coverage on your prints, try double printing: Print your photo, then place the paper back in the machine and reprint the image. This way, you have double the amount of toner on your page.

The more toner that's on the paper, the more that plastic layer is available to resist in your transfer. High-density print settings, double printing, and printing in color (CMYK) all add more toner—hence more plastic to the paper—and improved results.

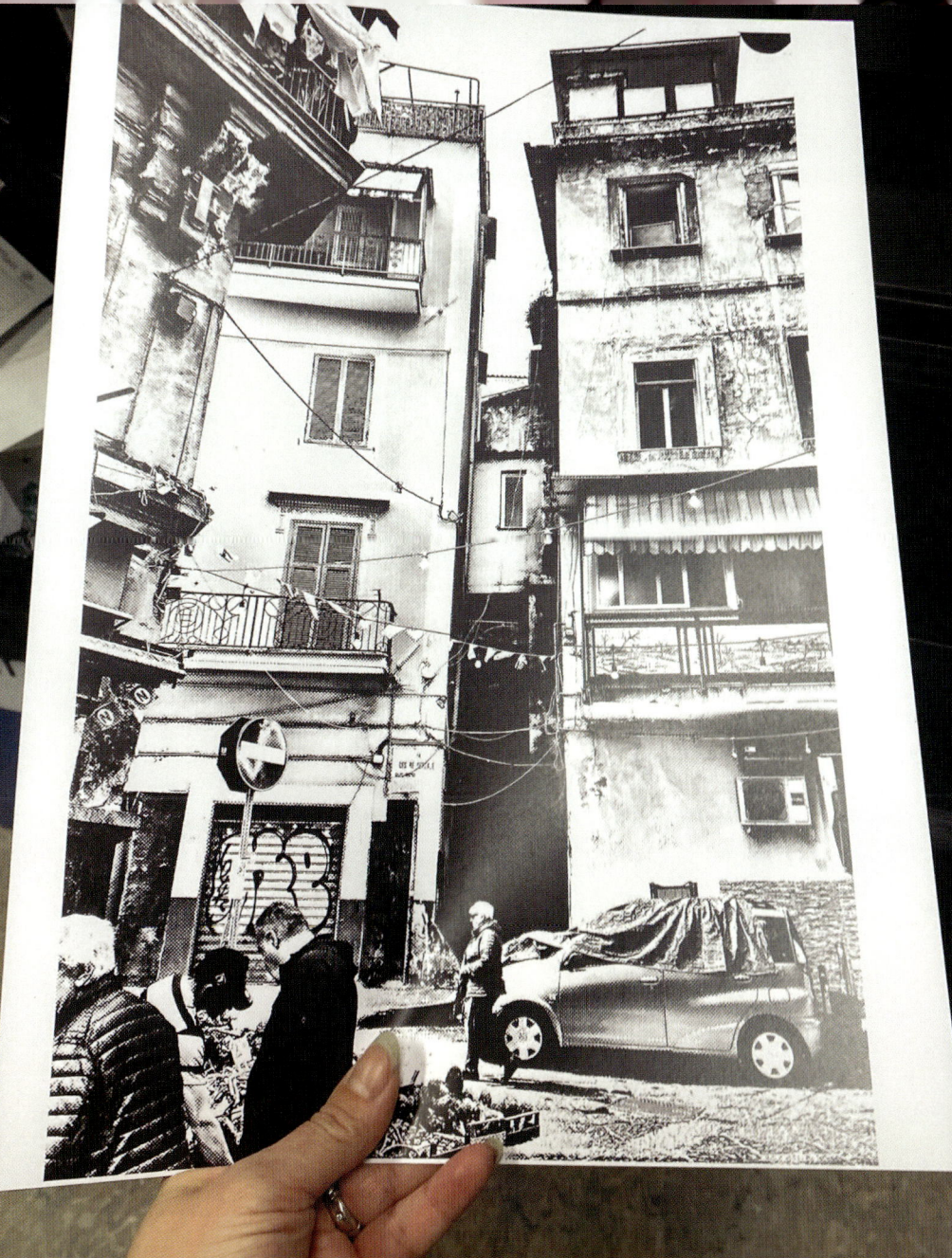

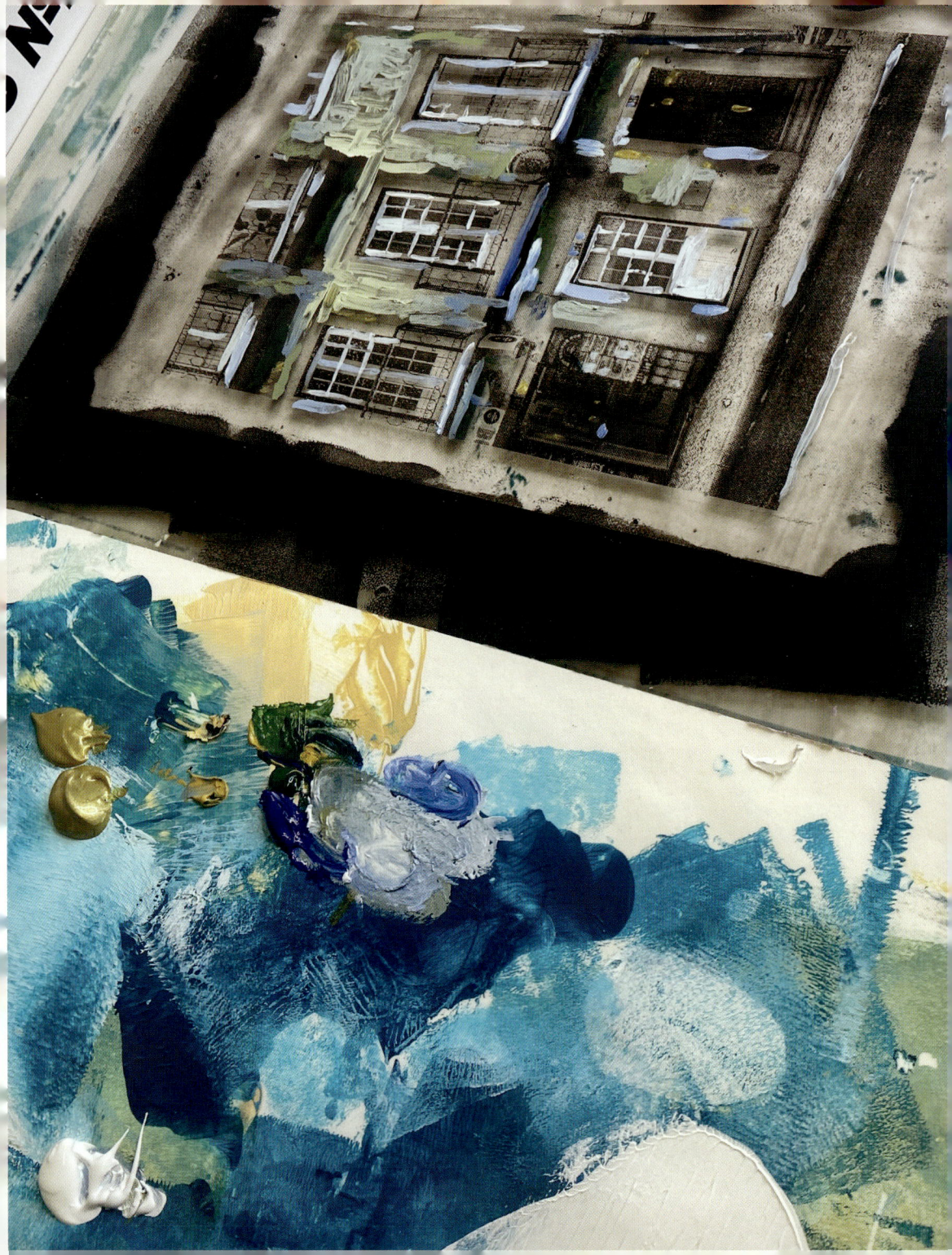

8
REVERSE PAINTING

Why limit yourself to just the transfer layer and the pickup layer when there is so much room for color and expression in between? If you want your image transfers to feel more painterly, layered, and deliberate, reverse painting is worth exploring. This method applies the same core principles of traditional painting but in a new order, allowing you to rethink how color, opacity, and texture interact beneath the surface of your final print.

Because much of the process happens face-down on the plate, there is always a degree of surprise when you lift the print. Once you become comfortable with the rhythm of reverse painting, however, it starts to open up new ways of thinking and making.

In this chapter, I'll guide you through how I approach the process, starting with an image transfer, and then working through palette decisions and color layering that build mood and structure. I'll also show you how these same foundational ideas can scale into more complex compositions. Finally, we'll look at how to select a pickup layer that enhances the overall piece, allowing just the right amount to come through and unify the print.

THINKING IN REVERSE

As the name suggests, reverse painting works in the opposite manner from traditional painting. In traditional painting, you typically start with a base or underpainting, block in shadows and highlights, build in your midtones, and finish with details. Reverse painting flips that on its head. Whatever you lay down first will be the top layer of your final print. Each additional layer sits behind the last, working backward from fine detail to broad background. After the image transfer is in place, you can lay in delicate

details with small brushes. These little pops of color sit on top of the surface when the print is pulled. Ready to see this in action? Follow me through a typical project.

I photographed some azulejo tiles while visiting Sintra, Portugal, a place where decorative tilework seems to cover every available surface, from palace walls to quiet city paths. The tiles I chose for the print have a stylized botanical motif, with interlacing shapes that suggest leaves, petals, and pine cones.

There's an elegance in the symmetry that I love. I edited the photograph to increase its contrast, which made the design bolder and more graphic, then I printed it using a CMYK laser printer to lay down more toner on the page (see right).

For the transfer, I used Black Oxide. With my hand I applied even pressure across the back of the print out and lifted it a few seconds later. Once the transfer was completely dry, I applied a thin layer of gel medium across the plate. This step helped the paint adhere smoothly and evenly, setting the stage for the subsequent reverse painting process.

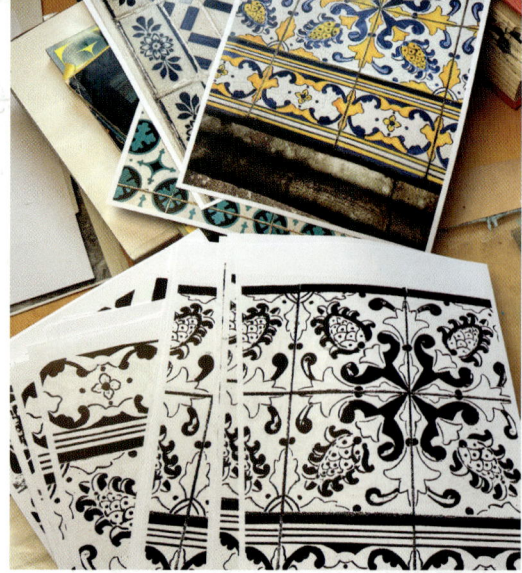

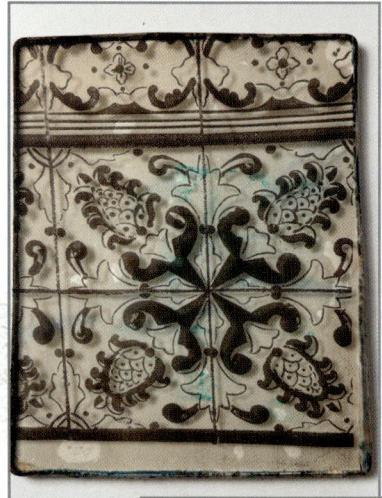

Although the tile came from Portugal, I wanted to reinterpret it through a different lens, one shaped by my years living in Florence, Italy. After nearly a decade in Tuscany, I've developed a strong connection to the region's color palette, full of earthy warmth and sun-soaked tones. To reflect that, I introduced warmer hues, especially Burnt Sienna, which helped shift the mood away from the original source and gave the image a new story to tell.

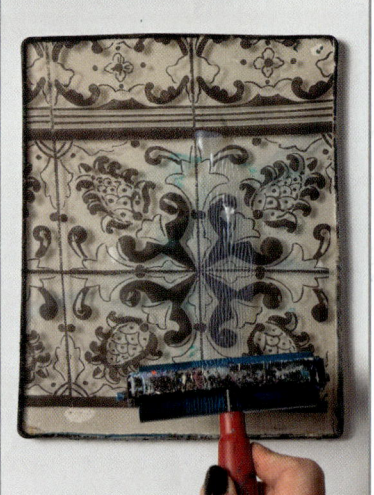

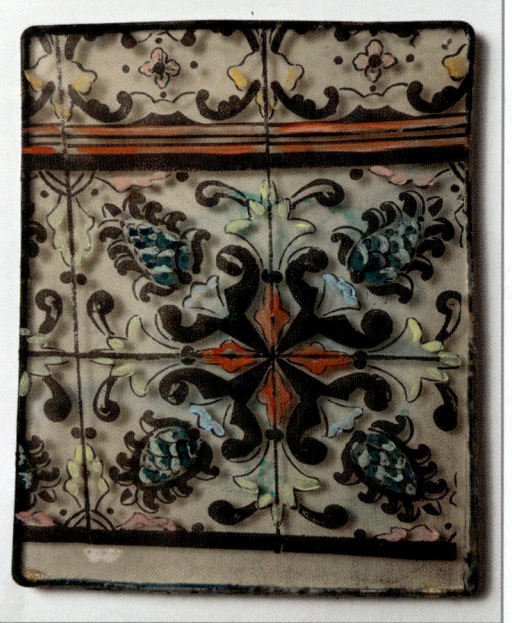

I worked around the tile, finding the small bits and detail areas first. Using a small brush, I started by adding lighter tints of Naples Yellow, Phthalo Turquoise, and Ultramarine Blue to pop as the highlights of the tile. I used a painterly approach, not just filling in shapes like a coloring book. I looked for places where I could intentionally build form through shading, such as those pine-cone-like Phthalo-Green shapes. I added a lighter Phthalo Turquoise on one side of each petal and a darker value on the opposite side to create depth, as if light is falling across them.

I continued to build color throughout the plate, adding whites and lighter hues to the tile's background, intentionally letting some areas overlap or spill beyond the lines. The overlap gives the final print a more expressive, organic quality. When painting, I don't always apply one complete layer before starting the next. Some areas have more buildup than others, depending on the details required for that part of the image. I do, however, let each layer dry before adding more paint on top.

Choosing when and where to let the pickup layer peek through can create subtle harmony in your work. It becomes a kind of underpainting, shifting the entire mood of the piece depending on its color. A warm tone will warm up the whole print. A cooler one will cool everything down. A bright tone will boost saturation, while a darker pickup will mute things a bit. Want to control that effect? You can apply a more opaque layer behind key shapes to protect them from the pickup's influence, giving you more contrast and clarity in those areas.

I added an additional layer of paint behind the cone shapes. This helped block out the pickup layer underneath so it wouldn't alter the tone of those specific shapes. In contrast, I left gaps around the edges of the tile, intentionally letting the pickup color show through. These areas act almost like glue, visually tying the piece together and creating unity and harmony.

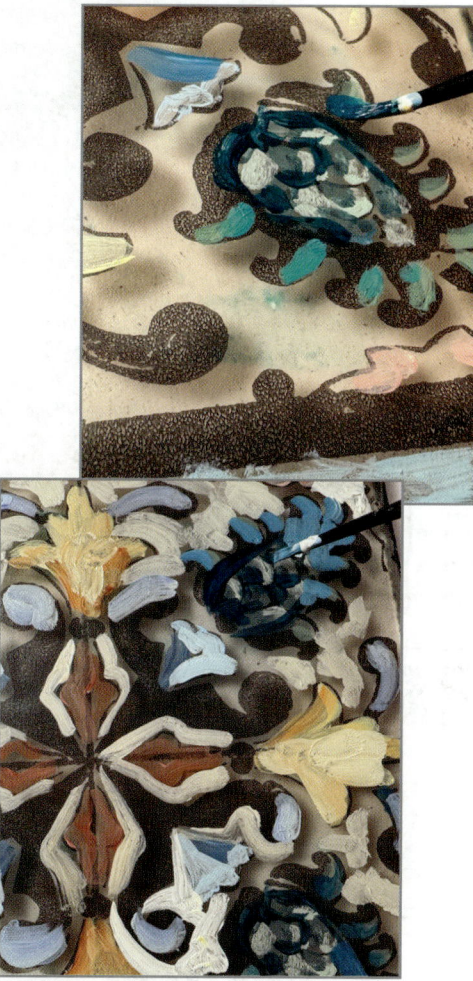

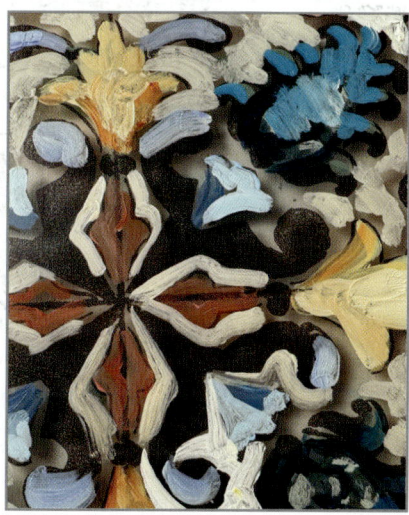

For reverse painting, I typically use a slightly thicker pickup layer than I would for a standard image transfer. You want this last layer to fully cover everything beneath it and adhere evenly. Work quickly so you can press your paper into it while it's still workable.

For this print, I used Bristol paper (250 gsm) and let it sit under two heavy books for about 25 minutes. It was a chilly night in my studio, so I worried it might not be ready, but when I tested the edge, it lifted beautifully and cleanly from the plate.

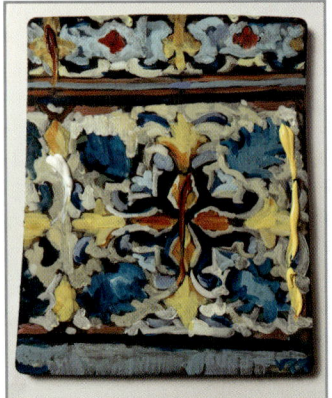
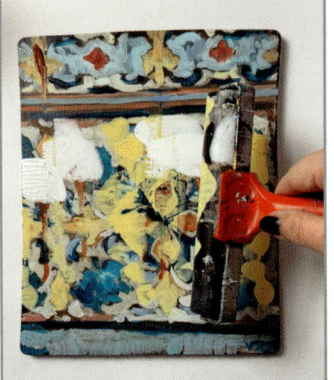
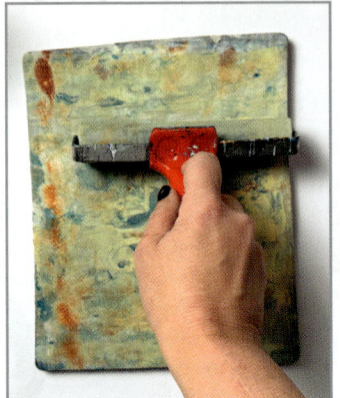

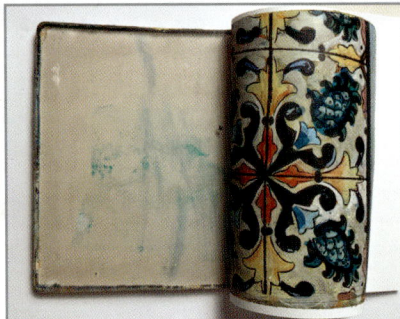
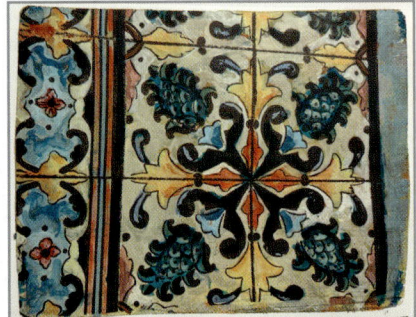

You can get a lot of mileage out of one photograph, depending on your color choices and how you approach painting it. Here is the same tile done with an image transfer in light blue and a slightly darker blue as the pickup layer printed on craft paper.

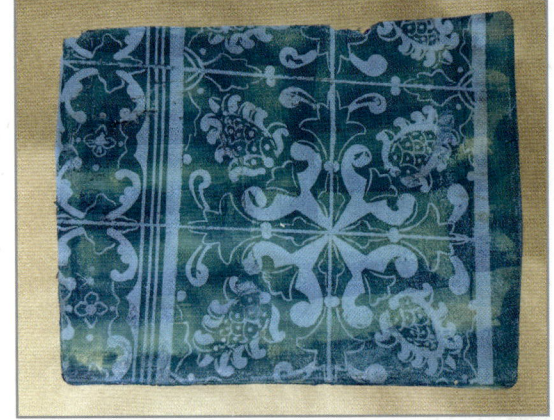

MAKE THAT BRUSH WORK

No matter what image you're reverse painting, the approach stays the same: Start with the finer details and gradually build up with broader brushstrokes. Because your strokes will be visible in the final print, however, you can use them to your advantage as a way to add texture, direction, and energy to the piece (below).

Consider this early evening scene of the Phú Quốc Night Market, for example. I paid attention to the direction of my brushstrokes, especially in the sky. I twirled my brushstrokes onto the plate, leaving the paint in more defined strokes angling through the sky. You can still see them clearly in the final print, giving the scene a sense of movement and atmosphere.

Try to avoid fully blending your colors on the brush before applying them. When you leave slight variations in each stroke, the paint carries a bit more energy. This can create a subtle impasto-like effect that adds depth and richness to your print. Even small shifts in hue within a single brushstroke can bring the surface to life and keep the image from feeling too flat or overworked.

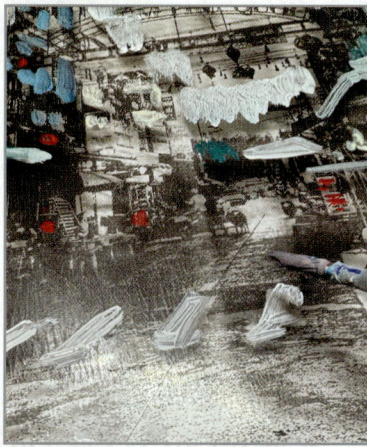

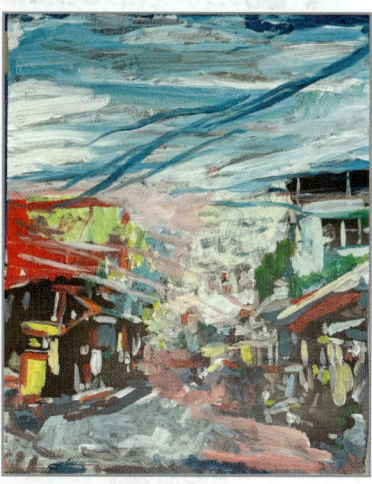

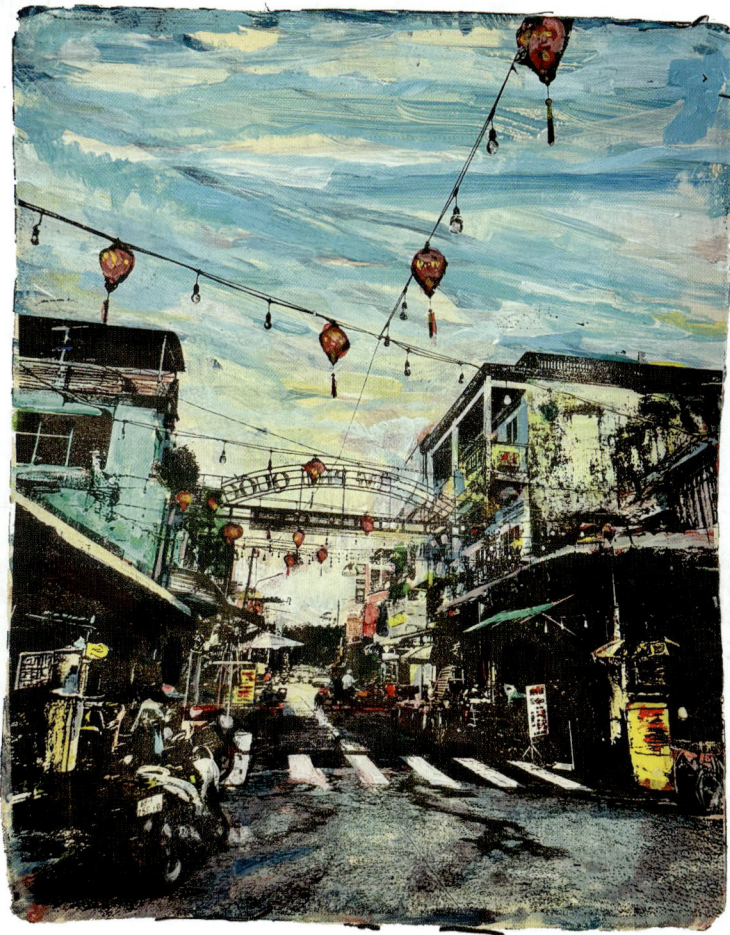

LEVEL UP YOUR LAYERS

This same reverse painting method can work beautifully on more detailed transfers. For example, I used this technique on a photo I took in Naples, Italy (below). I edited it with a halftone effect and high contrast in CMYK, then transferred it onto my 16 × 20-inch gel plate.

This image had way more going on, especially in the foreground, with layers of trash and street detail, so I spent a lot of time working from the original photo, carefully mapping out the visual story with color and brushwork. Even though it's a bigger piece, I approached it the same way: First, I worked on

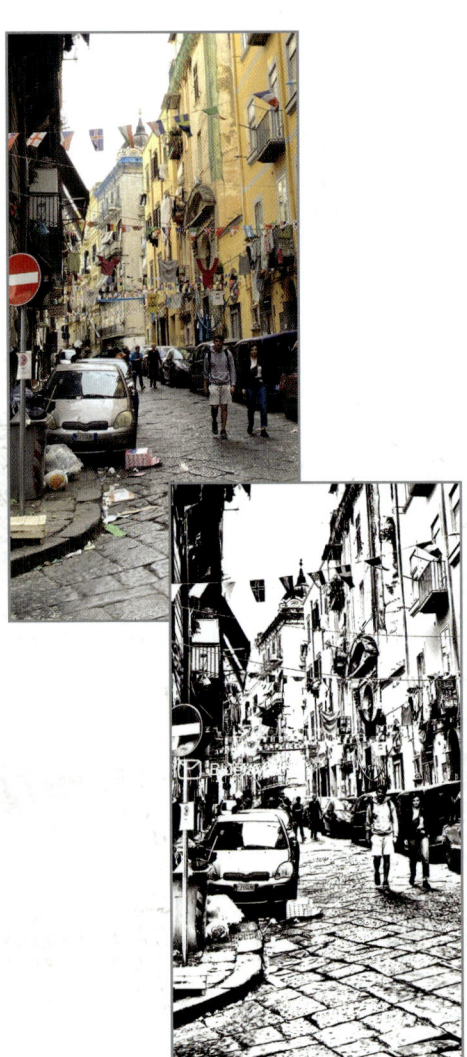

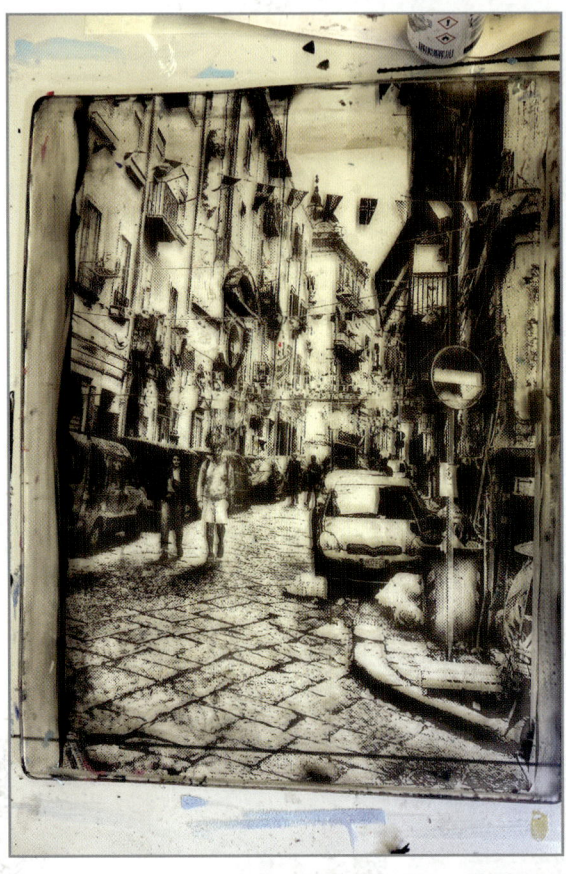

small details, then gradually built up the colors and broader shapes behind them. I worked around the entire composition rather than focusing on one area at a time. This is very much how I approach traditional painting on canvas. I added bits of blue throughout the composition to create some unity in the final print.

The image on the next page shows another print that I did with a similar approach and color palette.

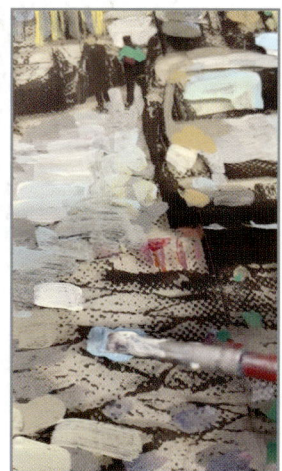

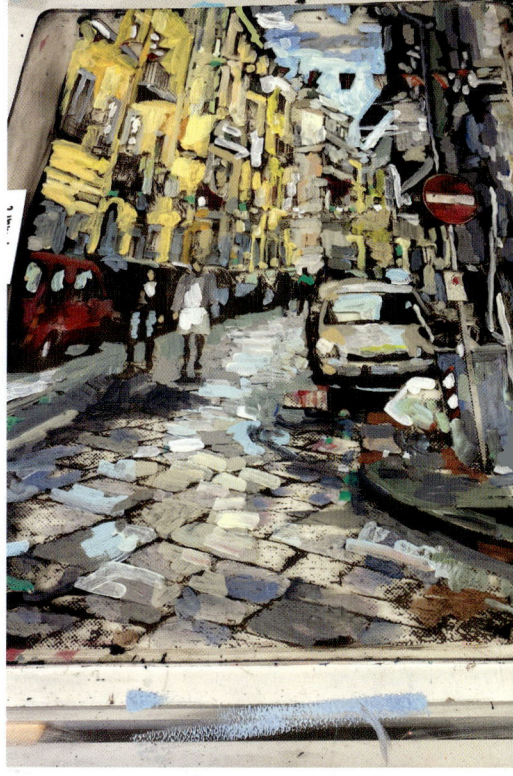

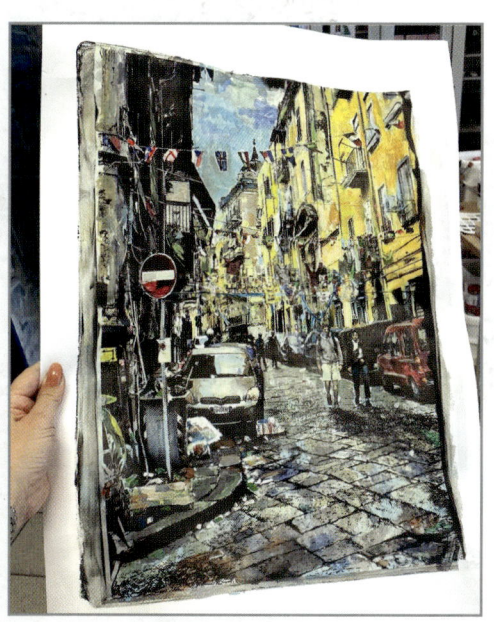

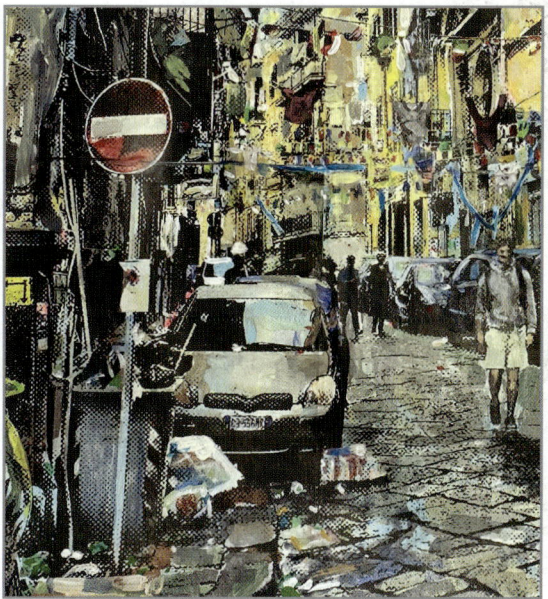

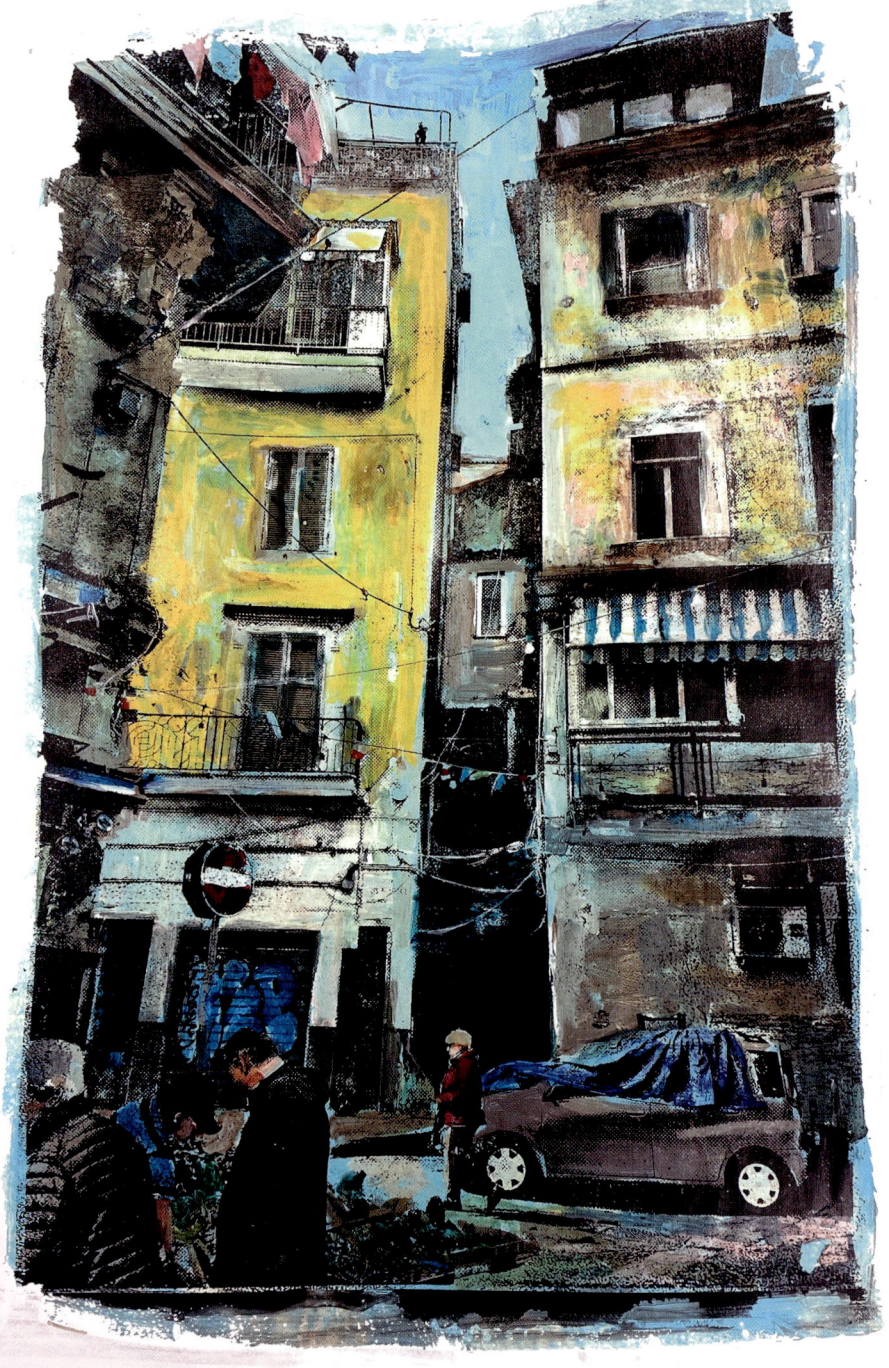

WHICH WAY IS UP?

It's totally normal to get a little turned around during the transfer process, and often, the final print turns out different than what you expected. Let me show you what I mean.

For this project, I started with a photo I took of the Hotel Poker in Naples, Italy. It's right across from the best pastry place I've ever eaten at, and I wanted to bring some energy and color into the print, even though the building itself was in fairly neutral tones. What I really wanted to capture was the vibrancy of the neighborhood, the constant line of people snaking around the corner, waiting for their number to be called so they could pick up their *sfogliatelle*.

The below left image shows what it looked like at the start of the reverse painting. I intentionally left some rough, raw edges around the sides of the transfer to let the city's texture come through. Naples has a way of making even grit feel inspiring.

Next, you can see the reverse painting as I was finishing it up (see below). I used tints of earthy yellow, warm blues, and magentas softened with white. Although it looks very pastel at this stage, the black from the image transfer will be the top layer of this print, and that will change the color relationships a bit by adding more contrast to the composition.

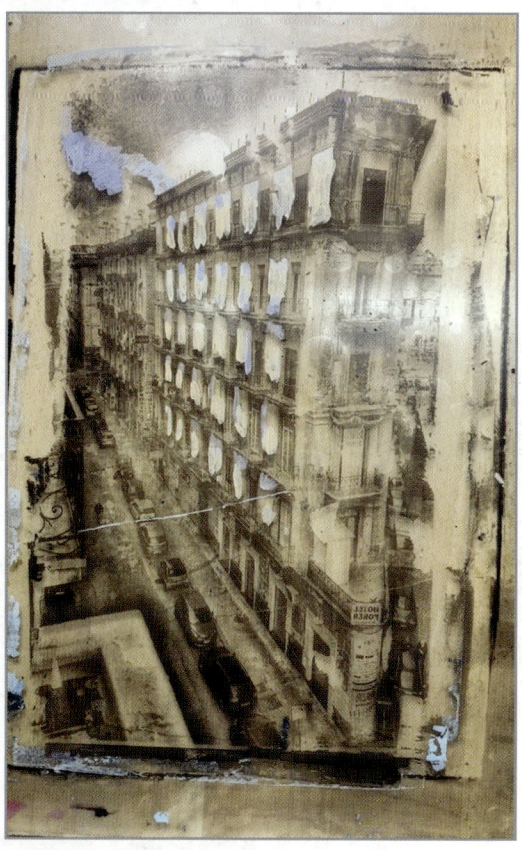

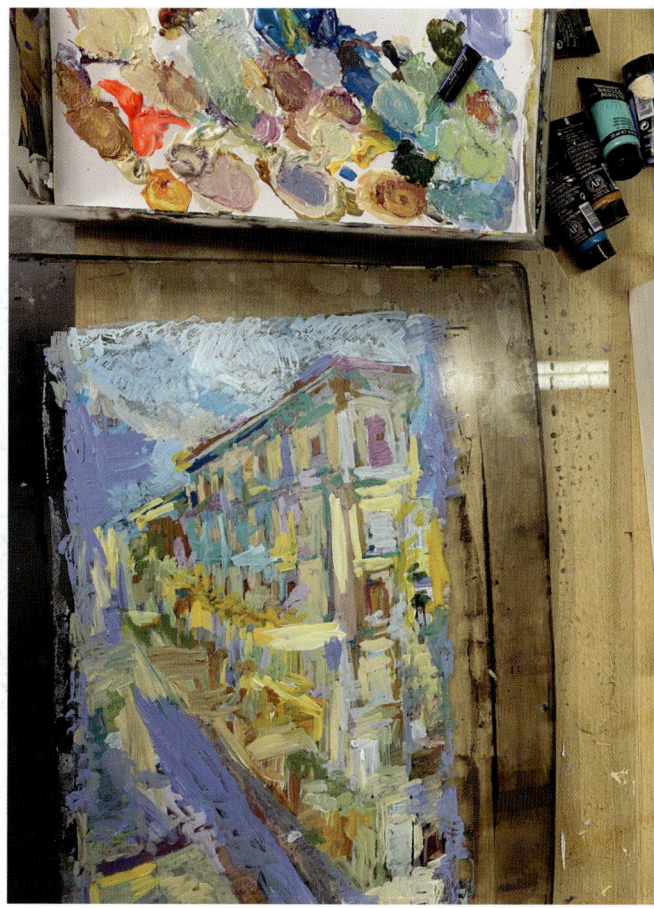

At this stage, I lifted the gel plate, which I had placed on a large sheet of acetate, so I could peek underneath and get a better sense of how things were coming together. This trick helps me decide which areas still need work before I move on to the pickup layer. Because the gel plate isn't totally transparent, the look of the colors is a bit dull. The view gives you a rough idea, but not the full picture.

To keep the palette feeling bright and energized, I added a mostly Cerulean Blue pickup layer. The pickup layer filled in the gaps between the sky and buildings and influenced all the colors already laid down on the plate.

Look at the final print after I pulled it off the plate. See how the colors shift, the textures change, and unexpected details emerge. That's all part of the process! Those little surprises are what make the reveal so satisfying.

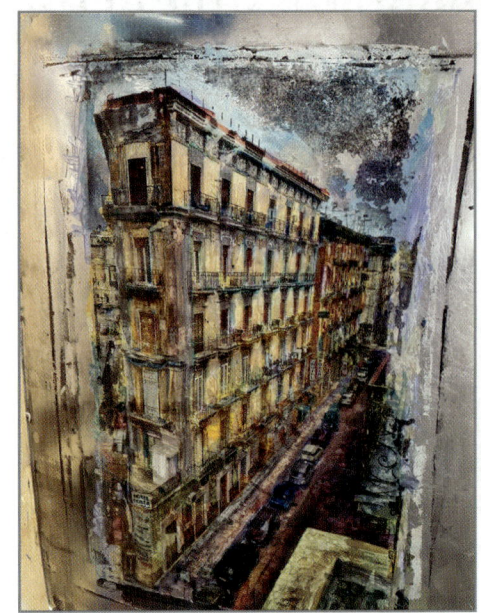

TOP FIVE TIPS FOR COLOR HARMONY

1. Stick to a Limited Color Palette.
Choose two to four colors that work well together and mix variations of those. Limiting your palette prevents things from getting muddy and creates visual cohesion, even when layering lots of textures or transfers. Look back at Chapter 4, "Making Colors Work for You," to get a better understanding of color relationships. Try working with analogous colors (colors next to each other on the color wheel) like blue, blue-green, and green for an easy, natural harmony.

2. Use a Mother Color.
Mix a touch of one base color into all the other paints you're using to create a subtle thread that ties everything together—even if your palette is diverse. For example, adding a little Burnt Sienna to each color can warm up the whole composition and keep it feeling unified. I do this in all my work. It mostly starts from me not washing my brush fully, but in the end, it works really well to create a more unified palette. If you overdo it, though, you could end up with muddy colors. Balance is key.

3. Repeat Colors in Different Layers.
Echo a color from your background in your transfer, or repeat a bold hue from one corner in another part of the piece. Repetition creates rhythm, and rhythm builds harmony. Even if a color shows up as only a faint ghost layer or edge bleed, it still counts!

4. Balance Warm and Cool Tones.
Too many warm colors can feel overwhelming, and too many cool colors can feel flat. Playing with both gives your work depth and vibrancy. If your transfer is cool-toned (like blue or purple), try a warm pickup layer or paper tone to balance it.

5. Be Intentional with Neutrals.
Don't underestimate the power of a soft white, gray, or even Buff Titanium. Neutrals give the eye a place to rest and help other colors shine. They can also pull together seemingly unrelated colors by acting as a bridge.

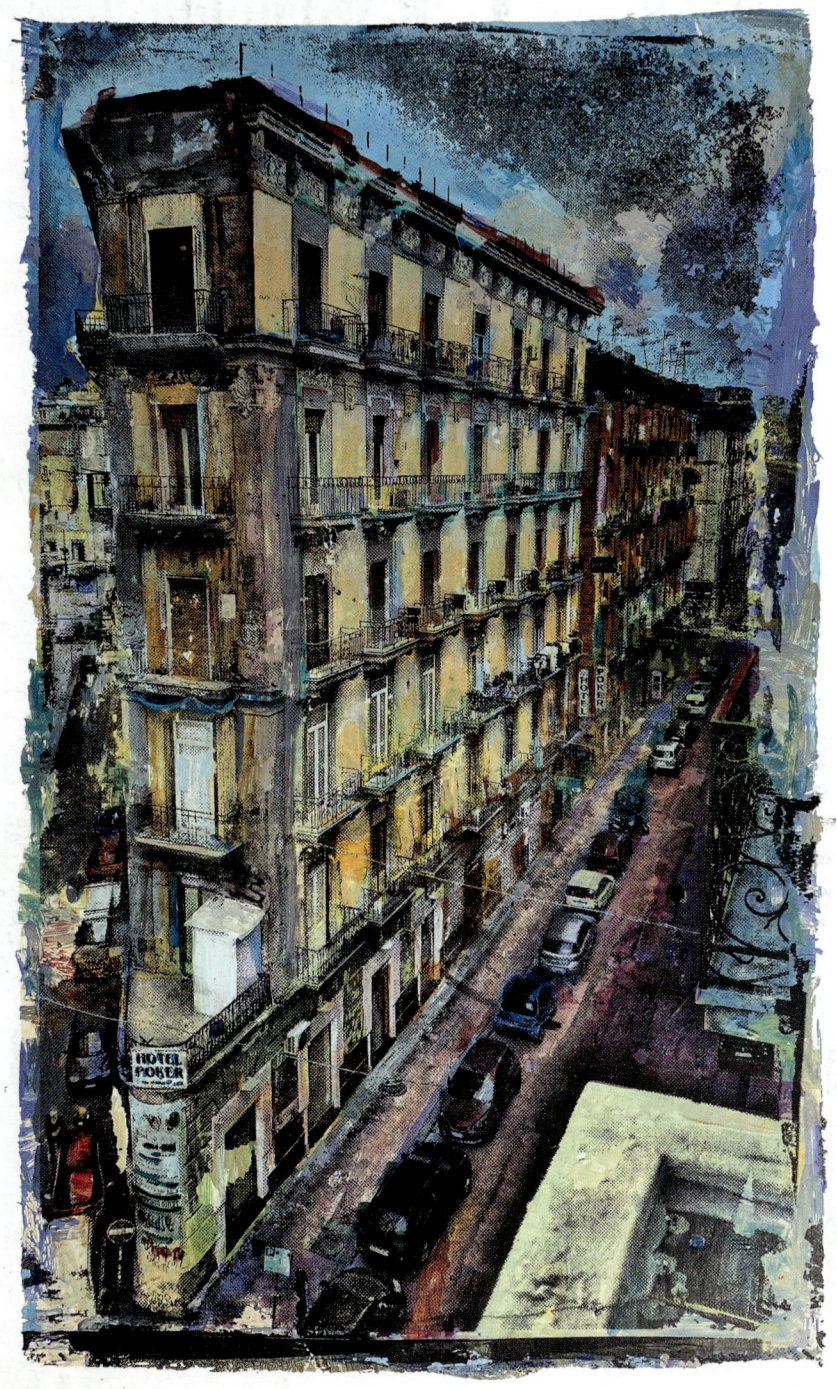

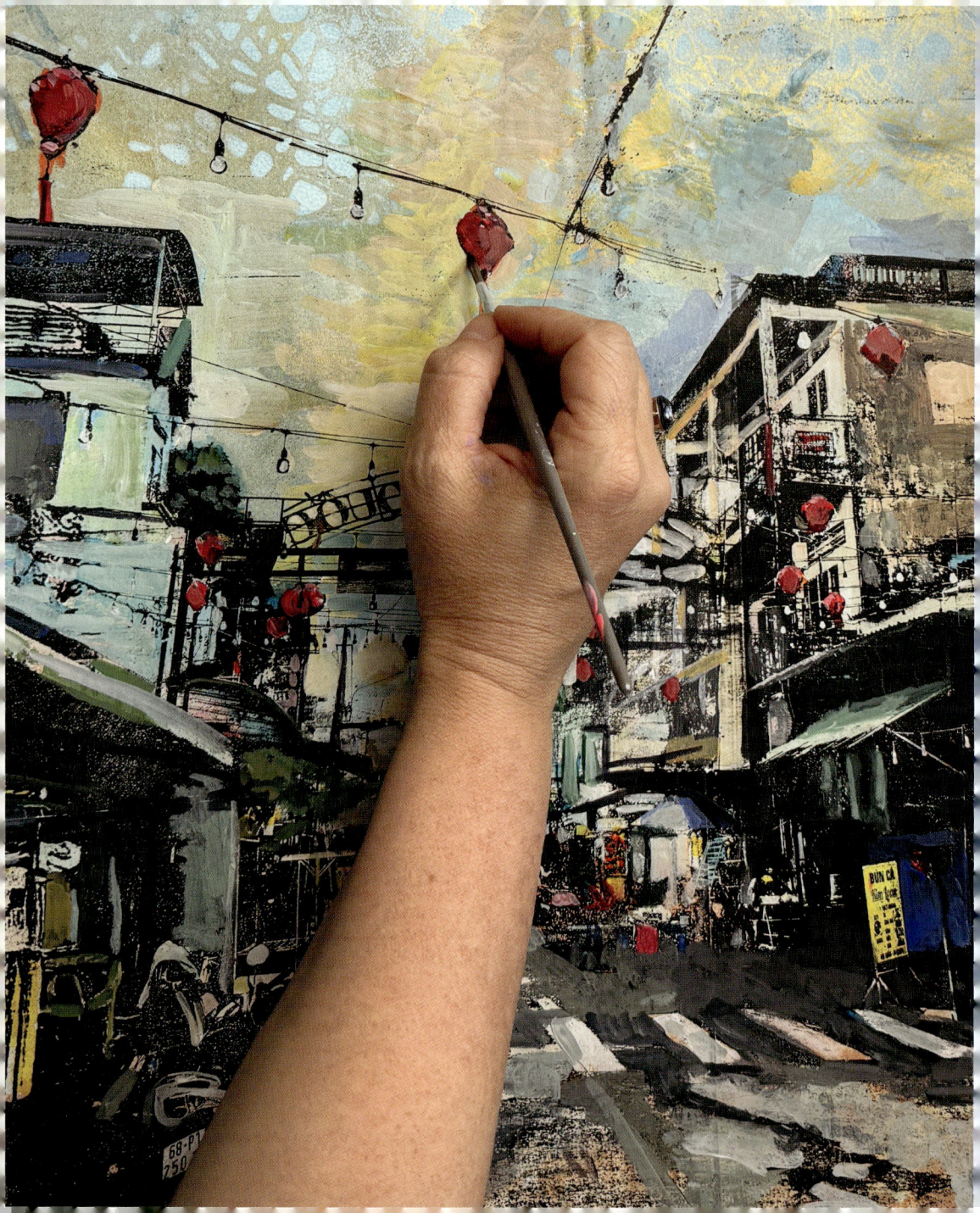

9
THE JOY OF ADDITIVE PAINTING

Who says the final pull of your print has to be the final version of your artwork? Absolutely not! One of the best things about gel plate printmaking is that you can continue building on your monotype even after you've pulled it off the plate.

WHAT IS ADDITIVE PAINTING?

You might hear printmakers talk about *overpainting*, *direct painting*, or *additive painting*. They all mean the same thing: painting directly on top of your pulled print. This technique, which I'll call additive painting, gives you a second chance to refine your work, whether you're fixing a botched transfer, sharpening details, restoring clarity, or building areas of color and complexity that weren't possible during the initial pull. Often, small details get lost during the

image transfer process and need to be brought back to life. While I like to use Black Oxide for image transfers because of its dependability, I don't like that it can make a final print feel somewhat static. Large black areas can look heavy, one-dimensional, or lacking nuance. Additive painting helps build depth, transforming flat, static areas into vibrant forms with just a few thoughtful brushstrokes.

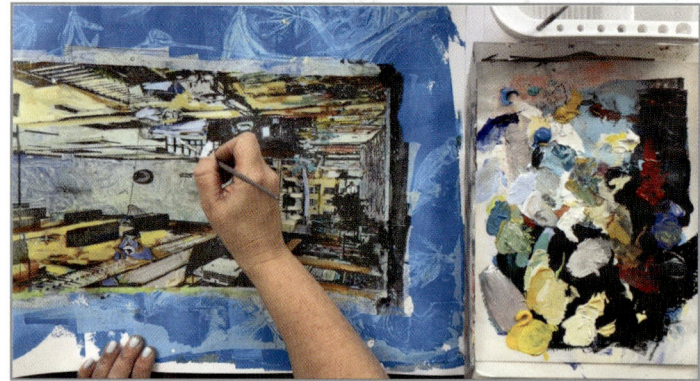

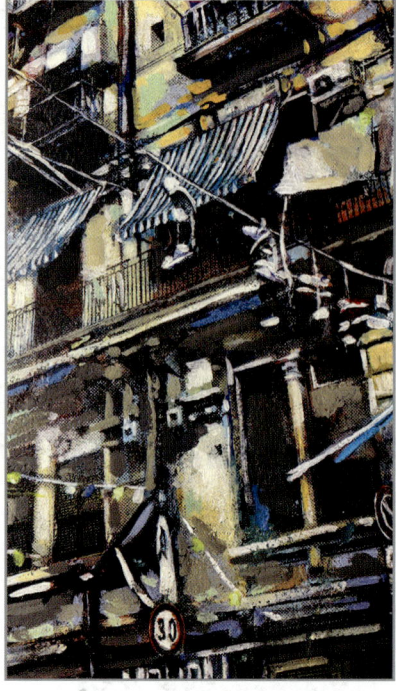

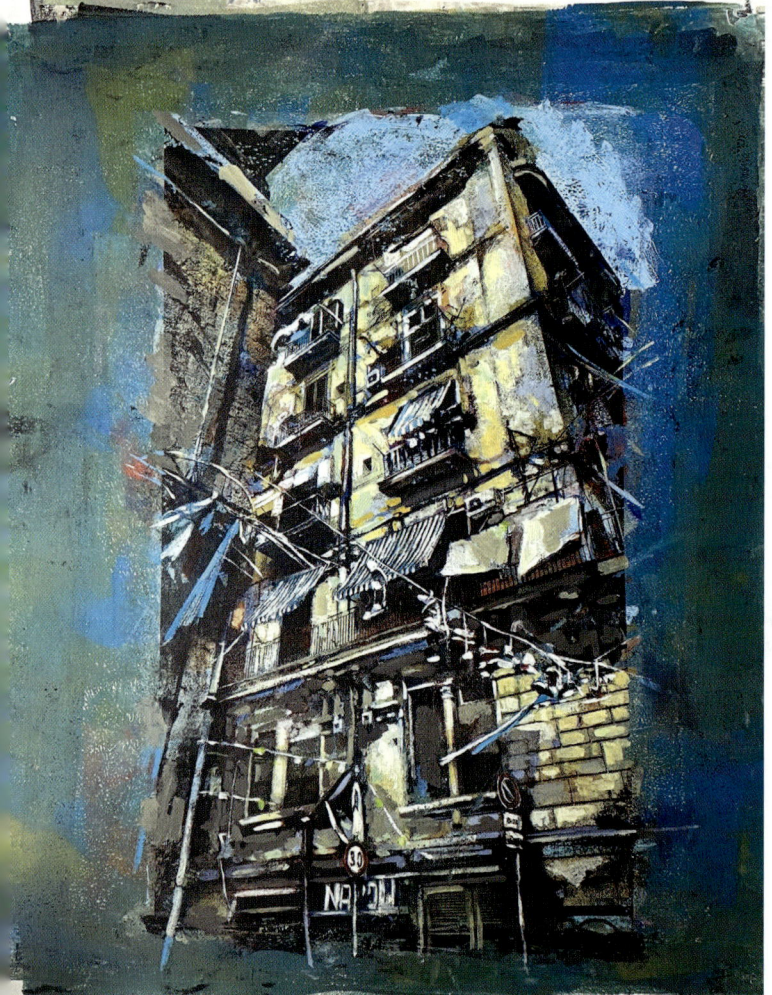

The figures shown here illustrate how just a few brushstrokes can shift the entire focus of a print. In this print, the shoes hanging from a line stretched across the street felt too subtle, almost lost in the background. But to me, they were the heart of the composition, the detail that gave the scene its personality. With a bit of additive painting, I was able to draw them out, refining their shape and contrast so they took their rightful place as the focal point. Additive painting bridges the gap between what the gel plate offers and what you want it to become.

CREATING A COHESIVE PALETTE

When painting on top of a print, I choose colors that echo the palette used during the reverse painting process. This consistency keeps everything feeling unified and intentional, rather than like separate elements competing for attention. Thoughtful color choices allow the added layers to blend seamlessly into the composition, enhancing the overall harmony.

Additive painting gives you the opportunity to refine and build upon what's already there. A print that once felt flat or unresolved can take on new depth, energy, and clarity through subtle shifts in value, contrast, and tone. By approaching post-print additions with the same care and intentionality as the reverse painting, you can transform your monotype into something that feels complete, cohesive, and a bit more painterly.

Consider another example: I did a lot of additive painting on my monotype of Piazza Libertá in Bassano del Grappa, a beautiful small town in northern Italy. The image transfer, done with Black Oxide, altered the light and bright color of the piazza despite the soft colors used in my reverse painting. By painting on top of the print with more of the pastel building colors that I used in the reverse painting, I was able to lighten the overall composition and have it reflect the vision that was in my memory from the afternoon I spent in this very piazza, doing watercolor sketches with my girls and husband—and eating some of the best pinsa pizza ever made.

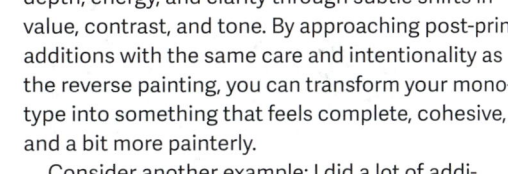

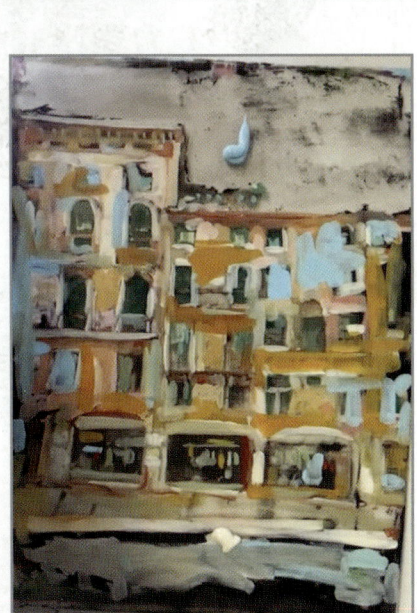

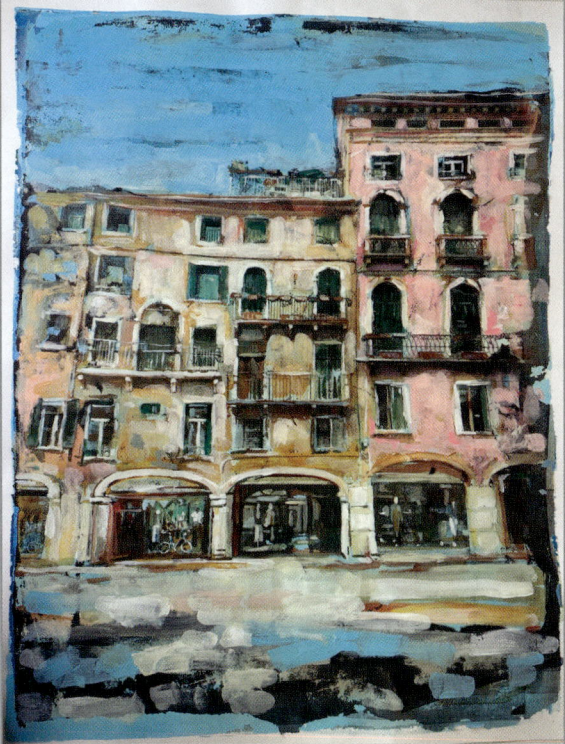

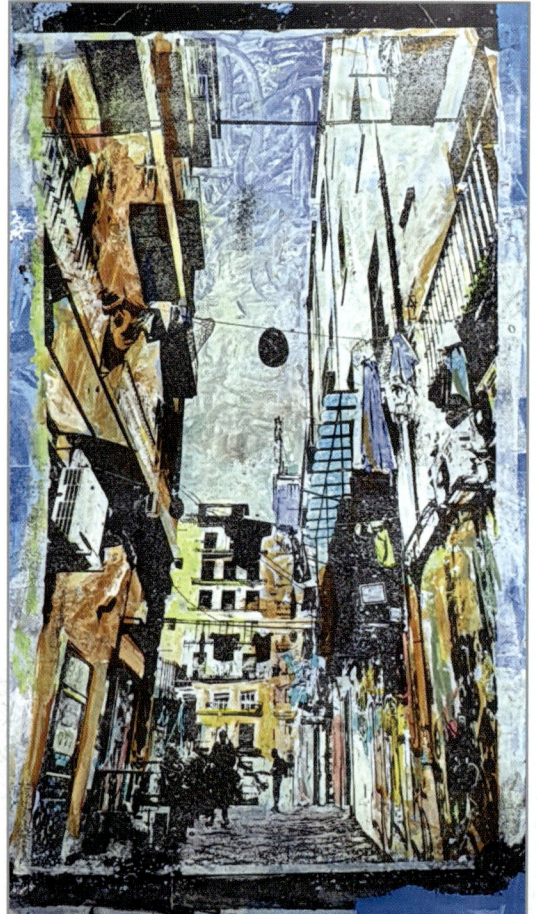
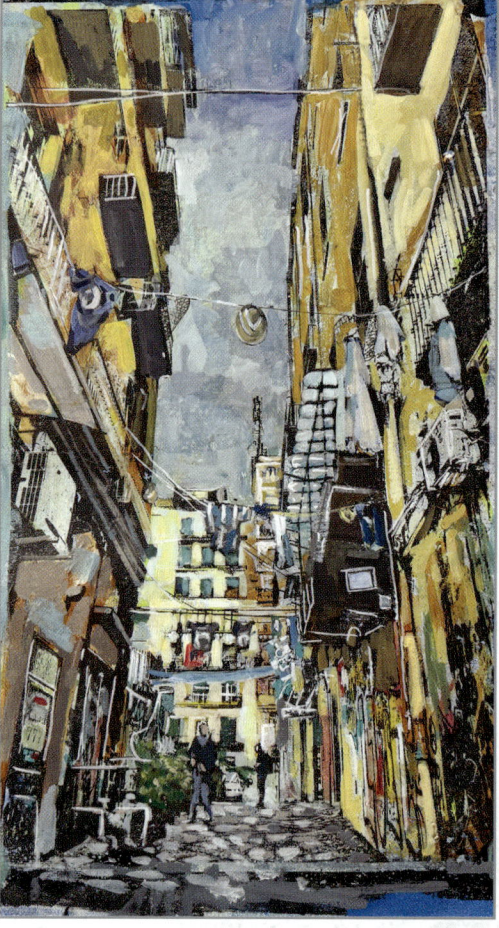

Here's a side-by-side look at additive painting in action. On the left, the silhouettes appear flat. On the right, additive painting brings in color and detail, helping the shapes stand out and resulting in a more finished, compelling print.

FIX BLEMISHES

Sometimes a print has quirks, hickeys, or other blemishes: a weird blotch of paint, a ghostly hint of a transfer, or plate tone where you didn't want it. Instead of tossing the print, reach for your brush. These blemishes are especially common with laser-print image transfers, with which paint doesn't always cooperate. Rather than fighting it, work with it like I do. A bit of additive painting can soften unwanted marks and integrate them into the overall composition.

A few thoughtful additions made all the difference in another street scene, as well. The original print had potential, but it felt somewhat unfinished. The figures were reduced to silhouettes, and the clotheslines strung across the narrow street lacked texture and definition. Using a brush, paint, and a white paint pen, I brought out the details I wanted to see. A few highlights here, some crisp lines there, and suddenly the scene had life, movement, and a stronger sense of narrative. Sometimes, adding those small touches can turn a decent print into a compelling one.

Additive doesn't have to mean just acrylic on acrylic. Feel free to mix things up. Paint markers, pens, and colored pencils all work beautifully on top of your monotype. Just know that drawing on acrylic isn't quite like working on paper; it's smoother and sometimes slippery. But once you get a feel for it, you'll start to see where, how, and when to use each tool. You can even add collage elements for an extra layer of texture and depth, as well as use tissue paper prints, bold cutouts, or scraps from other prints. It's a fun way to breathe new life into an image that might otherwise feel unresolved.

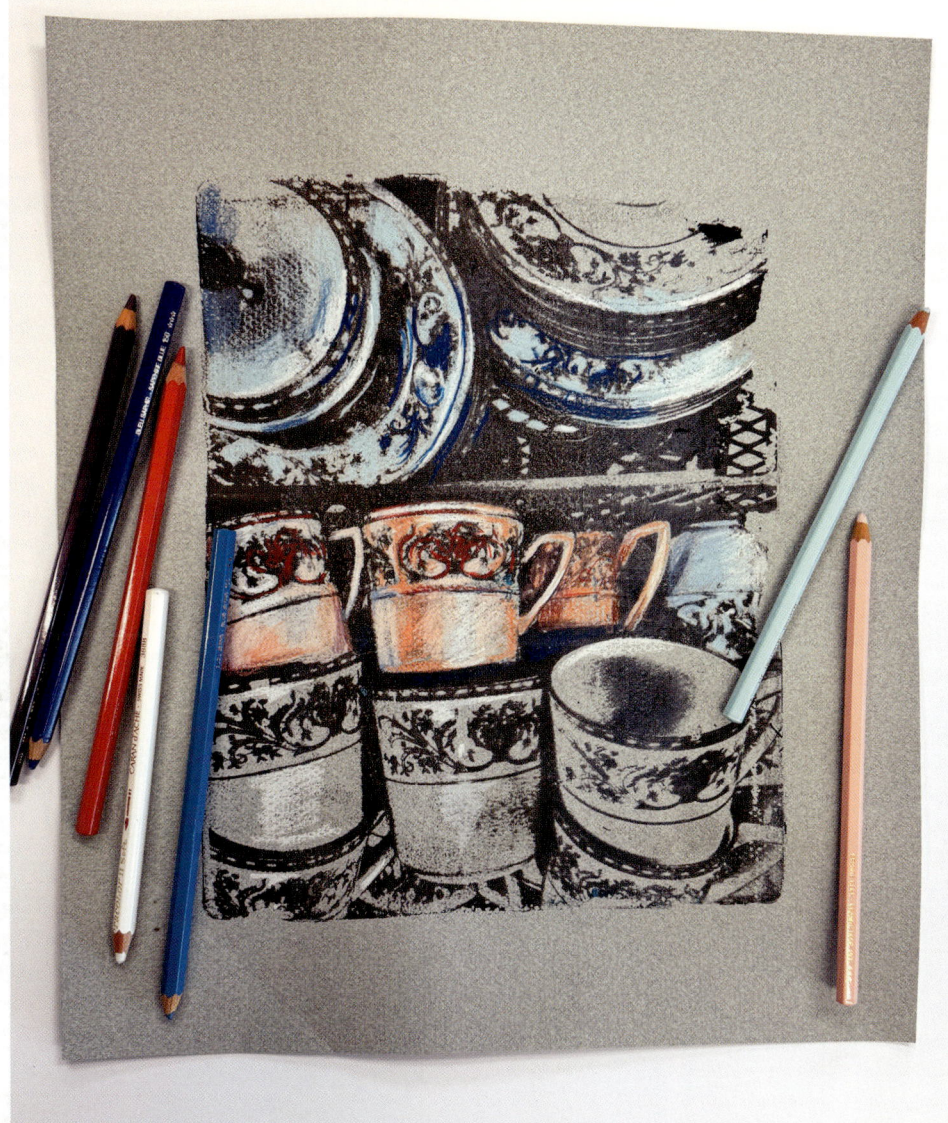

Here is a print that I did of a stack of dishes in a Danish thrift shop. The print was created using Black Oxide and Payne's Gray on soft blue Canson Paper. I then layered colored pencils on top.

RESCUE MISSION

Let's talk about those prints that almost made it. You know the ones. They've got potential, but they came out too light, too dull, or too patchy.

Here's an example: I recently pulled a photo transfer, but the plate didn't have enough Black Oxide to do the image transfer properly. The image came out super light on the gel plate. Rather than starting from scratch, I grabbed my Cerulean Blue acrylic paint and rolled it onto the plate as a pickup layer. Because my original photo was taken at night, the cool blue undertone actually enhanced the mood and gave the print a bit of cinematic drama. After pulling it off the plate, I layered lighter paint directly onto the print.

A few things to keep in mind when painting over a print:

- **Undertones matter.** My light yellows are translucent, and against that strong blue, they took on a cooler, more subdued vibe. It worked for the nighttime scene I was going for, but I had to build it up slowly with multiple layers to avoid letting the blue take over the entire scene.
- **Color relationships shift.** A warm color on white acts totally differently than that same color on blue. This can be frustrating when you mix the perfect color on your white palette, but when you lay it on your print, it looks different. If you have a swatch of the color in your sketchbook, lay colors on top to test how they look.
- **Paint behavior changes.** If you're thinning your acrylics with just water, they might bead up or pool on the surface of the print. To help your paint stay put, mix in a bit of gel medium. It helps thinner layers glide on smoothly and stay where you want them.

Whether for the final touches needed to help define your print or the start of creating a painting on top of your print, additive painting can help transform your work. I can't even begin to tell you how many layers I added to the print until it felt complete, but the persistence paid off. So, next time a print doesn't quite hit the mark, don't panic, grab a brush. It might just need a little love and a little layering to become one of your favorites.

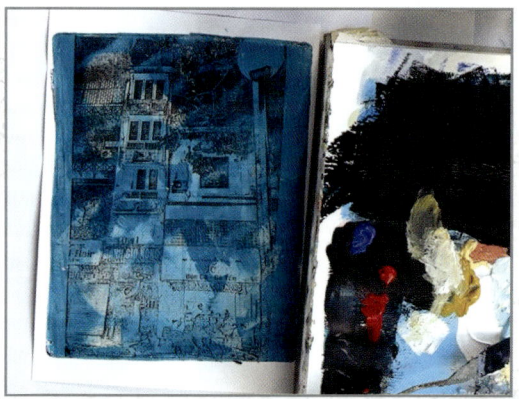

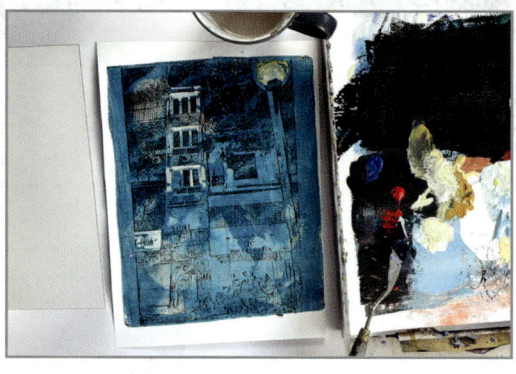

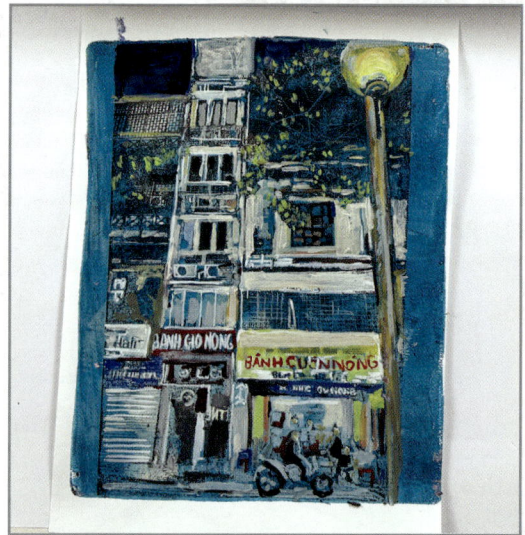

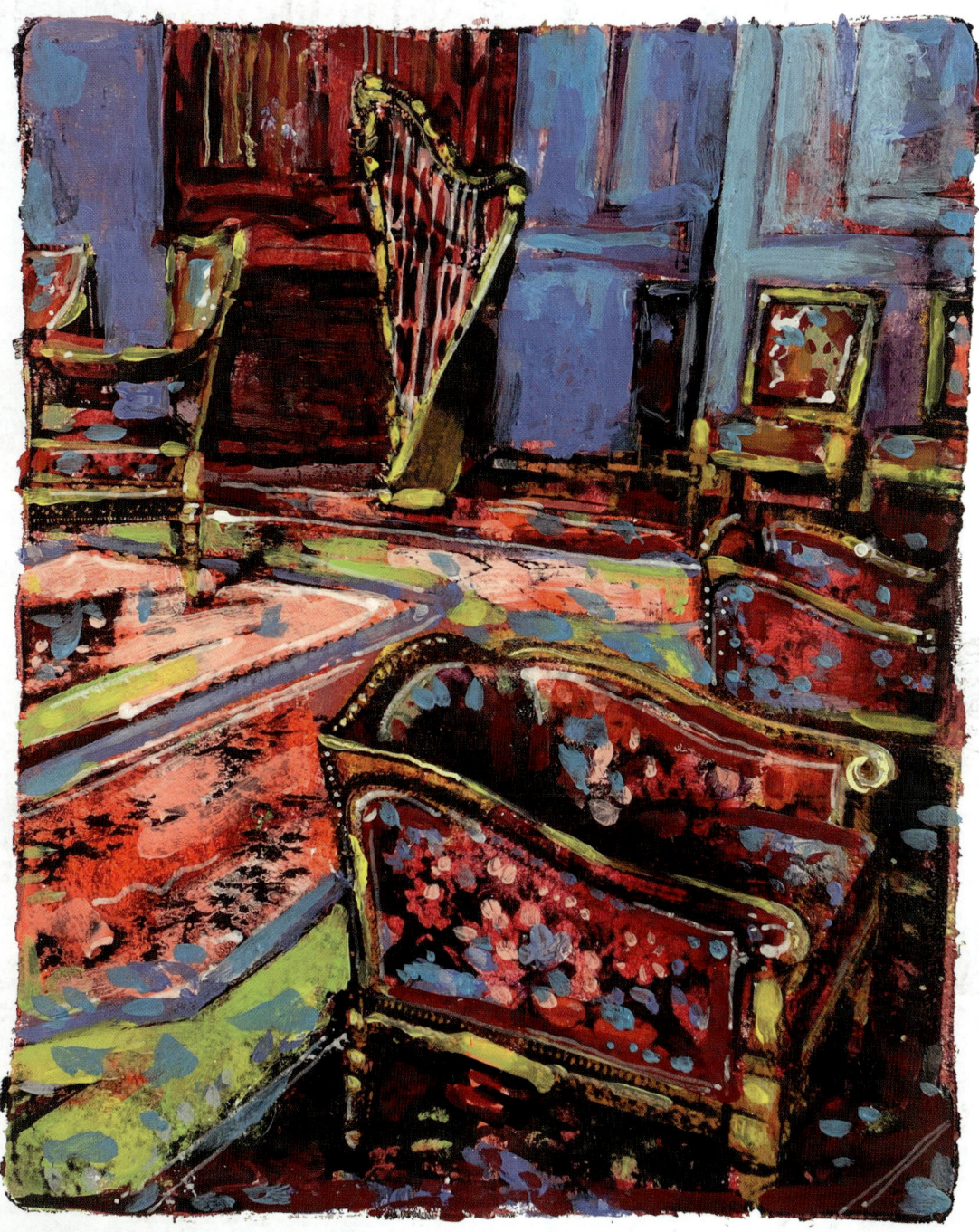

In this print, like the one of Bassano del Grappa, the black felt too heavy. Instead, I grabbed a bright and vibrant color palette to bring some ostentatiousness into this elaborate ornate room in the Palace of Versailles.

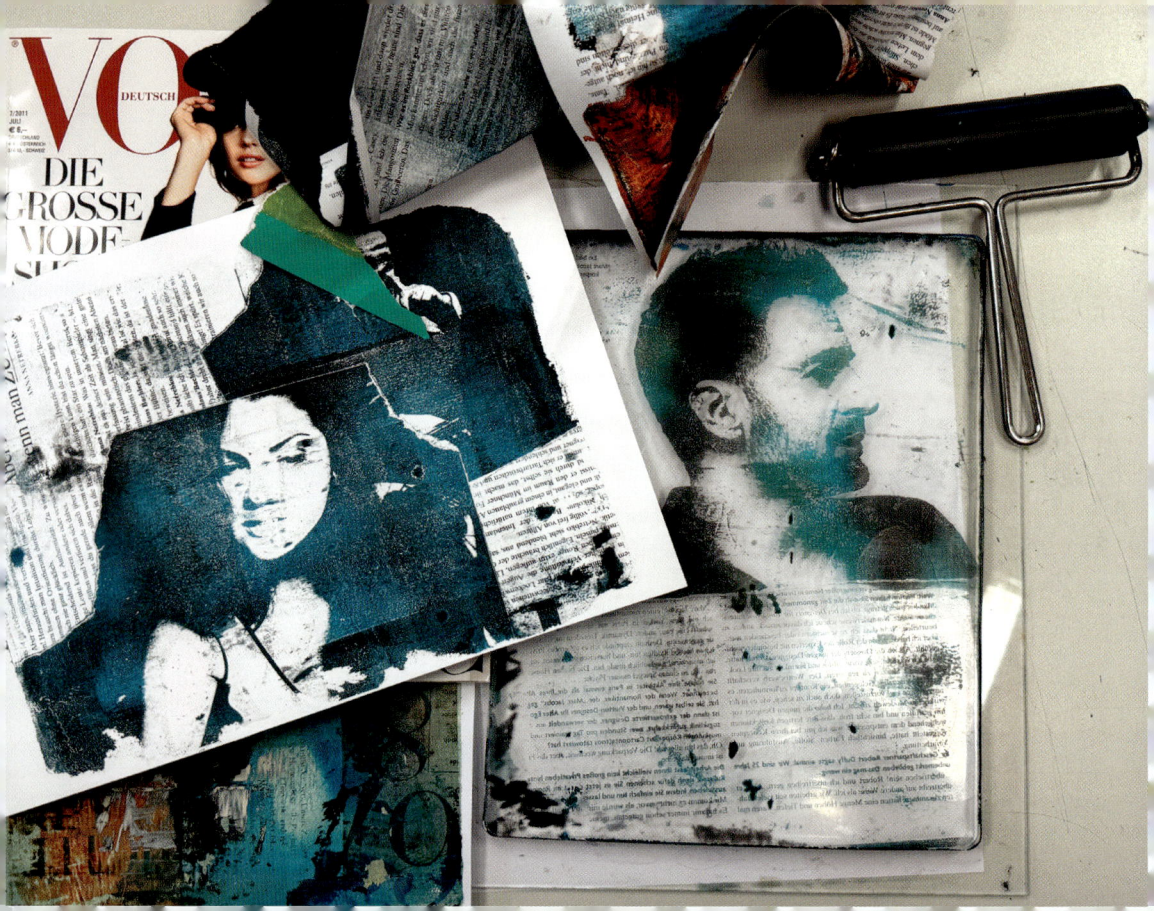

10
MAGAZINE TRANSFERS

Magazine transfers are unpredictable in the best way. They don't just replicate an image; they transform it into something that's individually yours. The process is quite similar to the laser-print transfers in Chapter 6 with a few differences in timing and pressure. Of course, you don't need an expensive laser printer or a trip to the copy shop. All you need is a gel plate, some acrylic paint, a brayer, some paper, and a good magazine page (see next page). This chapter walks you through how to get the most out of magazine transfers, including tips for picking the right publications, getting a clean transfer, and troubleshooting common issues.

CHOOSE YOUR IMAGE

Look for glossy magazine pages with a smooth coating and high-contrast photography. The best results come from images with rich blacks and bright highlights. Faces, bold patterns, and subjects with intense lighting usually transfer beautifully. Avoid using overly busy or low-contrast images, as these tend to produce muddy and indistinct results. I've found *Vogue, Elle, Architectural Digest,* and *National*

Geographic consistently provide strong, clean transfers (although older issues of *National Geographic* tend to work better). Avoid the thicker magazine pages. The ones that have the perfume samples folded into them don't work very well at all, probably because the magazine paper is too thick. The results depend on the type of ink the publication uses, so they can be hit or miss.

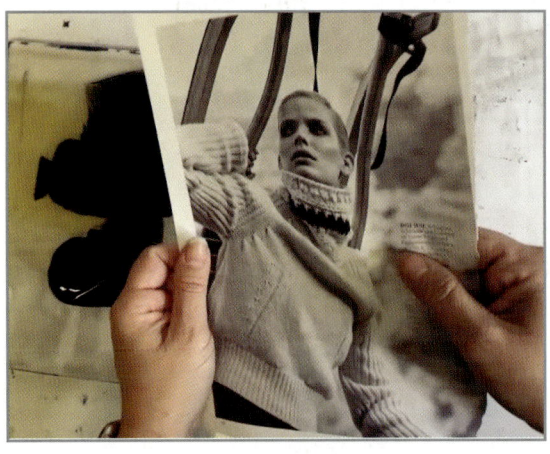

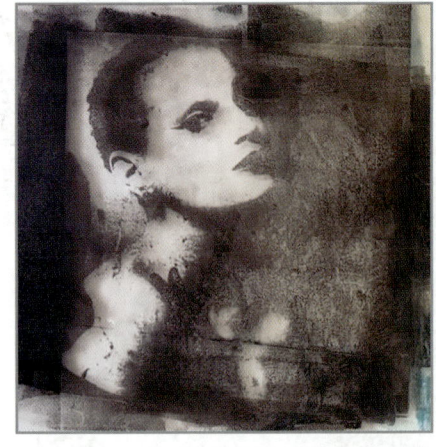

PAINT, LAY DOWN, AND LET IT SIT (BRIEFLY!)

Using a brayer, roll out a smooth, even coat of acrylic paint on your gel plate. Just like with laser-print transfers, I usually go with Black Oxide paint for strong contrast. Keep the layer thin to prevent smudging or sticking.

Place your magazine image face down onto the freshly painted plate. Rub gently but evenly with a brayer. I almost always use a brayer with magazine transfers because they typically need more consistent pressure than laser prints to transfer correctly. Let the magazine sit on the plate for 15 to 30 seconds. Timing will vary depending on humidity; on damp days, even 10 seconds may be enough. If left too long, the page can become stuck and torn. Keep in mind that magazine paper is less absorbent than

standard copy paper, so it takes longer for the paint to bond and pull the ink from the surface. If you leave it too long, the paper can stick or tear as you lift it. You'll develop a feel for the sweet spot with practice.

I like to peek under a corner before pulling the whole thing up. If the image hasn't fully transferred, gently lay it back down and apply a bit more pressure. The magazine paper might wrinkle a bit. When it's ready, carefully lift the page from one corner to reveal the image left behind on the plate.

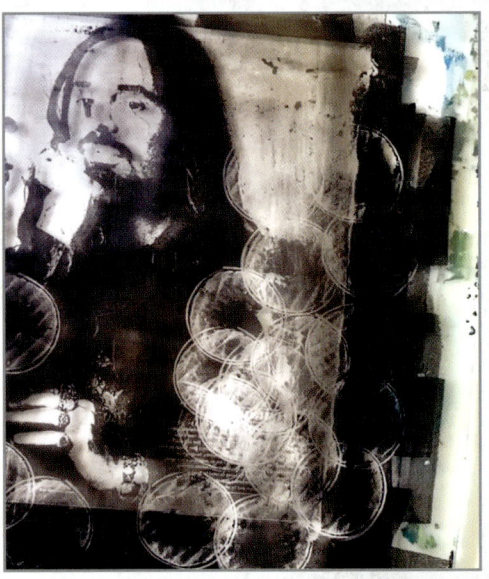

ADD DETAILS, TEXTURE, AND A PICKUP LAYER

Before adding anything more, let the transfer layer dry fully. Drying time varies depending on your climate, but typically one to five minutes is enough. If it's still tacky, wait. Adding paint layers, especially the pickup layer, too early can cause smearing.

Once your image transfer is dry, you can start layering colors behind it. Use more transparent paints to let the details from the transfer show through. I often lean into texture here, like using the edge of a paper towel roll to stamp circles or adding a bit of metallic paint for sparkle. Build up your layers intentionally, from detail to background, and remember to let everything dry thoroughly to avoid smearing.

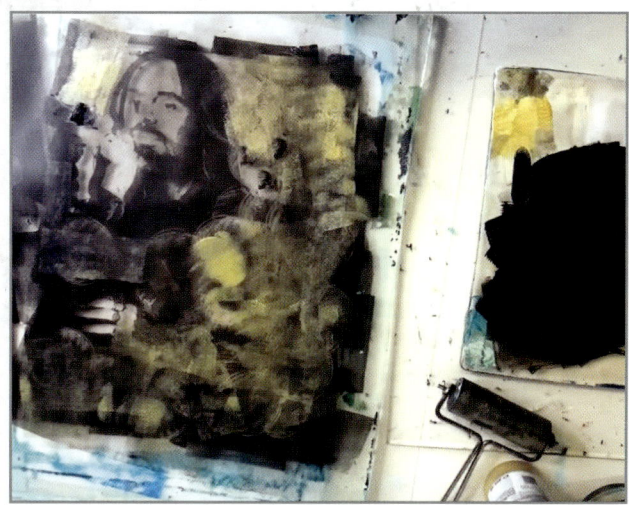

Roll a thin layer of contrasting color of acrylic paint or gel medium over the dry transfer. This will act as your pickup layer to pull the entire print off the plate. Pro tip: Using a lighter color over a dark transfer can create striking, high-contrast results.

Place your final paper (something sturdy, like Bristol) onto the still-wet plate. Press firmly and evenly over the entire surface; usually, this takes about one minute. For extra contact and pressure, I stack a heavy book or two on top and let it sit briefly.

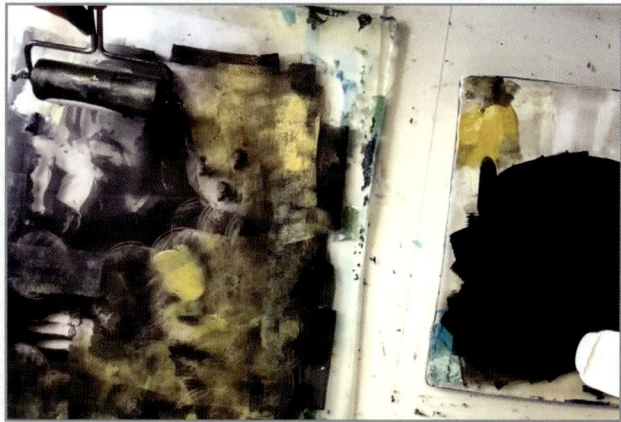

Once everything is fully dry, remove the books. Let it dry for a few minutes longer so air can circulate over the paper where the books were. Gently lift your paper from the plate. Start at the corner and work your way around releasing the paper from the plate. If it sticks, lay it back down to dry more. Voilà! Your transferred magazine image is now part of your layered, one-of-a-kind print.

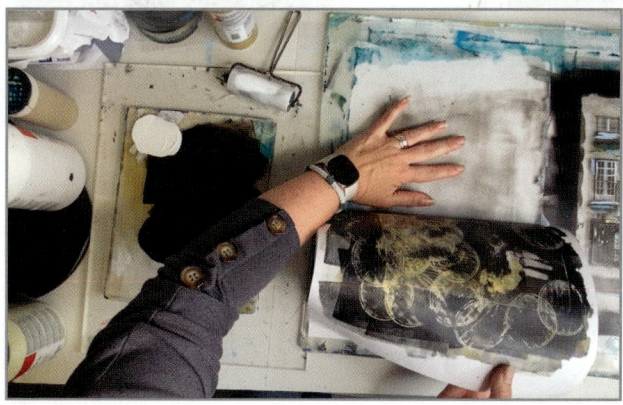

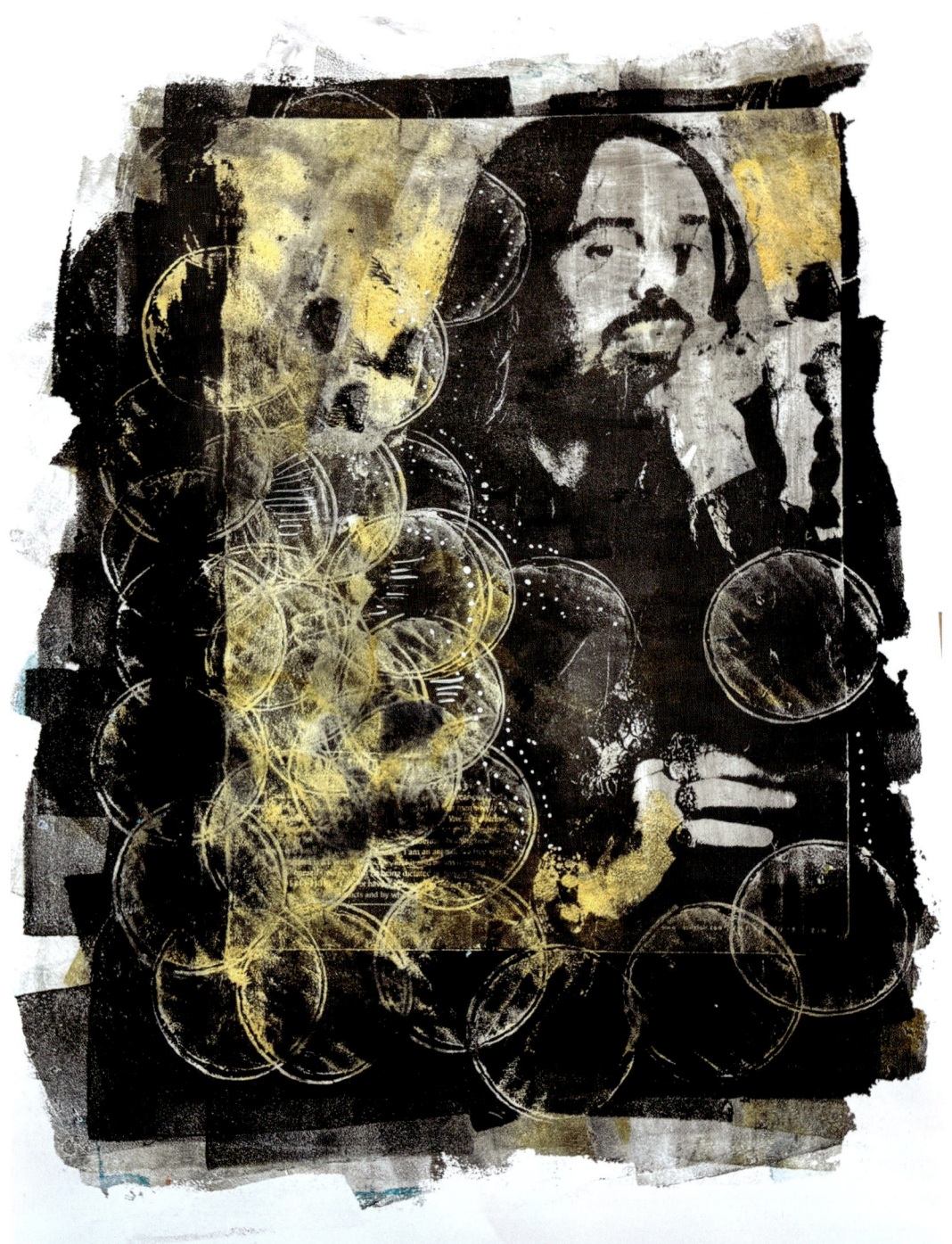

KEEP EXPERIMENTING

Magazine transfers are part science, part sorcery and entirely unpredictable. The only way to truly master them is through hands-on experimentation, embracing play, failure, and the occasional happy accident. Each pull from the gel plate is its own moment. These quirky pages can yield some of your most expressive, painterly, and richly layered prints, full of texture and unexpected detail. Try creating a print using only a text cutout or use three layers of transfers to tell a story.

Even the so-called "failures" hold creative potential. Partial or ghosted transfers are perfect starting points for mixed media, additive painting, colored pencil, collage, or embellishment with paint markers that can breathe new life into them. So, next time you're flipping through a magazine while waiting at the dentist's office, keep your eyes open. You might just stumble on your next perfect image source.

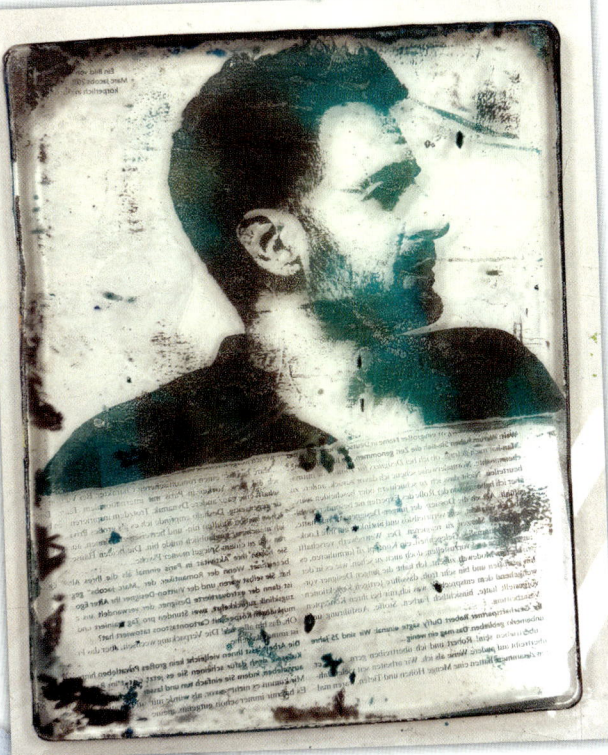

A NOTE ON COPYRIGHT AND FAIR USE

Before you start tearing through magazines, keep in mind that many of their photos are protected by copyright. Whether or not you can legally use them in your artwork often depends on how much you transform the image, whether you plan to sell the work, or whether you keep it for your personal collection.

If you're adding your voice, changing the context, or combining images into something new, you're more likely to stay on the safe side of the law. Some artists consider this kind of work "fair use," especially when the image is heavily altered or used in a noncommercial, experimental way. But copyright laws vary by country, and what's acceptable in one place may not be in another. Always be mindful of local laws, use your best judgment, and do what feels right for your practice.

Remember, you should be creating your own art, not just replicating someone else's work. So, transform your prints into something that is amazing and super individual!

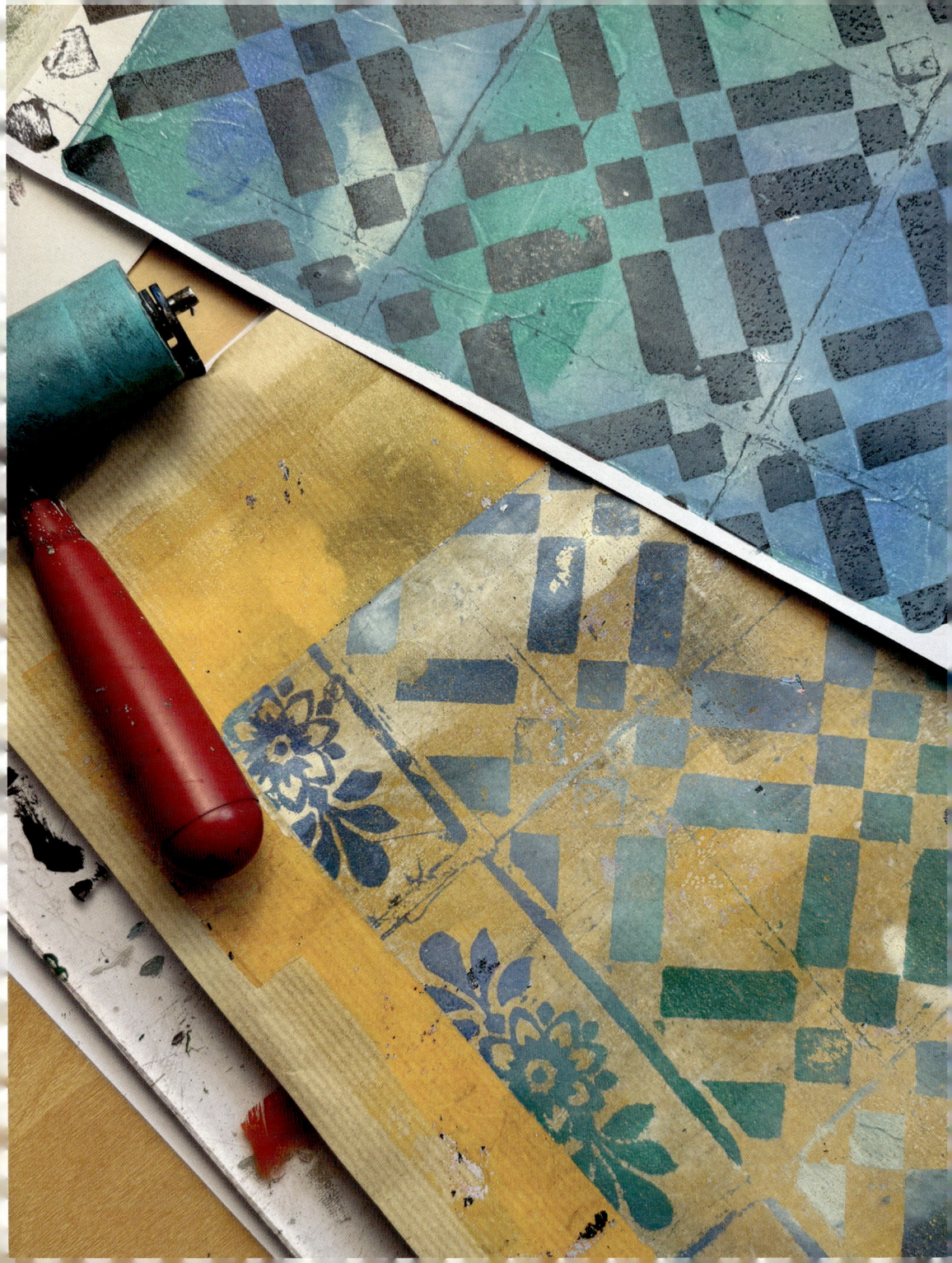

11

BEYOND BLACK IMAGE TRANSFERS

So, you've gotten the hang of image transfers with trusty Black Oxide, that reliable workhorse that delivers crisp, high-contrast results. Now what? Black is an excellent starting point to build confidence and an understanding of how details translate onto the gel plate. Having found your footing, however, you may now crave more nuance, mood, and color. You've come to the right chapter.

Switching up your transfer color can completely change the emotional tone, texture, and impact of your prints without changing the image itself. From soft vintage feels to rich jewel tones, subtle gradients, and vibrant ombrés, color opens the door to new expressions. Follow me on a tour of some of my color-boosted projects and tips for experiments of your own.

A TALE OF TWO TRANSFERS

One of my favorite parts of gel plate printing is how a single image can take on entirely new energy depending on your palette. For instance, I photographed the intricate blue-and-white vase shown on the next page at a riverside temple in Trang An, Vietnam. It was nestled among incense offerings and stone carvings—quiet, beautiful. The design on the vase shows a winding mountain path, echoing the spiritual journeys so many visitors make in this region, surrounded by misty karst peaks and sacred caves. I cropped and boosted the contrast of the photo to make it work as a bold transfer.

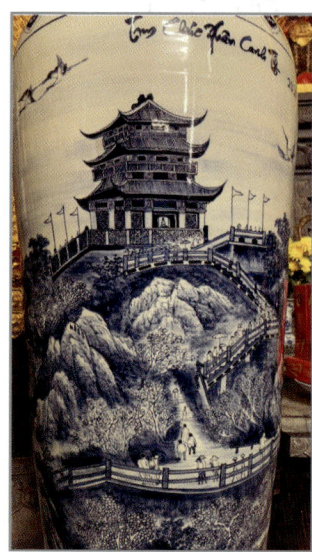

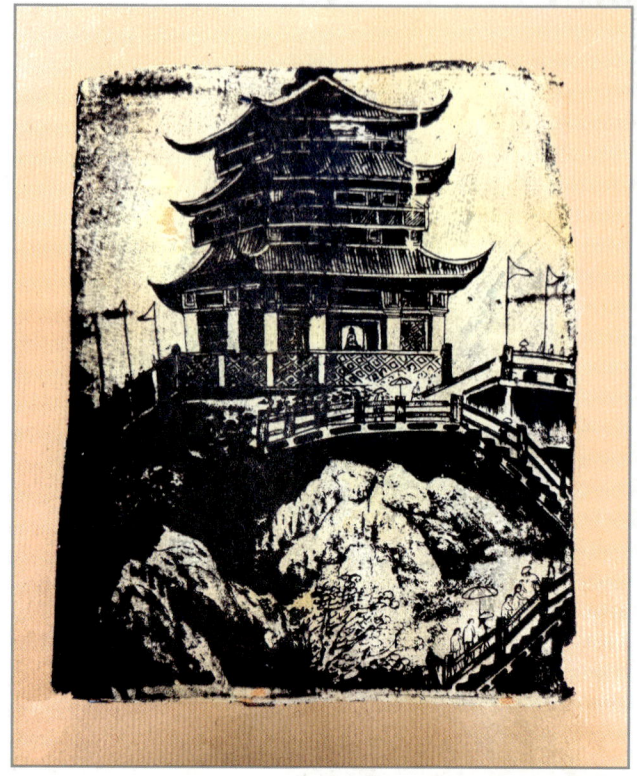

Compare the prints shown here. Both began with the exact same materials: identical laser-printed photos, the same pickup layer, identical paper, and the same paint brand. The only difference? I used dependable Black Oxide for one and Ultramarine Blue for the other.

In the black version, notice how the tiny figures in the lower left and the intricate architectural details stand out. Everything looks sharp and defined. Although the ultramarine version loses some of that definition, it gains something else entirely: mood. A dreamier, more atmospheric tone emerges—same print, different vibe.

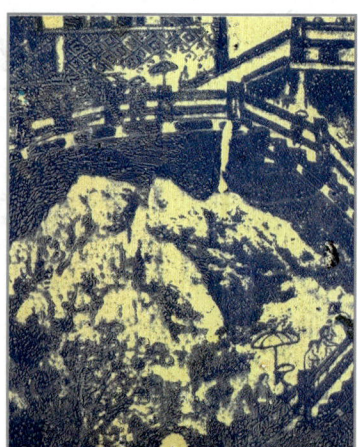

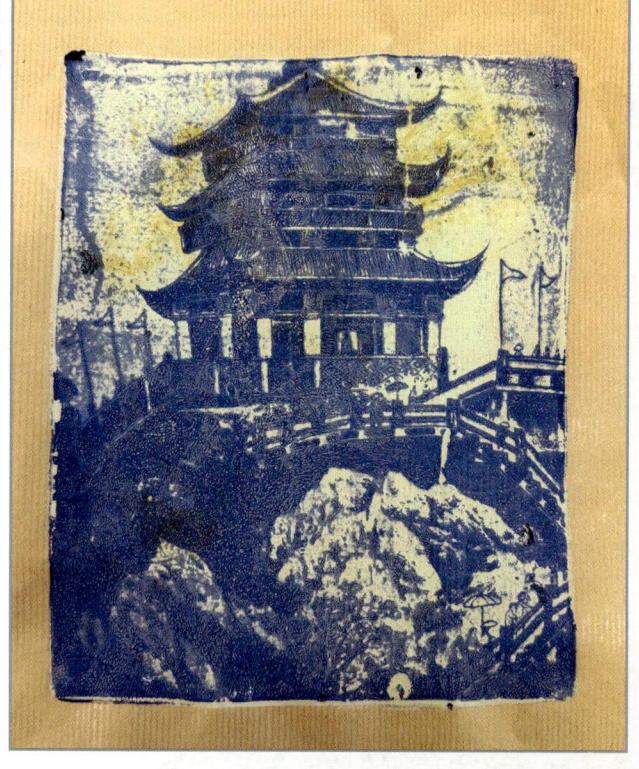

WHEN TO USE COLOR

Photos with large areas of black are a good option for switching out the black for another color. While walking through the cobblestone streets of Lisbon, Portugal, I took a photo of a stunning blue door. As I often do, I converted the image to black and white. I then used Black Oxide for the transfer, and the door became an imposing void, weighty and flat, losing some of its original charm.

This photo was a good candidate for a color image transfer. I tried again using a fluid Phthalo Turquoise with a hint of Yellow Ochre unevenly mixed in to create some variation. The Phthalo Turquoise was fairly thin and translucent, and the Yellow Ochre added a bit of opaqueness to the color and kept it from beading up too much. When you look at the image transfer on the gel plate itself, you can see how translucent it is, even with the Yellow Ochre added.

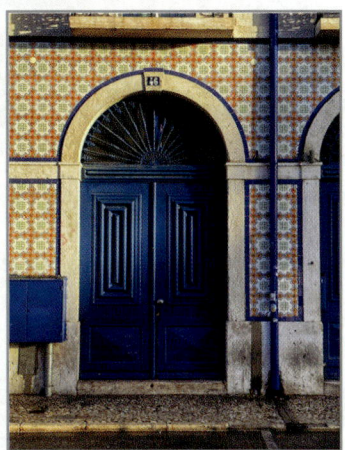
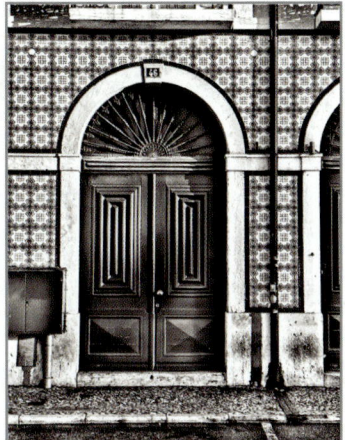
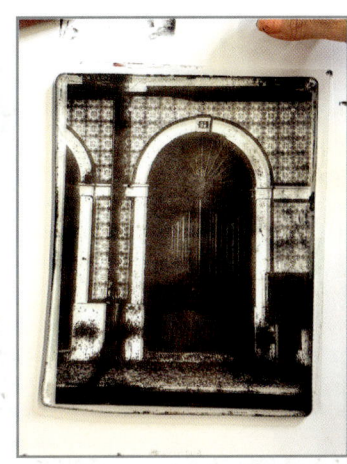

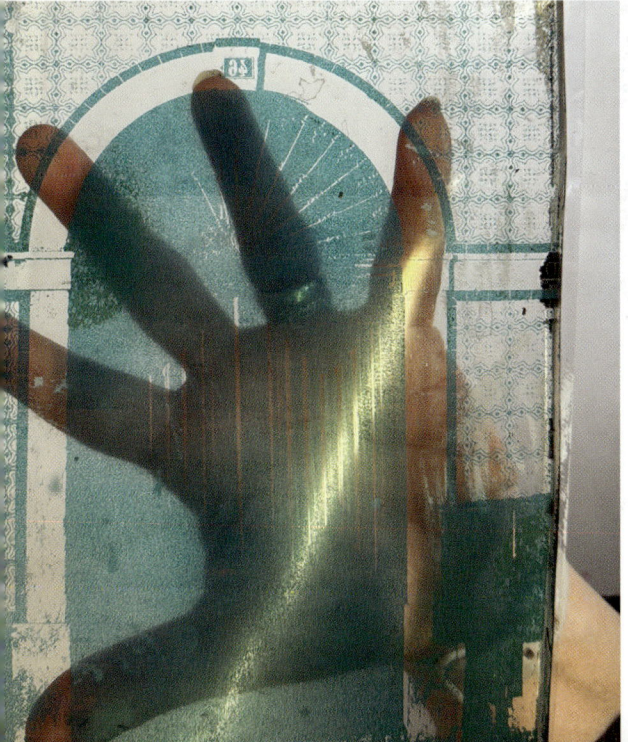
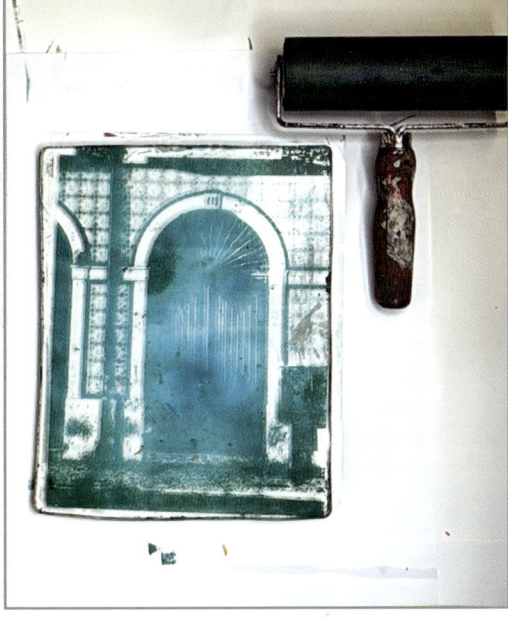

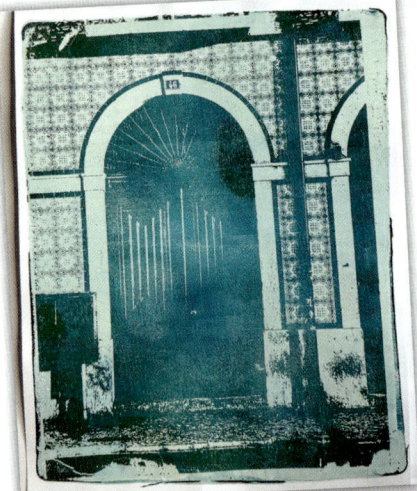

The color transfer shifted everything. The door now emanates a soft, ethereal quality. It's the same image, but with a totally different energy. I opted not to use reverse painting for this one, as the color was already so vibrant. For the pickup layer, I chose Naples Yellow Green to complete the color story. It's the same door, exact composition, but an entirely different emotional experience. The second image below features another Lisbon architecture print done with a similar image transfer color, but with a Titanium White pickup layer.

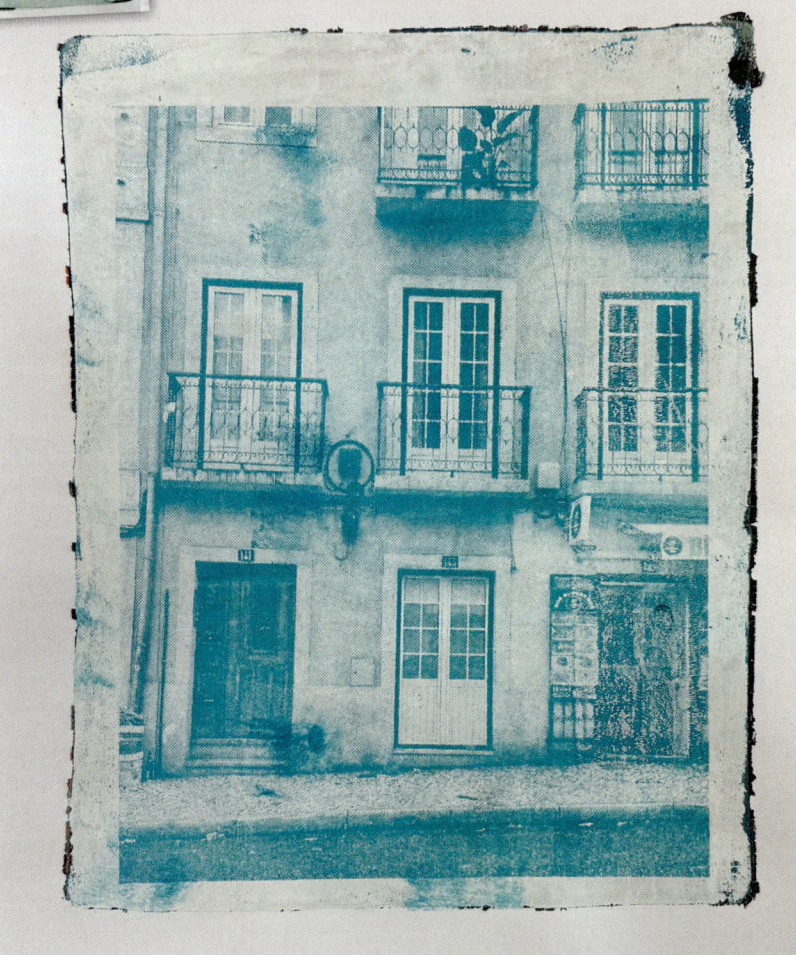

VINTAGE FEELS

For my series of Vietnamese street life prints, I wanted
a vintage analog vibe. To help create this feeling, I mixed
Burnt Sienna, a warm, slightly transparent pigment, with a
touch of Black Oxide to give it more opacity. I didn't thoroughly mix the colors, so the transfer has subtle variation
and visual texture. The result brings me back to my days in
a dark room working with negatives.

The pickup layer? Buff Titanium. It is perfect for that
soft, aged photograph feel. I left the edges rough and torn,
also evoking darkroom prints from decades past. Likewise,
using Pthalo Turquoise makes the final transfer resemble a
cyanotype while still maintaining a hint of that vintage feel.

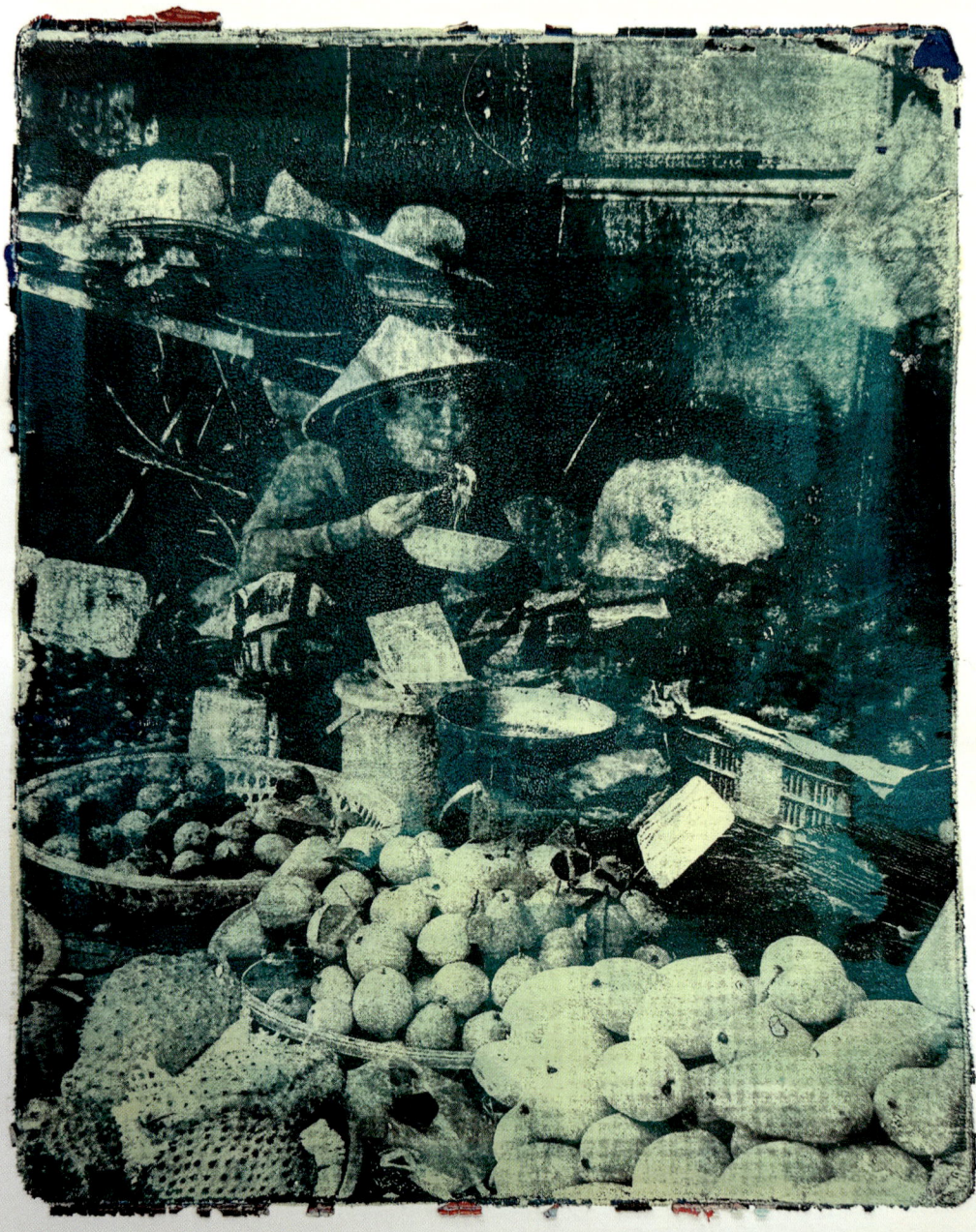

OMBRÉ AND GRADIENT TRANSFERS

One way to bring movement and life into your transfers is to use more than one color without over blending them. Let your brayer carry streaks and swirls of each color. The slight separation can create marbled effects, surprising gradients, and beautiful unpredictability. If you want to lean into softness and gradient, try laying down two or more colors in a horizontal or vertical ombré. Blend them gently with the brayer (again, not too much!), and pull your transfer from that. For example, I used a blue-green gradient for a photo of the Naples, Italy, skyline. I liked the softness of these colors, paired beautifully with the strong geometry of the buildings.

For the transfer in the image below, I began with a high-contrast, close-up photograph of a patterned vase. The black-and-white version was already bold and graphic, so I wanted to play with color, specifically jewel tones like blue and purple, without thoroughly blending them. Both paints I used were fluid and slightly translucent, which meant the paint tended to bead up a bit on the image. That might seem like a problem at first, but I've learned to embrace it. The speckled texture that comes from beaded paint can actually add a lot of character and visual interest to the final print.

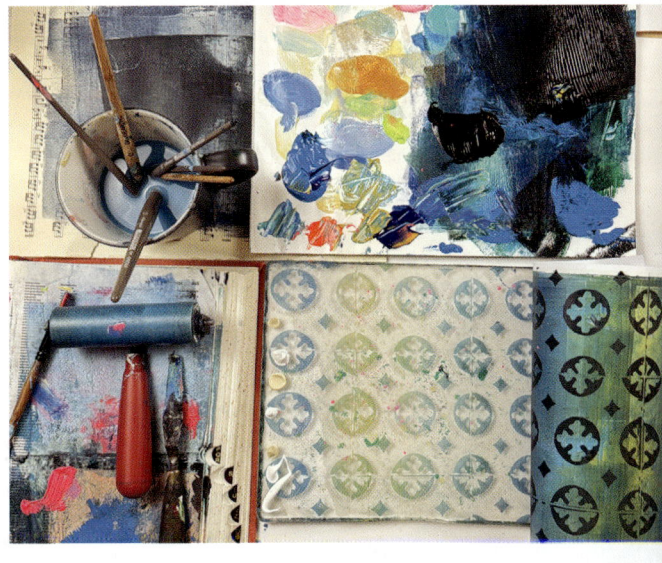

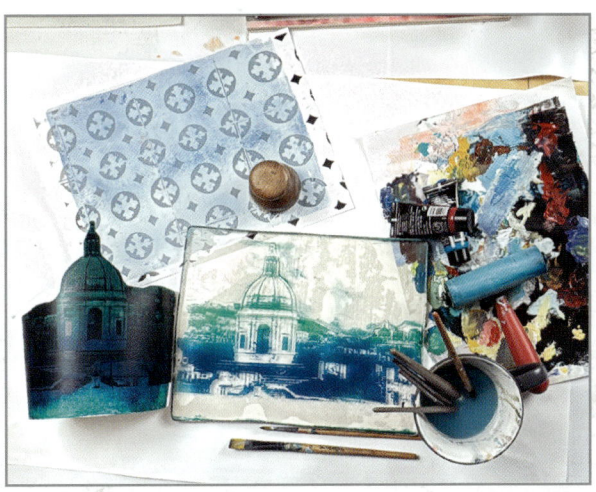

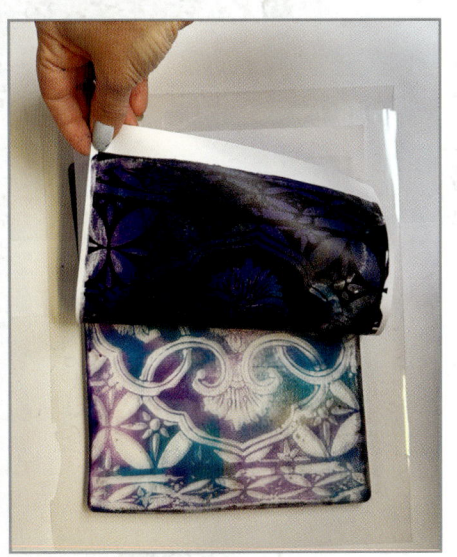

Left: I created this transfer with a mix of Permanent Blue Violet and Phthalo Turquoise. The pattern is from a porcelain vase. Like the earlier one, it was taken in Vietnam. However, this one was not in a beautifully adorned temple but rather in our hotel lobby.

Because of the translucency of the image transfer colors, I knew the pickup layer would show through. So, I chose Naples Yellow Green as my background. It's soft and neutral, playing nicely with the richer colors without adding to their intensity.

The result? A transfer with a beautiful dappled texture and spontaneous depth. As a bonus, the image didn't need to come out perfectly. The distressed, uneven areas actually added more personality to the final piece, enhancing its overall feel rather than detracting from it.

The image below shows some other versions of the same laser-printed image, transferred using a variety of colors and papers, including recycled sheet music.

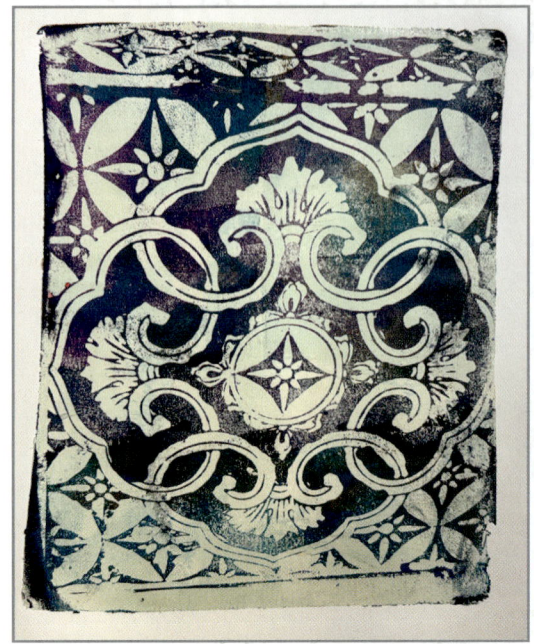

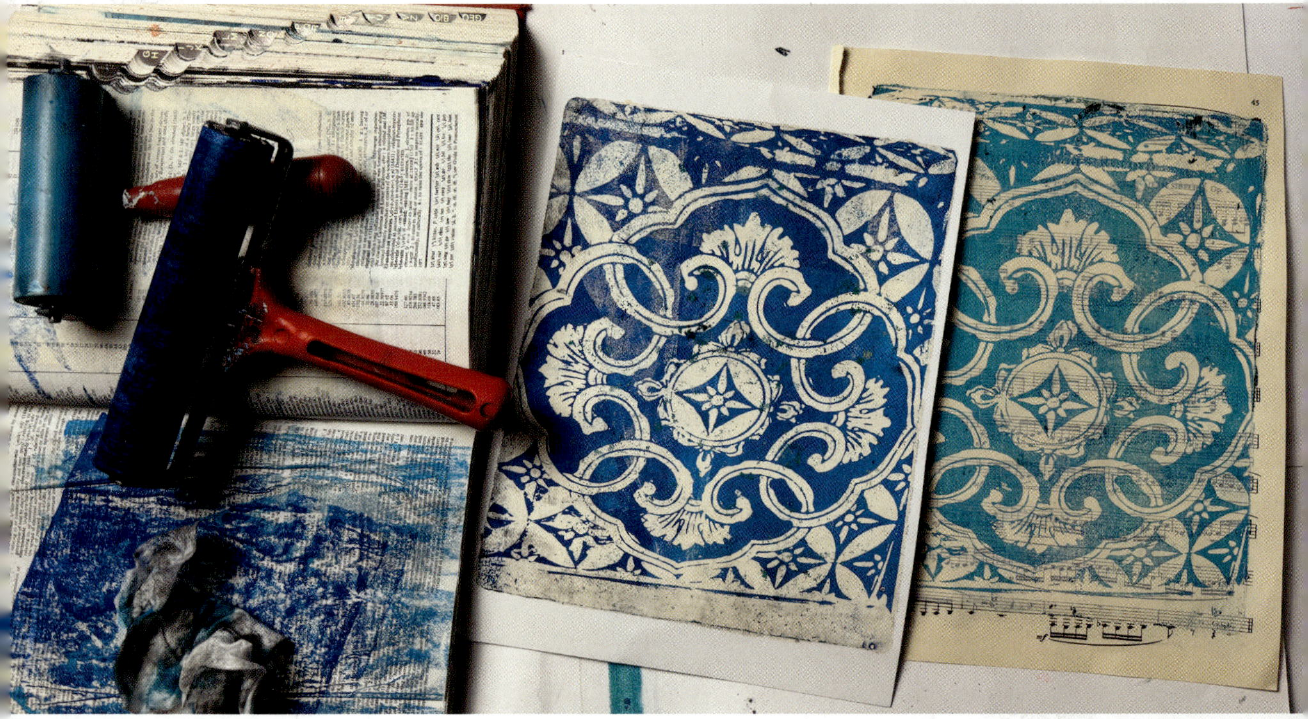

MORE COLOR OPTIONS

Color doesn't stop with your paint. Try experimenting with colored paper and gel medium. Just like your pickup layer's tone, the color of your paper can subtly influence the overall color story of your print. Or you can use gel medium to lift the image transfer and let the color of the paper peek through for a more direct effect. Try printing on warm-toned paper for a nostalgic feel, or opt for a cool gray to soften harsh contrasts and create a more dreamy, atmospheric quality to your work. The same transfer will look completely different depending on the base you pull it onto. Or you can switch things up and use a dark paper with a light color for your transfer. All of these options can give a new look to your transfers.

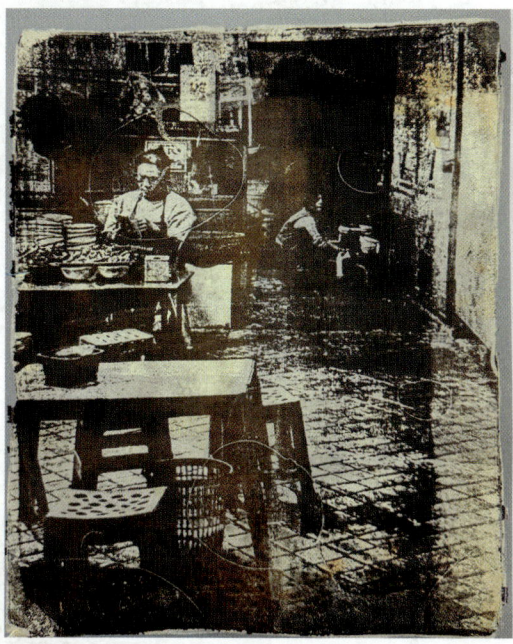

This was printed on a cool gray Canson paper.

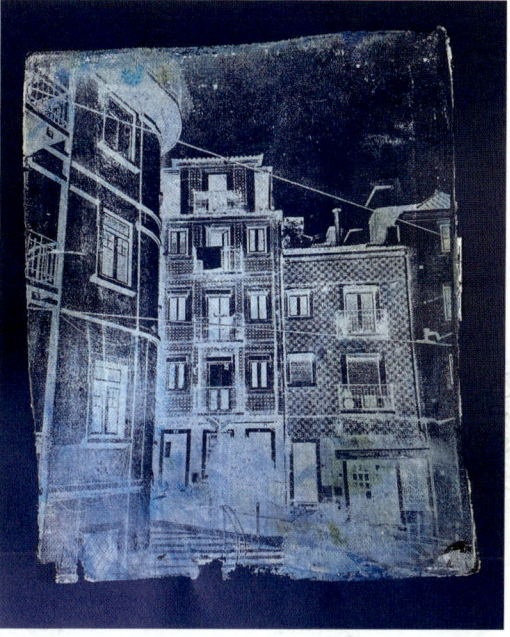

This street view of Lisbon was printed on a dark blue Canson paper.

WHEN IT DOESN'T WORK

Sometimes, things don't go as planned, and that's okay. Failed transfers teach you just as much as successful ones. Set a piece aside, figure out what didn't work, and try again with more contrast, a different color, or another type of paper. I often mix in a bit of Black Oxide to add opacity and anchor delicate colors when things feel too light. Embrace these two quotes to help you get through the struggles and remember it is all part of the learning process.

"There are no mistakes, just happy accidents." —Bob Ross

"Every artist was first an amateur." —Ralph Waldo Emerson

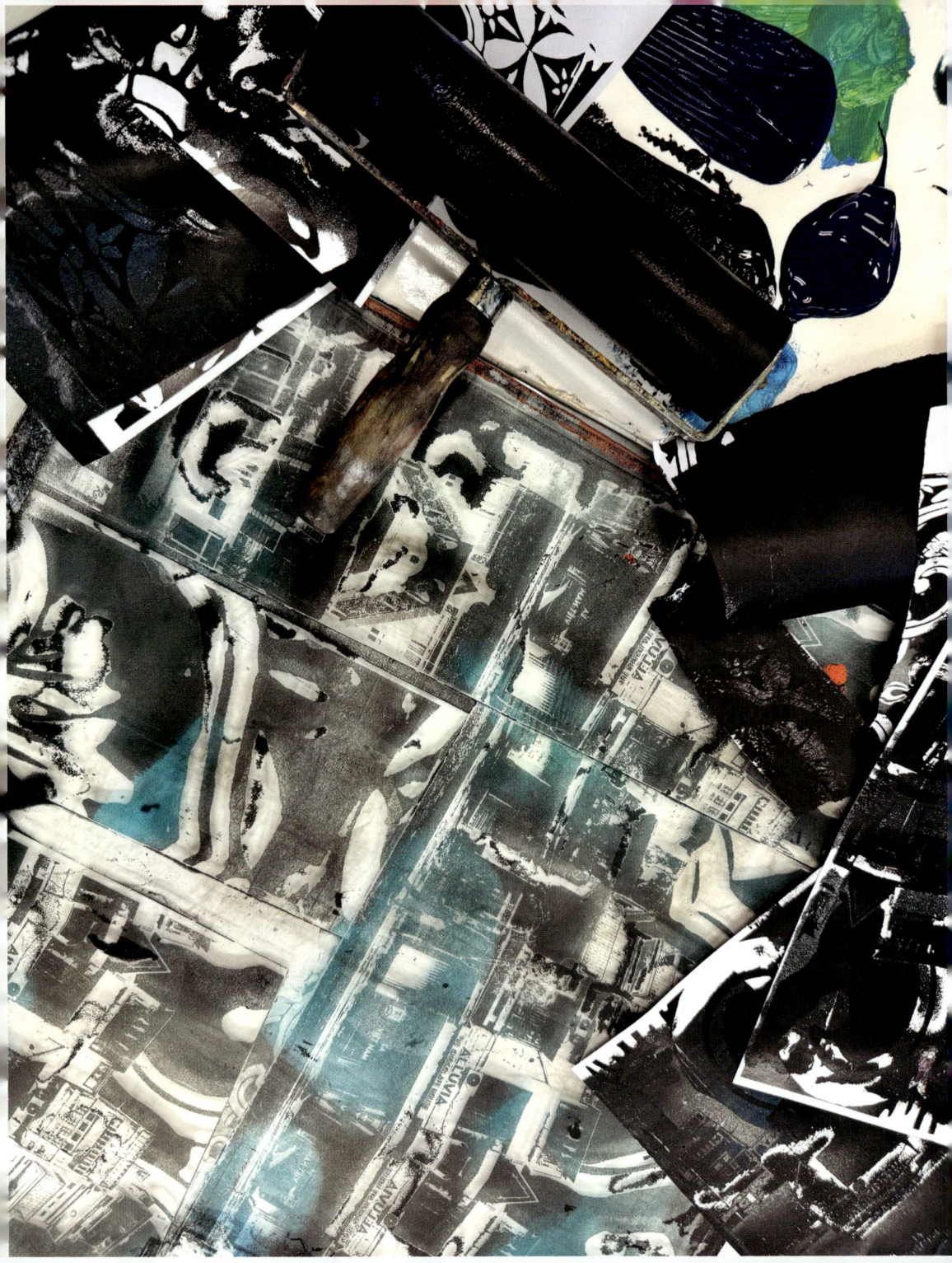

12
LAYERED TRANSFERS

If your gel plate practice has started feeling like a paint-by-numbers exercise (remove colors here, add them back there), this chapter is your permission slip to break out of that cycle. We're about to start an adventure that'll make your usual image transfers look like warm-up exercises!

LAYER UP

In my work, whether it is painting, collage, or printmaking, layering is more than a visual choice. It's how I make sense of the world. I've lived in many places, and navigating the cultural nuances of each has shaped how I see and what I make. Gel plate printmaking gave me a way to bring identity, place, and memory into a single image.

In this chapter, I will show you how these same techniques can help you explore your ideas to build a narrative into your layers. I'll break down my process so you can see how to bring in your perspective, one layer at a time.

COMBINING IMAGE TRANSFERS

You can approach multi-image transfers in lots of ways, and each method has its own effect. One technique is to roll acrylic paint over your entire gel plate and lay down several photos at once. This lets you combine multiple images in a single transfer. Another method is to create one image transfer, let it dry, mask it off with a layer of paint or paper, then apply another layer of paint and add a second transfer behind it. The tricky part? Sometimes, the first transfer will lift when you add the next one, but hey, that's part of the process and can give you a double exposure effect.

SILHOUETTES

I played with silhouettes by cutting out the dome of Santa Maria Della Pace and the skyline of Naples, Italy, and then layering a laser-printed tile image in the sky. This kind of layering can add depth, contrast, and storytelling elements to your prints. I started by cutting out the silhouette of my high-contrast photo of the skyline. Covering the plate with a darker green, I placed the skyline at the bottom third of the plate and then laid a larger A4 laser-printed photo of tiles from Portugal over the silhouetted photo and the rest of the plate. After pressing down on the paper, I lifted the tile image, followed by the skyline image. The tile image was able to transfer everywhere the skyline photo was not. I added Titanium White to the same color I used for the transfer layer to create a much lighter tint of that hue for the pickup layer, then I pulled the print onto Bristol. The final image juxtaposes the delicate lines of the skyline with the bold graphic lines of the tile.

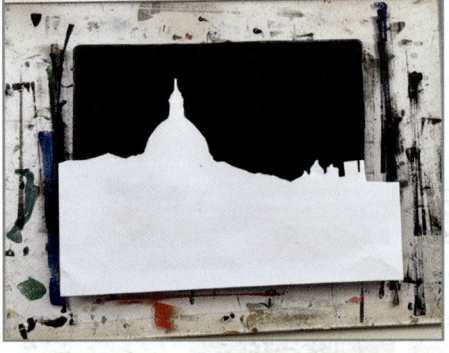

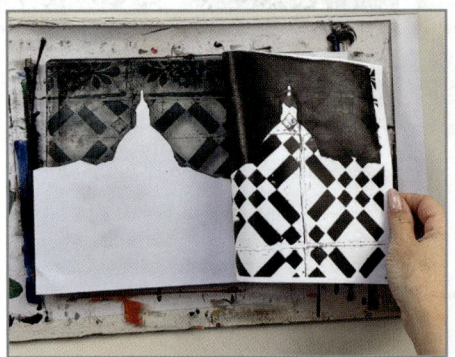

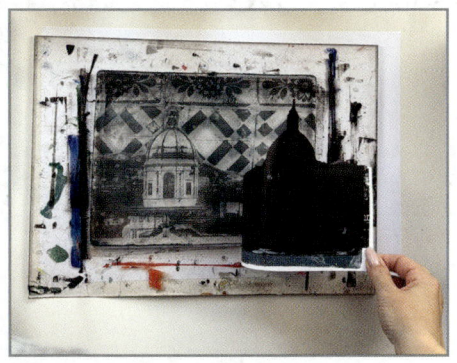
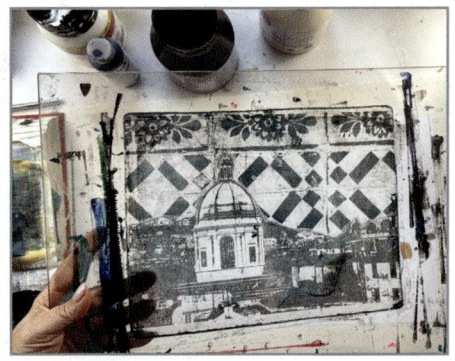
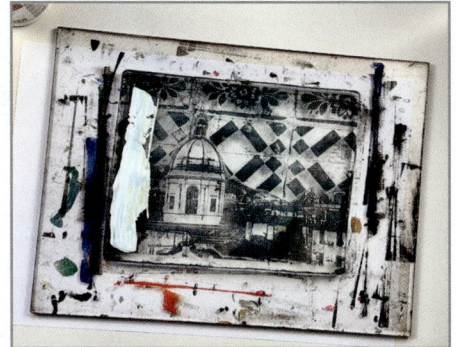
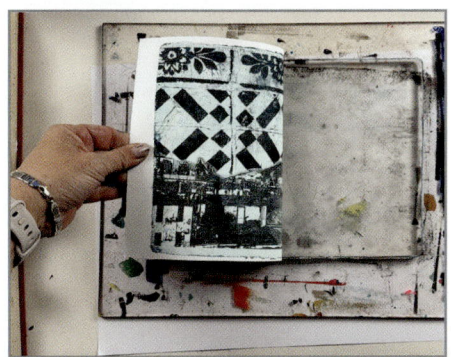
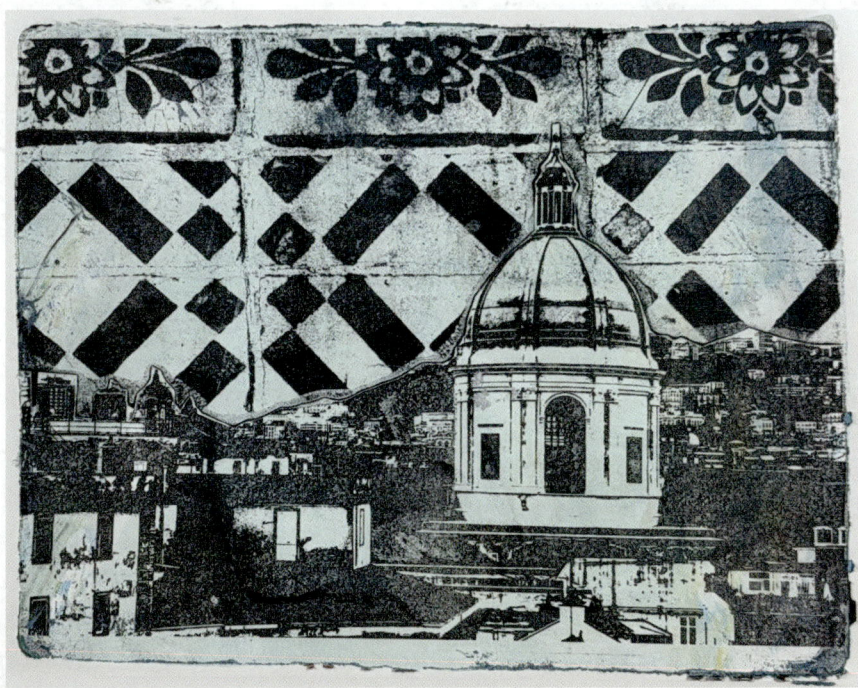

STAMPS

You can also use your laser print like a stamp, repeatedly transferring the same image to build up a distressed, layered effect. This method works exceptionally well when combining multiple photos or even mixing text into your composition. Try starting with one image transfer in a bold or dark tone, then layering a more transparent color over the top. This can create interesting dimension in your print.

OPACITY

Don't forget about opacity. Mixing in a gel medium or using a more translucent paint can shift how the underlying image shows through. Play around! You'll start to get a feel for which colors push forward, which recede, and how they interact with the image itself.

LAYERS AND MIXED MEDIA

Layering several image transfers can add depth, and a fun variation is to blend magazine image transfers with your own photography for a mixed-media feel.

For instance, I combined a photograph of the Church of Santa Maria Novella in Florence, Italy, with tiles from Lisbon, Portugal, and Tam Cốc, Vietnam, on my 16 × 20-inch plate. By stacking the image transfers on top of one another, I created depth and layers. By using similar colors in the transfers, I helped harmonize the overall composition.

Being experimental like this takes some risk-taking; you have to be prepared to have it not work out. Let loose, enjoy the process, and see what you learn in the making.

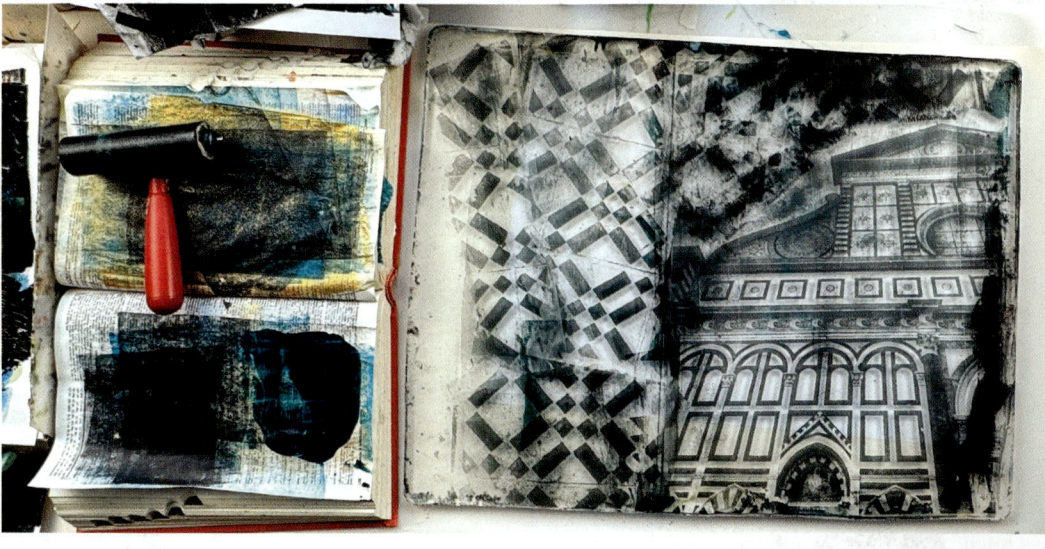

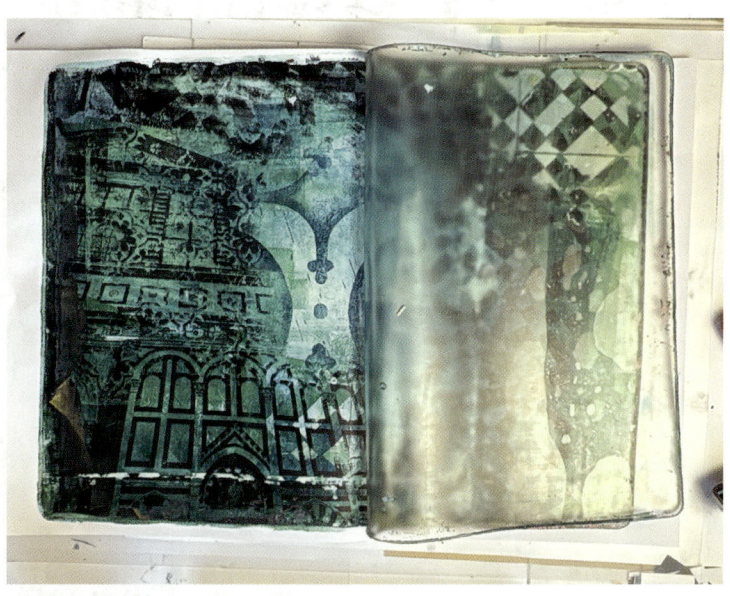

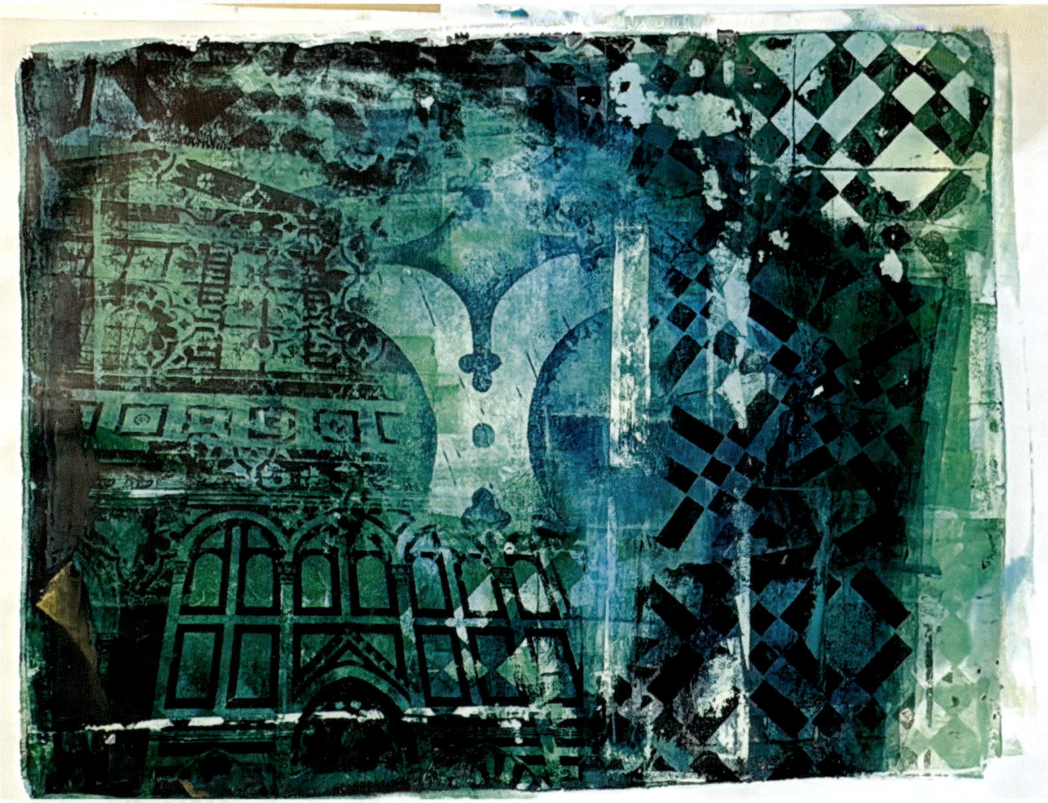

WASTE NOT, WANT NOT

Do you have scrap laser prints around? Doubles of prints or trimmed off pieces? Start putting them together in interesting ways to create new compositions.

Your stack of laser prints is a treasure trove; don't toss it! Some images work beautifully when transferred multiple times, each pull a little more faded and textural. Others are perfect for cutting up and weaving into a mixed-media collage (see below).

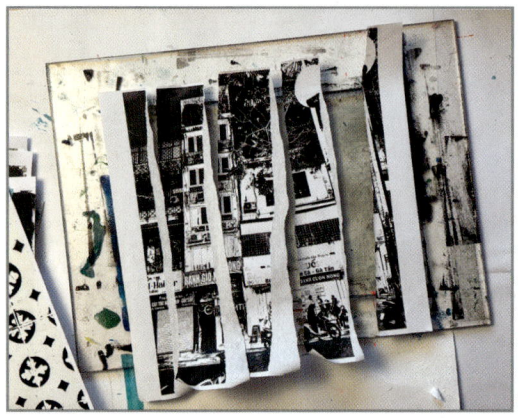 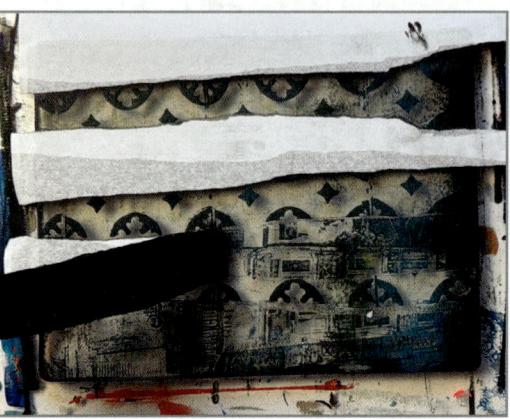

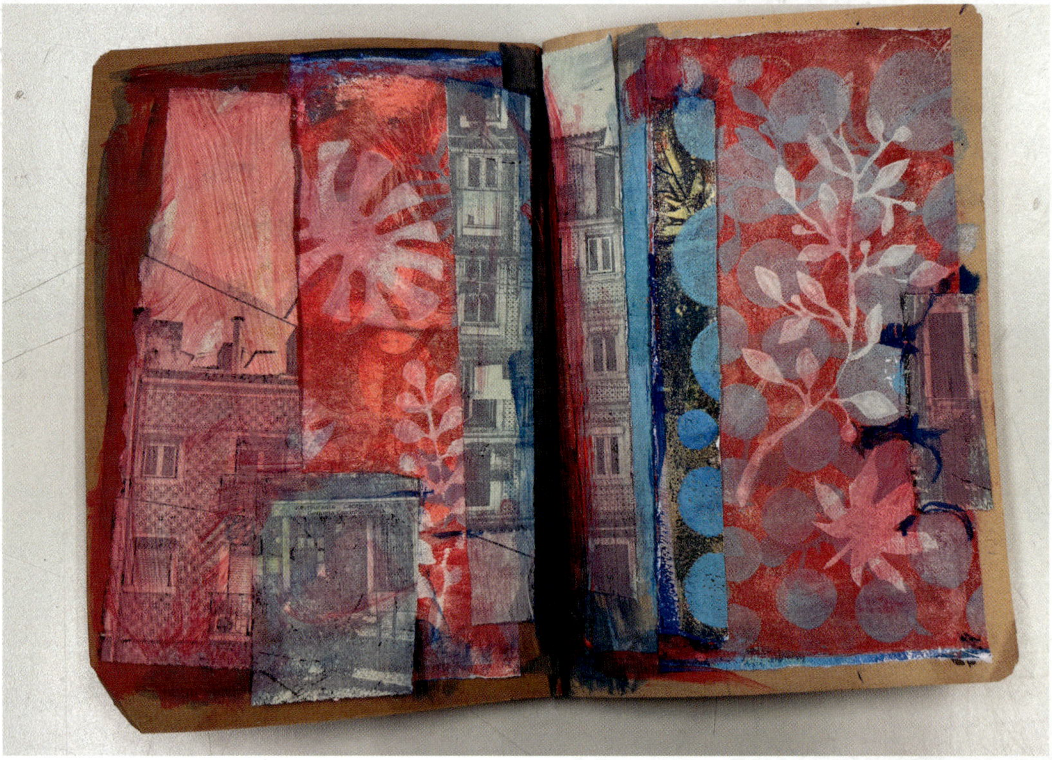

This was made from used laser transfers, stencil prints, and a variety of scraps from my studio.

COLLAGE FLOW TIPS

Everyone has their own style of working, but here's what I like to do with my collages:

- **Mix it up:** Combine large, bold elements with smaller, detailed ones.
- **Rotate for balance:** Turn vertical pieces horizontal and vice versa.

- **Repeat:** Repeat elements, even if you change their scale, to help create harmony and keep the viewer's eye moving around the composition.
- **Stick to a color palette:** Use a consistent palette to create harmony, especially when working with a variety of textures and styles.

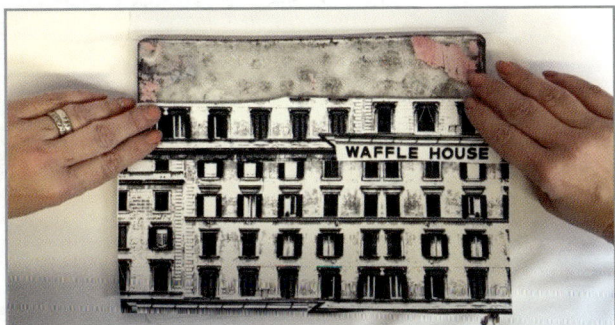
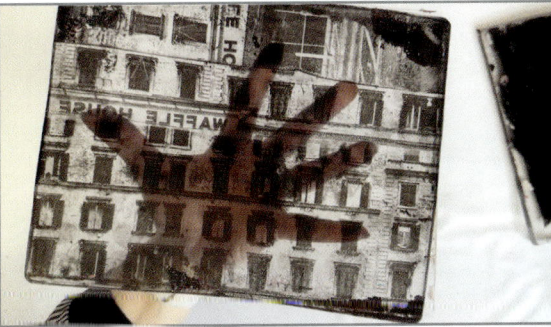

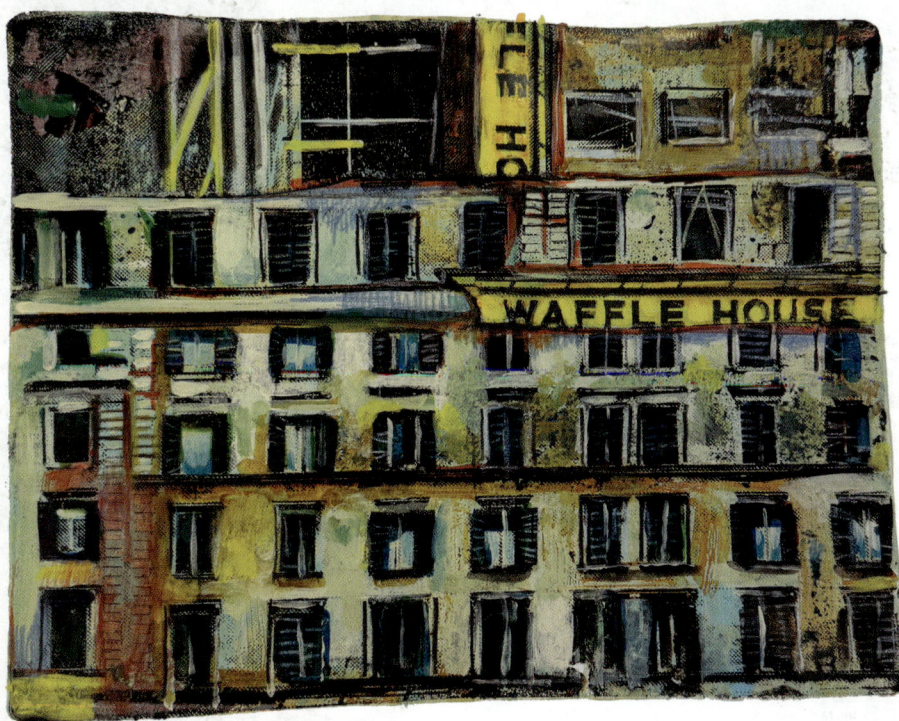

SEAMS AND EDGES

One challenge that often comes with layering and collage work is the appearance of visible cut lines or seams between your image pieces. If those edges feel distracting, you can easily soften them by gently applying a cotton swab and a touch of baby oil or hand sanitizer to the image transfer. It's a simple way to blend the surface without damaging the image. That said, I often choose to keep seams visible. To me, they add a sense of structure and history to the work, proof of the process. In the print below, I pieced together several scraps from my laser prints to create a larger, collaged image. The seams are clearly visible, and I leaned into them, letting them become part of the visual rhythm and texture of the final piece.

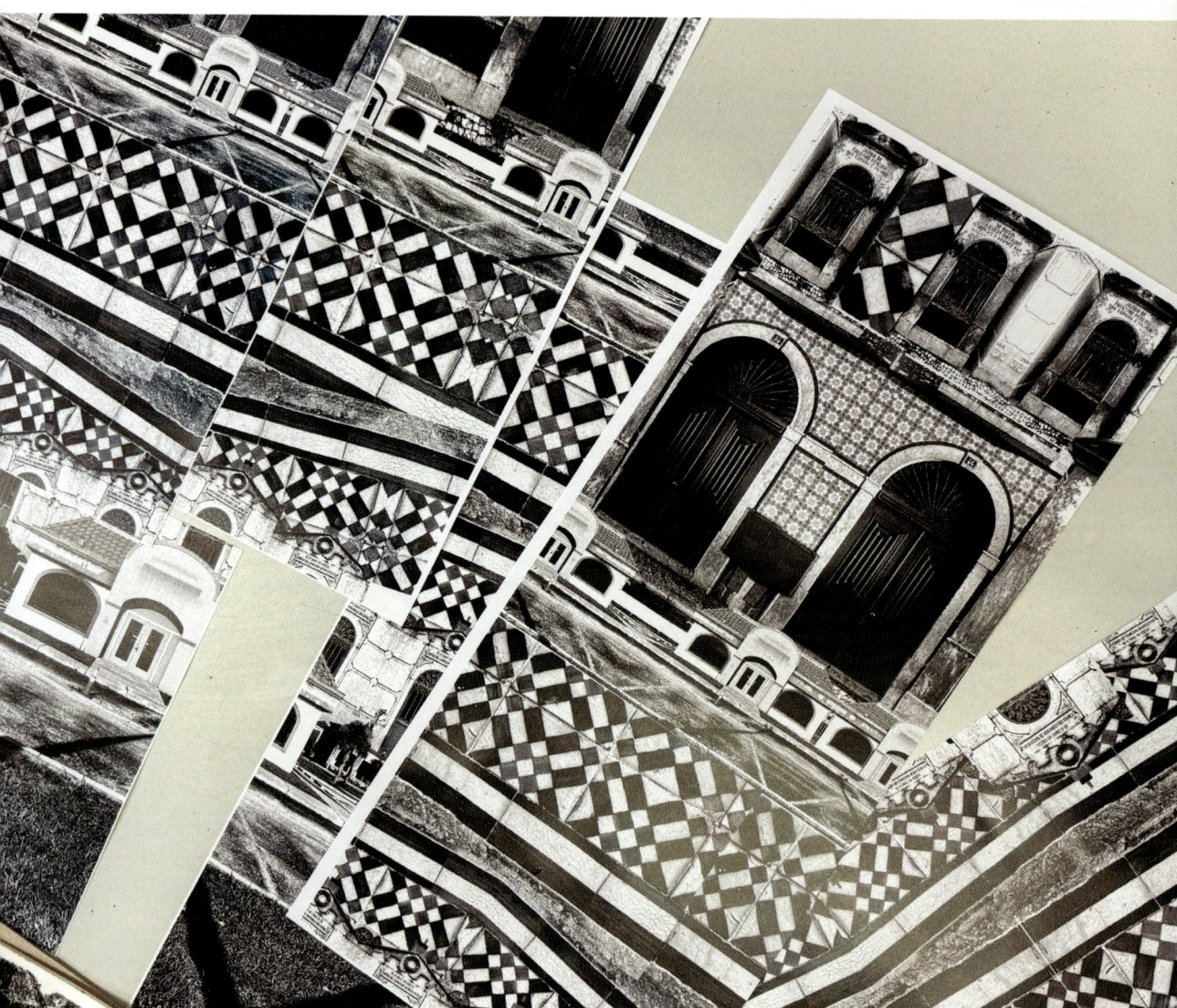

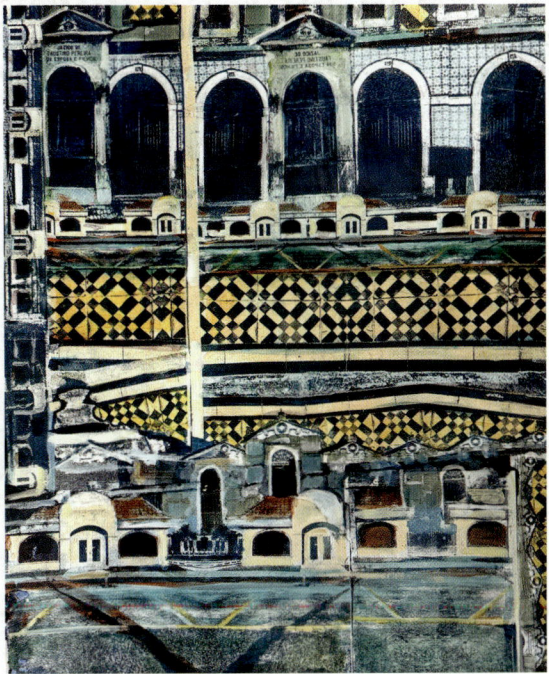

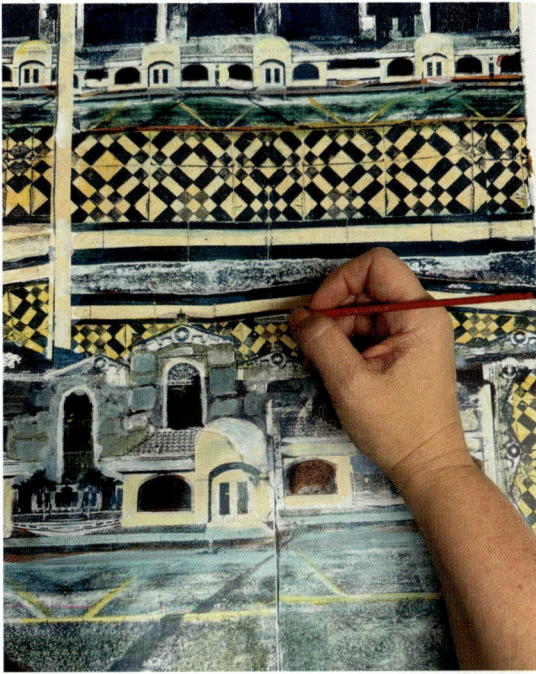

RECYCLE SURPRISES

When a transfer doesn't go as planned? No problem! It is not a mistake, but a surprise. Cut it up and start fresh. These "mistakes" often become the best collage elements later. I compare it to working on a jigsaw puzzle. You pick up a piece, turn it around, and feel your way into where it fits. It's both grounding and freeing. With the right color story and a bit of play, you'll discover new combinations that surprise even you.

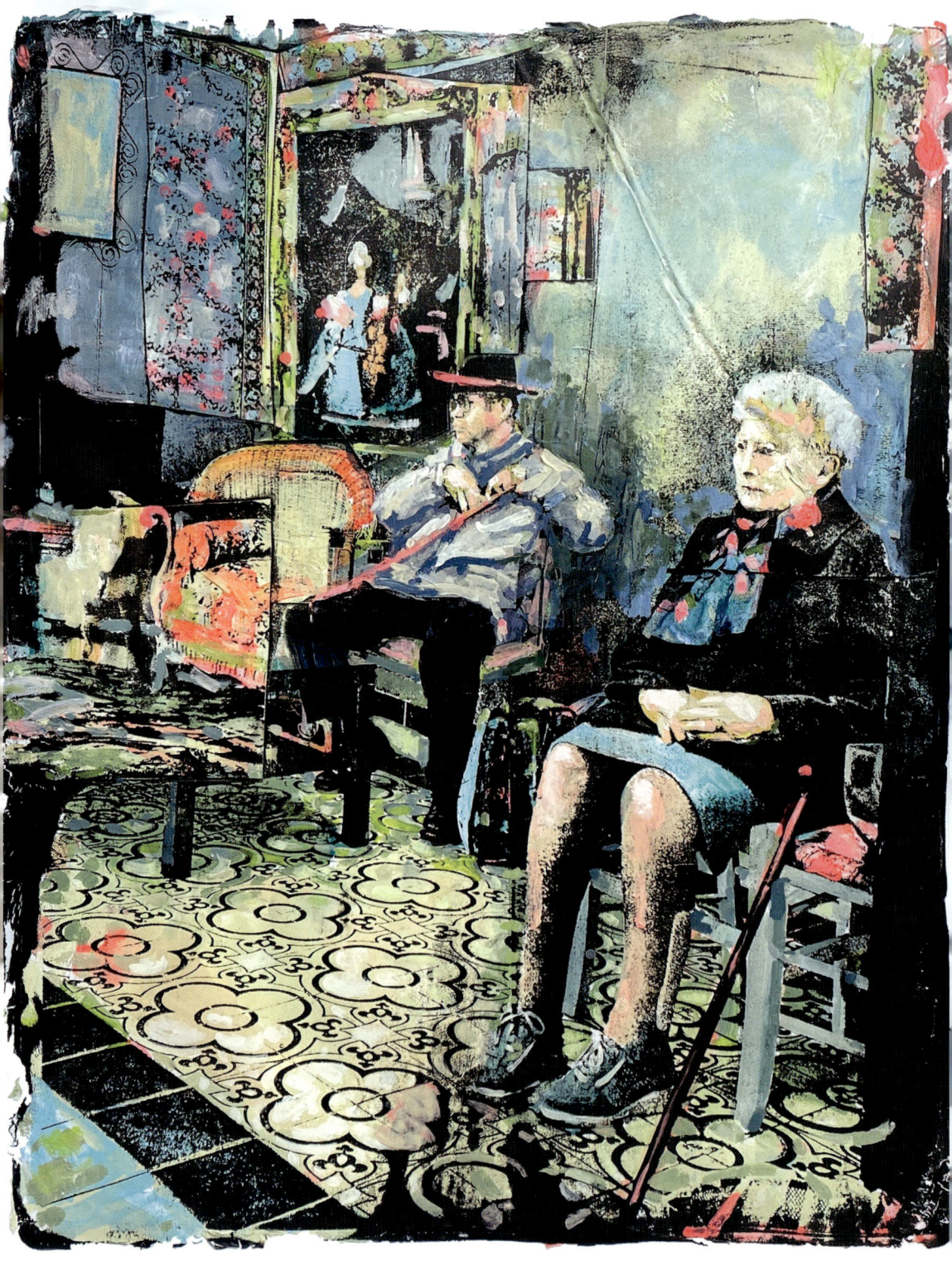

13
IMPOSSIBLE POSSIBLE WITH DIGITAL COLLAGE

By now, you've worked with image transfers, played with layering, and started developing your approach to color. Maybe you've even begun combining transferred images for a more collaged aesthetic. This chapter builds on that foundation and takes you further toward creating compositions that feel expansive, intentional, and full of narrative.

You'll learn how to take disparate elements and bring them together to construct scenes that don't exist in the real world yet still feel emotionally grounded. I'll walk you through how I combine architecture from different cities, layer personal memories with unlikely pairings, and use symmetry, rhythm, and contrast to build a visual language that feels both surreal and oddly familiar.

INVENTING NEW WORLDS

Consider the image on the opposite page, for example.

I combined my photographs from the Palace of Versailles with another photograph of elegantly dressed older people waiting at a market in Strasbourg, France. The juxtaposition of ornate elements with everyday moments captures a quiet kind of presence and timeless style, unified by soft, cool tones and the occasional pop of hot pink.

This work came from a desire to create a setting that couldn't exist in reality, but still carried a sense of truth. At first glance, most people don't realize that it's a composite image. That's the power of collage. It gives us the tools to reassemble the world in a way that speaks more to our feelings than to facts.

COMPOSING WITH PHOTOGRAPHS

Creating unexpected dialogues between images and my photos are a central part of my process. It allows me to create visual narratives from real places, giving me the freedom to recontextualize them entirely. By playing with scale, context, and juxtaposition, you're not just making a collage; you're crafting new narratives.

You can combine printed images by hand through traditional collage or use digital tools to explore compositions more fluidly. I often use photo-editing apps to test ideas, saving multiple versions as I play with scale and placement. This digital sketching phase helps me solve composition problems before I ever touch the plate. It's like writing a draft. You can rearrange, delete, duplicate, and test possibilities without wasting materials.

For the image below, I started with the photo of a Vietnamese vase, then layered in photos of Portuguese tiles and French graffiti. The intention was to build a scene that couldn't exist in any form other than through the intersection of my experiences and my own photos. Each piece, drawn from the places I've been, guided me toward this particular composition. Instead of assembling components, I begin constructing environments.

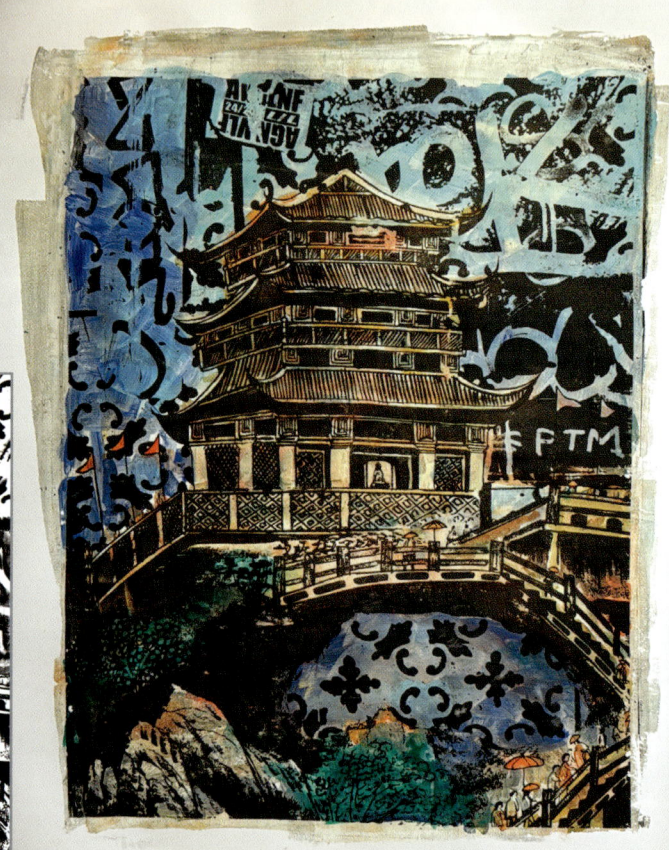

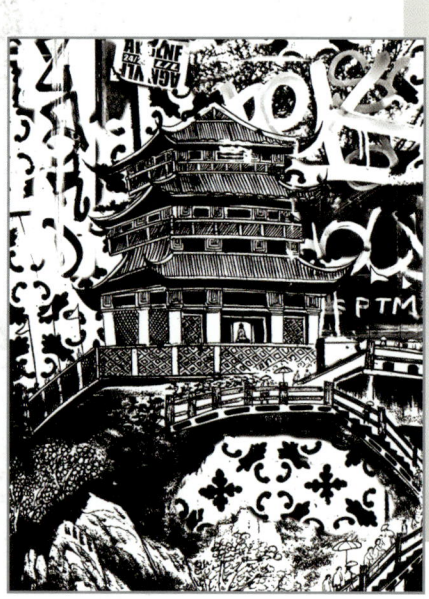

PLAYING WITH SYMMETRY AND REPETITION

For the next example, I combined images from the United States, Italy, and Germany before printing. Aesthetically, I wanted to create a layered cityscape. The result is a seemingly realistic yet surreal landscape, blending diverse architectural styles in a way that would be impossible in real life.

I also love working with symmetry and mirrored elements, using them to emphasize patterns and repetition. Those blue and black striped peaks? They're beach cabanas from Versailles! And yes, I did stick a Waffle House sign on a building near the Rome Termini train station, with some traditional German half-timbered houses peeking out above, while a street from Naples, Italy, towers behind them, adding another layer to the composition.

When I was satisfied with the composition, I edited the final photo to make it high contrast and converted it into a halftone (below). I laser printed my collage on A4 and A3 laser paper. I chose a slightly heavier paper (120 gsm) for added durability because I needed to align multiple sheets on the gel plate, and I used CMYK print settings to ensure the most concentrated toner for the prints. I loosely taped them together to do the image transfer.

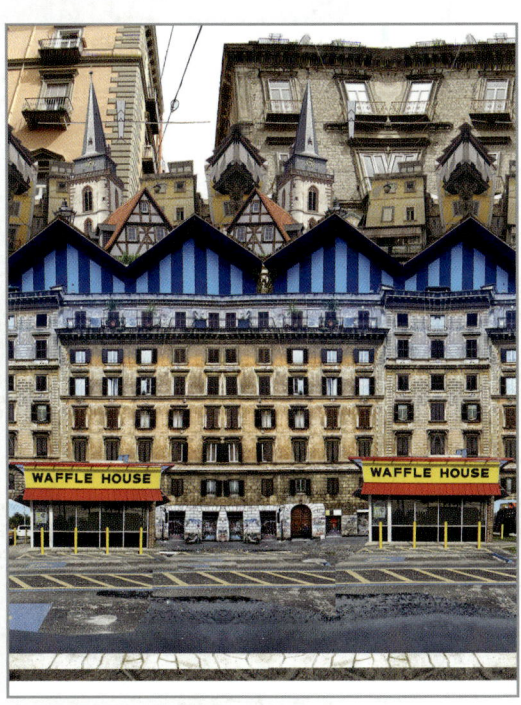

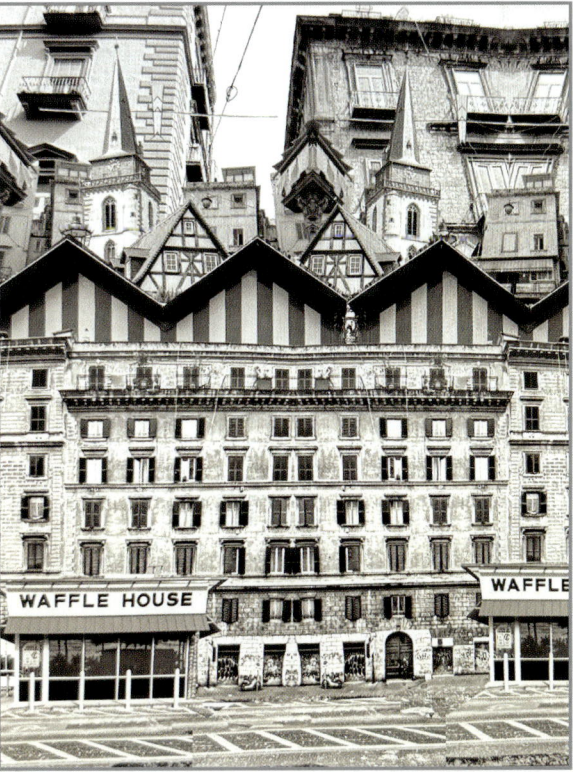

Halftone for better texture.

SEAMS A BIT OFF? ROLL WITH IT!

Now, let me tell you about my first attempt at transferring this massive image. It was a total fail! I laid a thin layer of Black Oxide over the plate. I tried to do the image transfer all at once, and the Black Oxide dried too fast. The second try went much better. I broke the laser print down into two sections and rolled out the paint on half of the plate at a time, starting with the bottom half before adding the upper half. When working on a large scale, seams between papers are inevitable. You can either embrace them as part of the texture or find creative ways to disguise them. If you prefer a seamless look, consider having your collage printed as a full-size laser print. I enjoy the organic, textured quality

that seams and unpredictable lines add to the final piece. You can soften any overly distracting areas with a cotton swab or even paint over them once your monotype is complete.

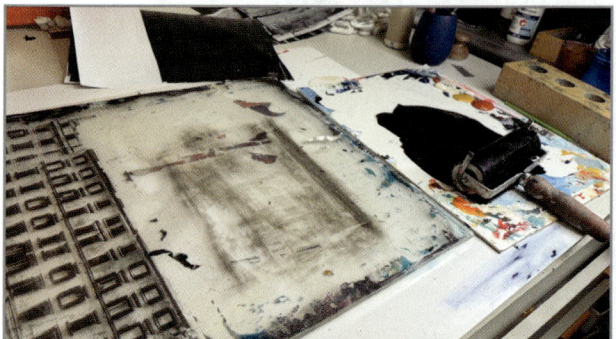

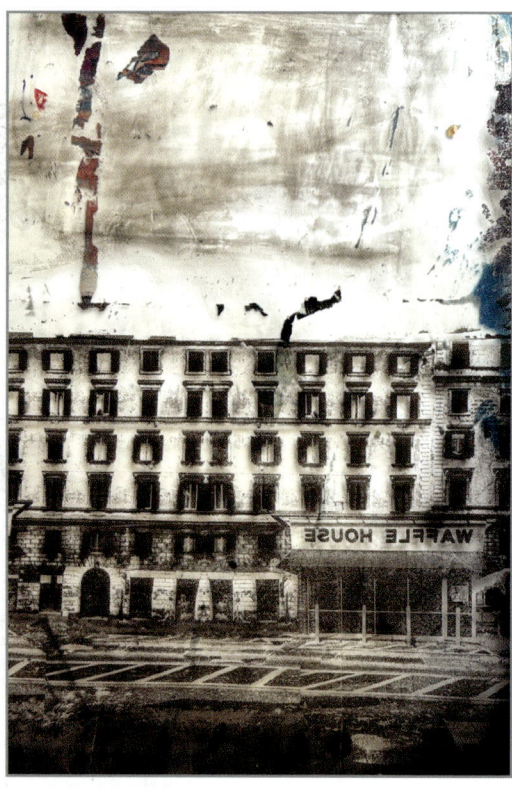

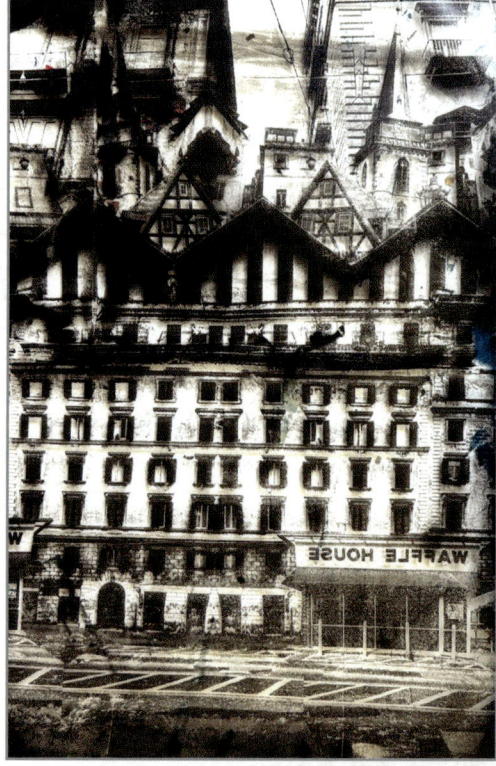

BUILDING LAYERS

After transferring my image, I laid down a coat of gel medium to help grip the following layers. I waited a few minutes for it to dry, then moved into the reverse painting stage, focusing on balancing detail with color harmony.

Typically, I start reverse painting with the details and then expand into the larger areas, but for this piece, I switched things up. I needed to block in some of the bigger color areas first to see how they would interact and how I could create variations to build my composition. (For more detail on my approach to color in this print, see Chapter 4, "Making Colors Work.")

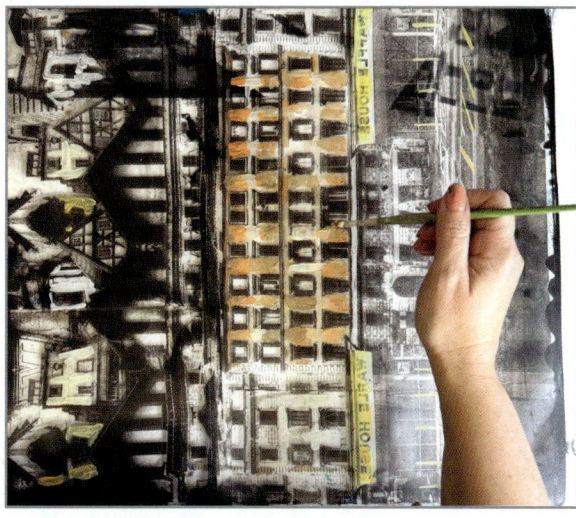

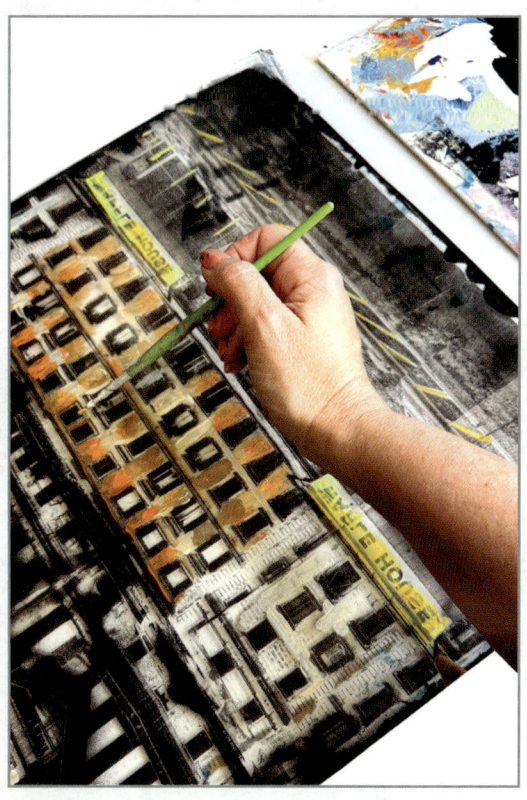

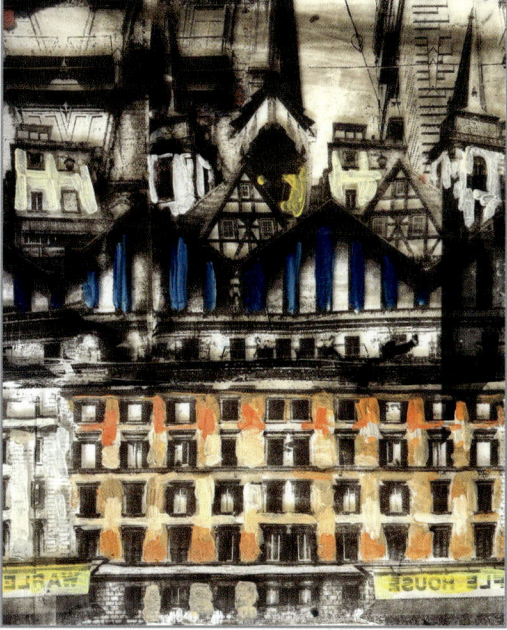

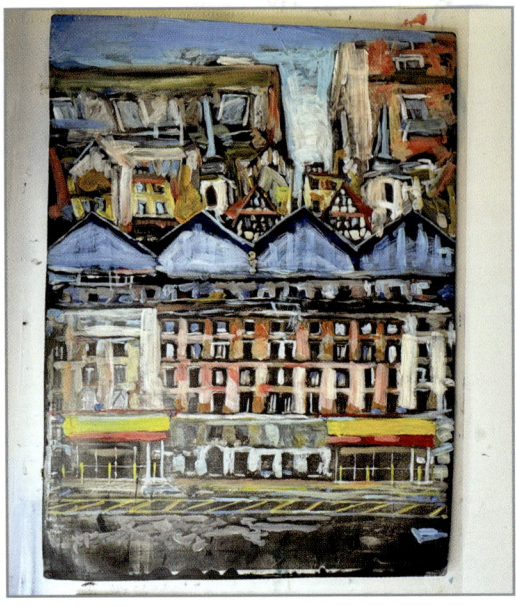

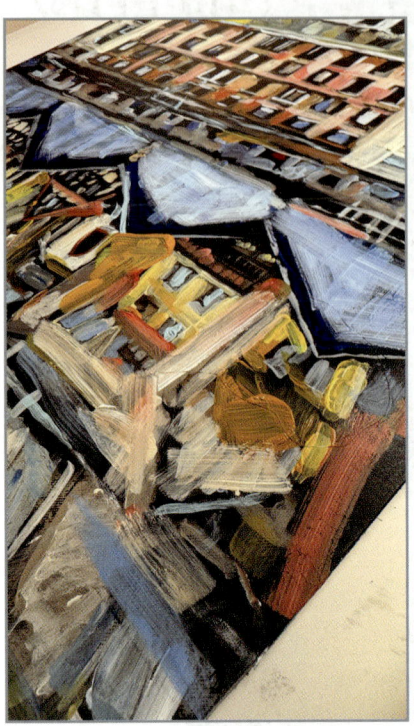

I worked on the reverse painting for some time, aiming to get the colors just right and working all around the plate to help create harmony. Sometimes, working with reverse painting might feel like coloring in a coloring book, but slight variations in brushstrokes and color layering create depth and a painterly feel.

Understanding relative color perception is essential when working with paint. Colors appear different depending on their surroundings. For example, placing blue next to bright white makes it look more intense, whereas putting it next to orange changes its perceived warmth. I used this principle to adjust values and create depth within the composition.

PICKUP LAYER

When I was satisfied with the color layers, I applied a final pickup layer using a light blue tone similar to the sky. This unified the print and subtly cooled the warmer colors near the bottom. I pressed Bristol board (205 gsm) onto the plate, placed books on top for even contact, and let it dry overnight.

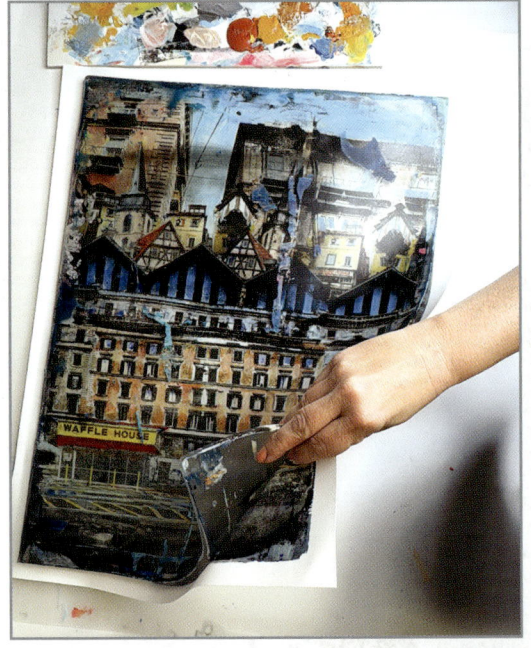

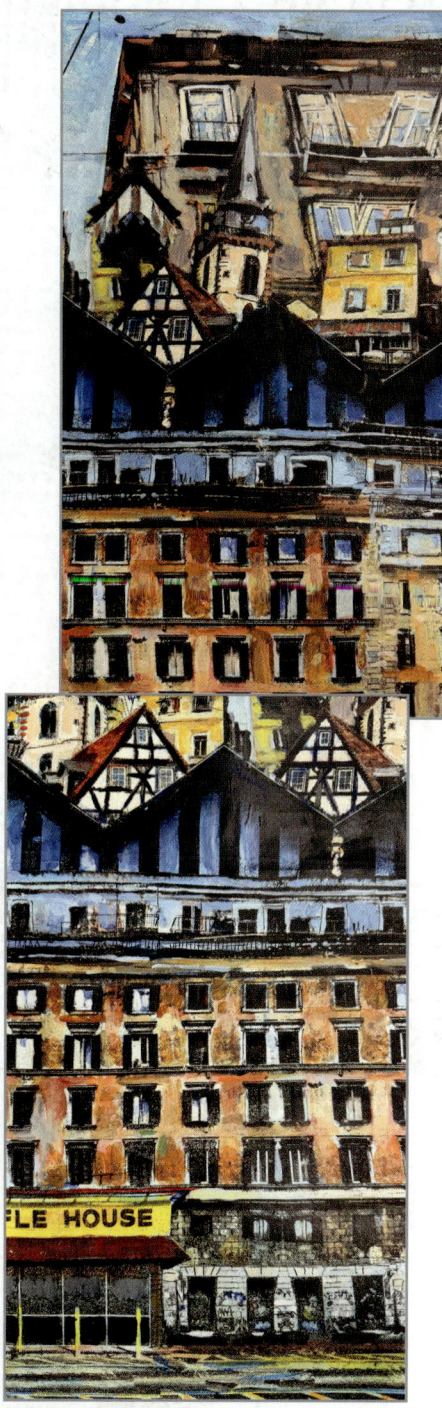

PROBLEM SOLVING

Peeling the print off the gel plate the next day required patience, but the result was worth it! I needed to make only a few touch-ups. The Waffle House sign lost an *F* in the transfer process, and a seam line ran through the center of the image. I softened these with paint while keeping the natural, crusty textures around the edges intact. Ultimately, they added character to the print.

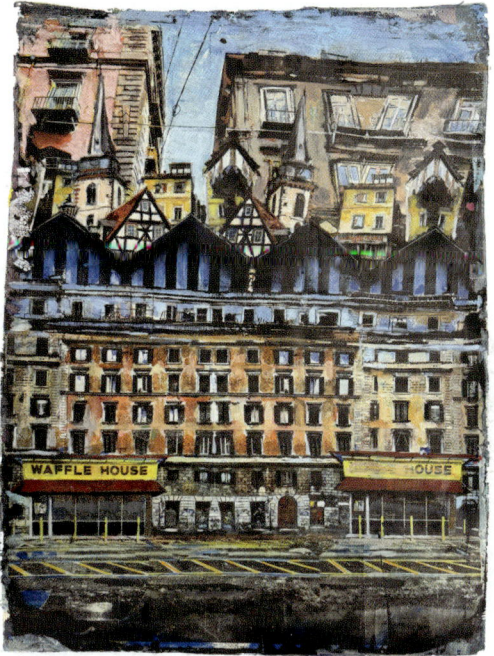

YOUR TURN

When you create your layered prints, remember that it's not about perfection. It's about exploration and happy accidents. Experiment with combining different images, explore color relationships, and don't be afraid to break up patterns to keep things interesting. Add those little variations in color and brushwork that make the work uniquely yours.

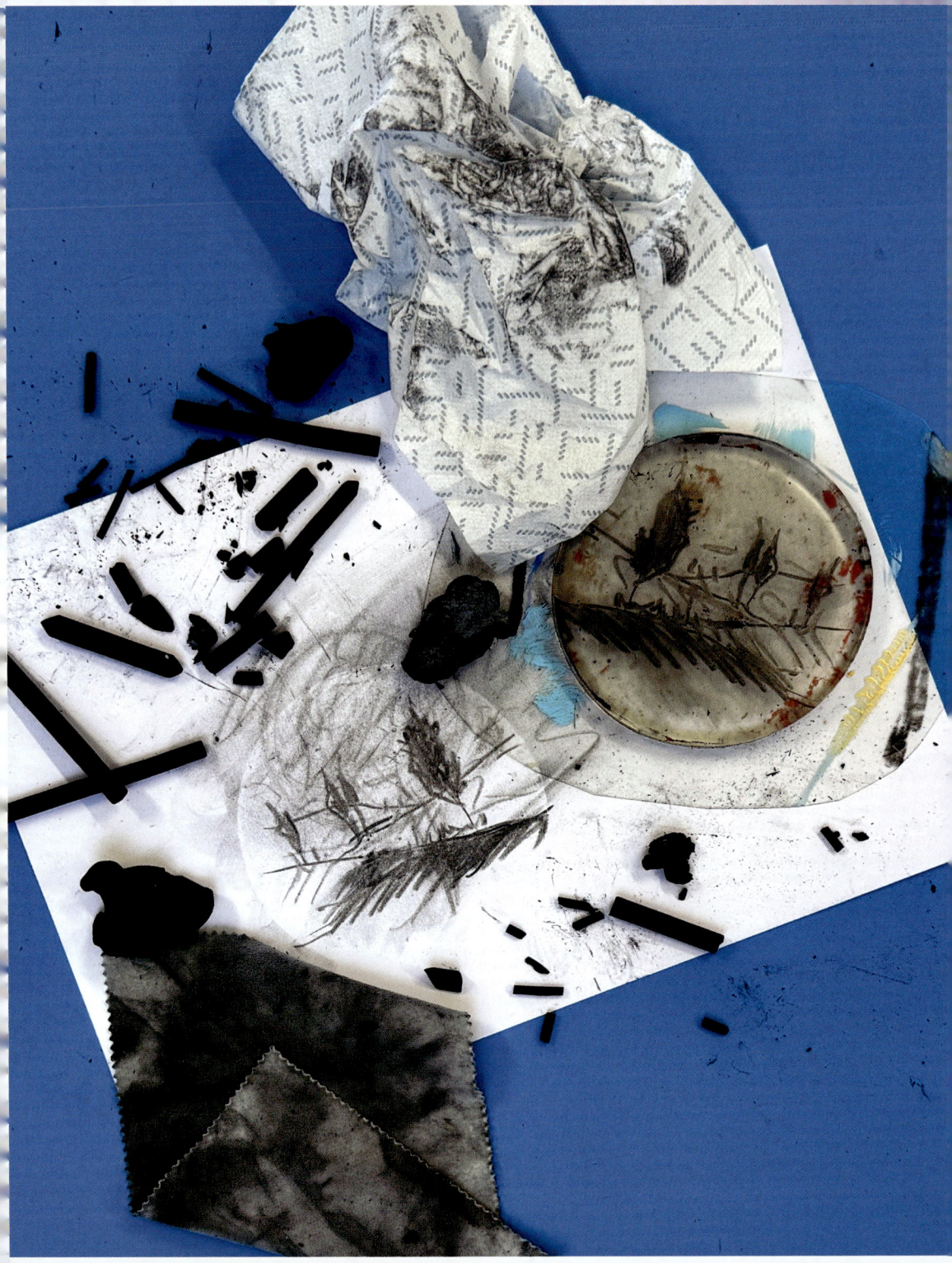

14
CHARCOAL TRANSFERS

It image transfers are feeling a little too rigid or mechanical, charcoal might be your new favorite detour. Charcoal drawings done with soft vine (willow) charcoal can be beautifully and easily transferred onto a gel plate. Vine charcoal provides light, gestural marks, which give your prints a more intuitive and expressive feel. Plus, the level of detail the plate can pick up from a charcoal transfer is simply incredible.

THE BASIC PROCESS

Let's walk through the process with a quick demo.
Sketch a charcoal drawing. In this case, I made some quick lines and shapes using vine charcoal on smooth, 90-gsm recycled printer paper. Usually, I prefer a paper with a little more tooth to catch the charcoal when I draw, but for this test, I went for the scrap paper that was at hand. Shake or blow any excess charcoal dust off your paper. Place your drawing face down onto a bare gel plate. No acrylic or gel medium is needed to do the transfer.

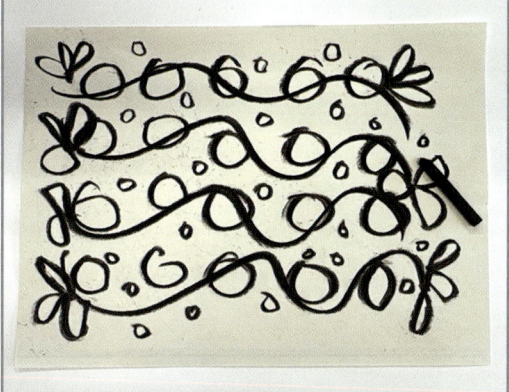

Apply firm but gentle, even pressure over the back of the paper. Lift to reveal your transfer. The charcoal will appear slightly darker on the plate than on the paper.

This dusty layer adheres to the plate without any fixative. When I first tried this, I assumed the charcoal would smudge or lift as soon as I added paint. But once transferred, it holds beautifully. For this test print, I added Quinacridone Magenta, followed by a bright yellow pickup layer. Even though I didn't let the Quinacridone Magenta fully dry (which caused some color blending), the charcoal remained in place.

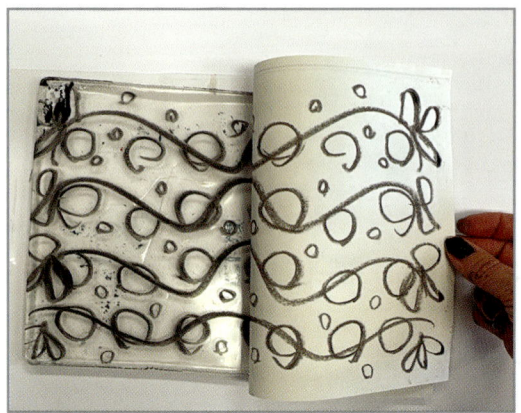
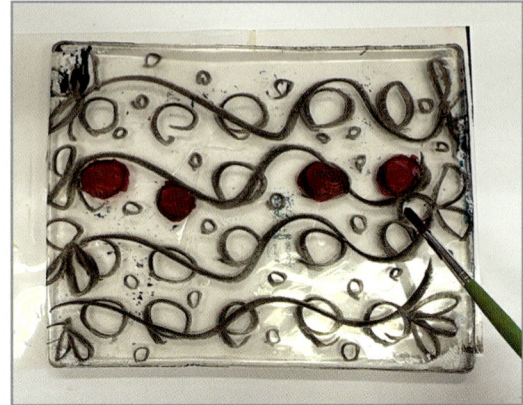
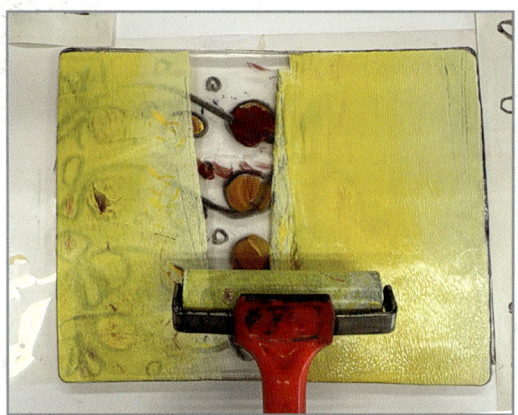
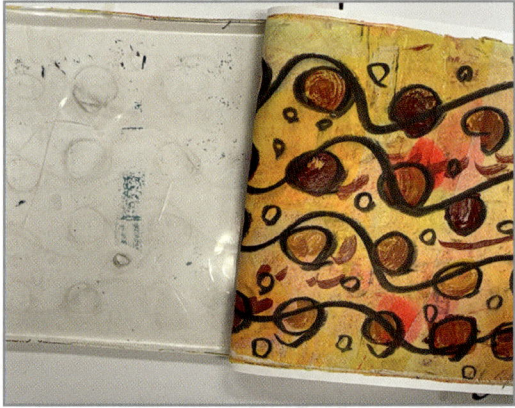

SCALE IT UP

Now, let's scale up the process. This time, I created a large gestural drawing of a tree using vine charcoal on 100-gsm charcoal paper. This paper had a bit more texture, which helped with tone. I worked the drawing with a chamois cloth to soften transitions and used an eraser to pull out highlights and reshape areas until the balance of energy and detail felt right.

I shook off the drawing to remove excess charcoal, gave the back a gentle tap, and then pressed it firmly onto my 18 × 24-inch gel plate. I checked the transfer by lifting a few edges, and when everything looked great, I lifted the drawing off of the gel plate. The tonal variations were clear, and even the erased highlights in the trunk stood out.

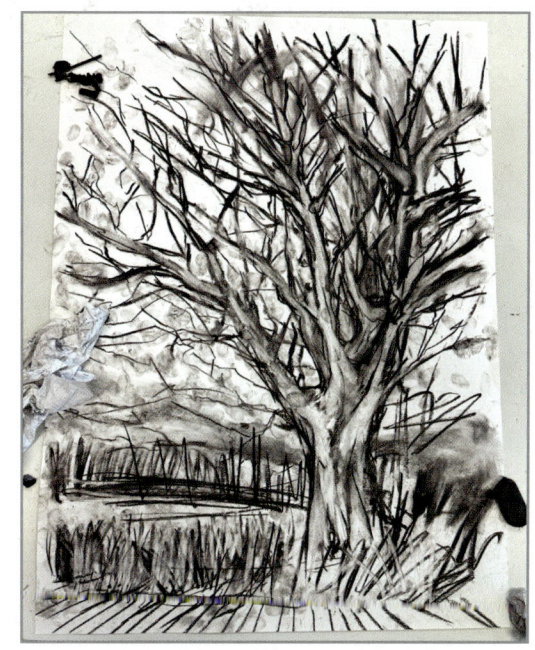

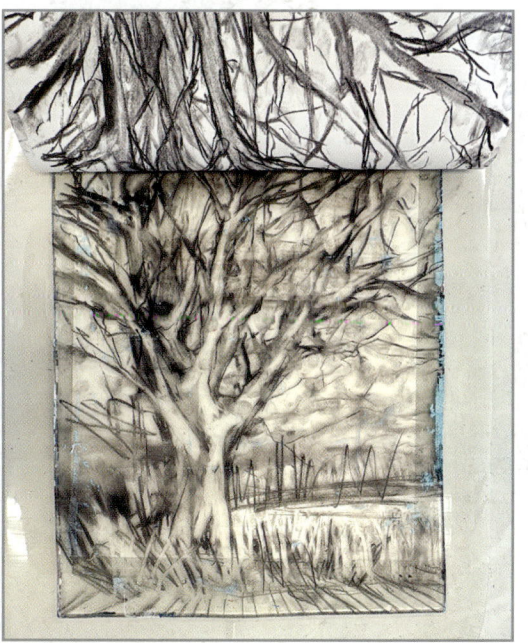

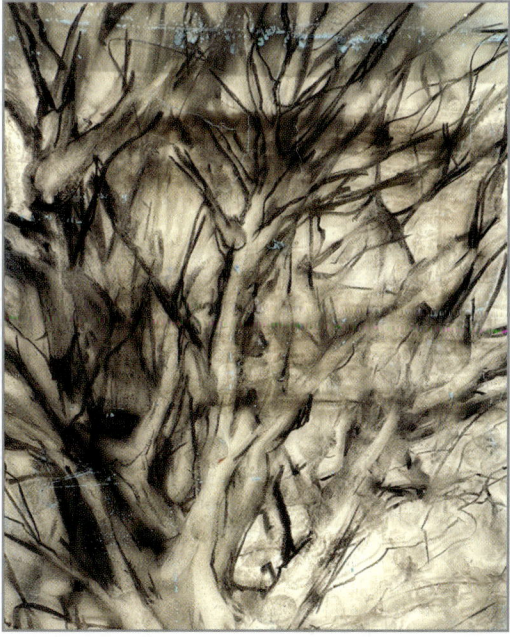

REVERSE PAINTING

Once the charcoal is down on the gel plate, you can add a layer of gel medium to lift your drawing off the plate onto the paper of your choice. However, I wanted to add color. I began reverse painting by focusing on the trunk and branches, starting with smaller brushes and layering in strokes of warm and cool wood tones. I used a mostly analogous palette to keep the piece harmonious but played with split-complementary hues to create contrast.

I kept my light source coming from the upper-right corner of the gel plate (opposite from the original charcoal drawing). I worked with slightly thicker, almost impasto-style brushstrokes and didn't wait for each layer to dry before moving on. Acrylic dries quickly on the plate, but thick strokes give you a little wiggle room.

The idea here was to stay loose and painterly and not to color within the lines, but to think about value, flow, and visual movement. I wanted the brushwork to feel active and layered.

Next came the sky and foreground. I left intentional gaps between the branches and the sky to let the bright Cerulean Blue pickup layer peek through. I painted the sky gradient directly onto the plate, using more saturated Cerulean at the top and lightening it with Titanium White as I moved downward. I laid it in with a brush, then rolled it with a brayer to even out any thick strokes.

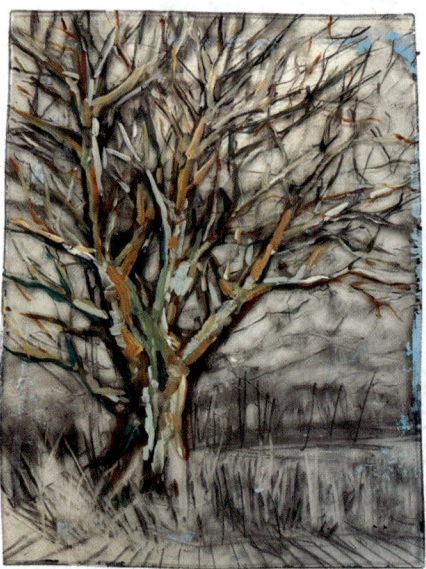

DIRTY PLATE?

You might have noticed that my gel plate isn't pristine. That hazy gray black? It's from past image transfers. This happens from time to time. It doesn't lift, and it doesn't interfere with my prints. But paint on the plate *will* influence my print. For example, some light blue acrylic lingered from a previous piece while I was working on the tree. I could've cleaned it off with tape or mineral oil, but I liked the surprise it might bring, so I left it.

Also, after a transfer, charcoal will linger on the plate. That is okay. Use mineral oil to gently work out

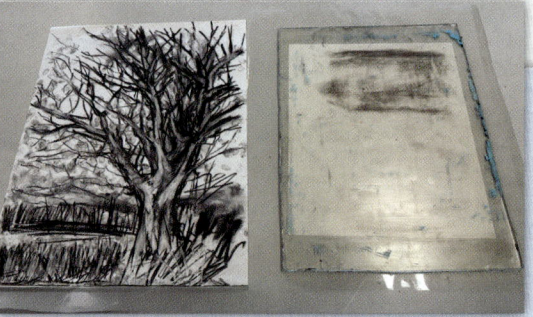

the leftover charcoal. There still may be a haze or ghostly imprint of the charcoal, which most likely will not transfer.

THE PICKUP LAYER

For the final pull, I used 205-gsm Bristol board, which is thick enough to hold up against heavier paint. I spent a lot of time smoothing the paper onto the plate, making sure it had solid contact across the entire surface.

Then, I placed a large piece of cardboard over the print and stacked books on top. The cardboard helped distribute the weight more evenly. Because of the thick layers of paint and the high humidity in my studio, I let it sit for 48 hours. I probably could've pulled it after 24, but I wanted to be safe.

When it was time, I lifted off the books and cardboard, flipped the plate, and began peeling it away from the Bristol. The adhesion was strong, but the Bristol held up just fine.

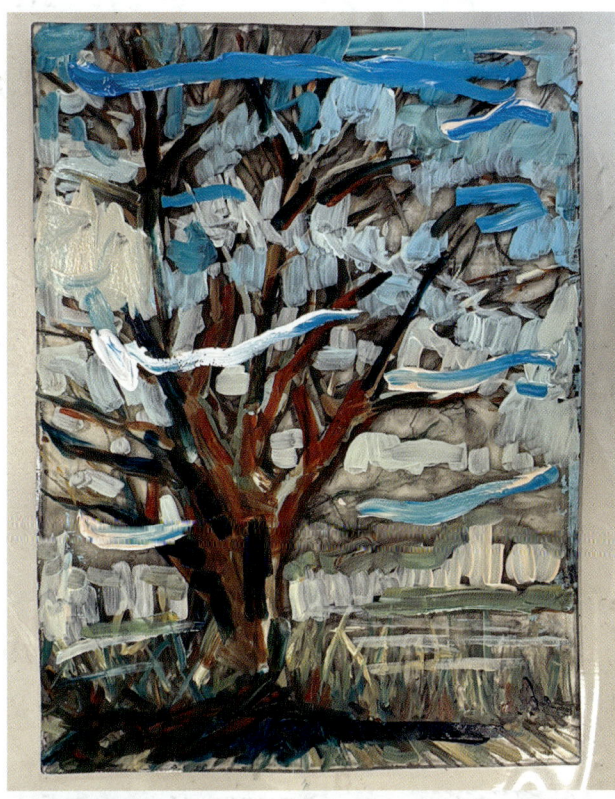

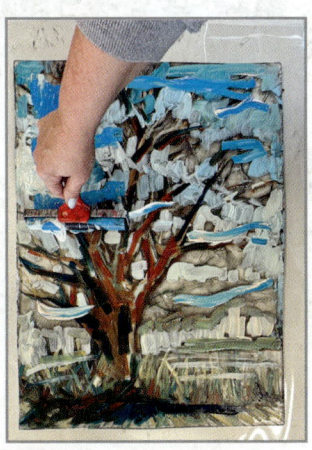

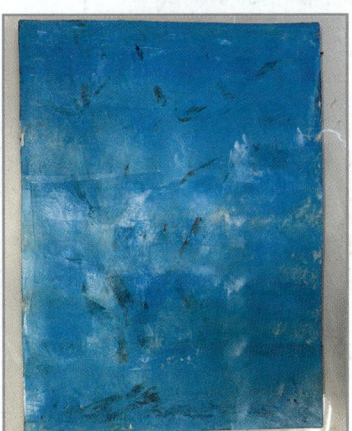

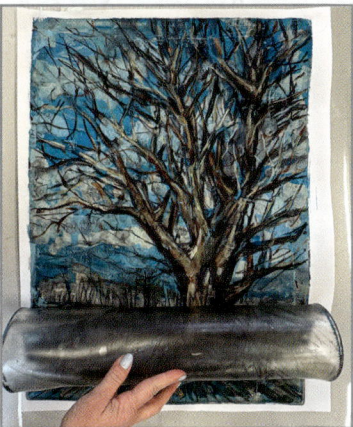

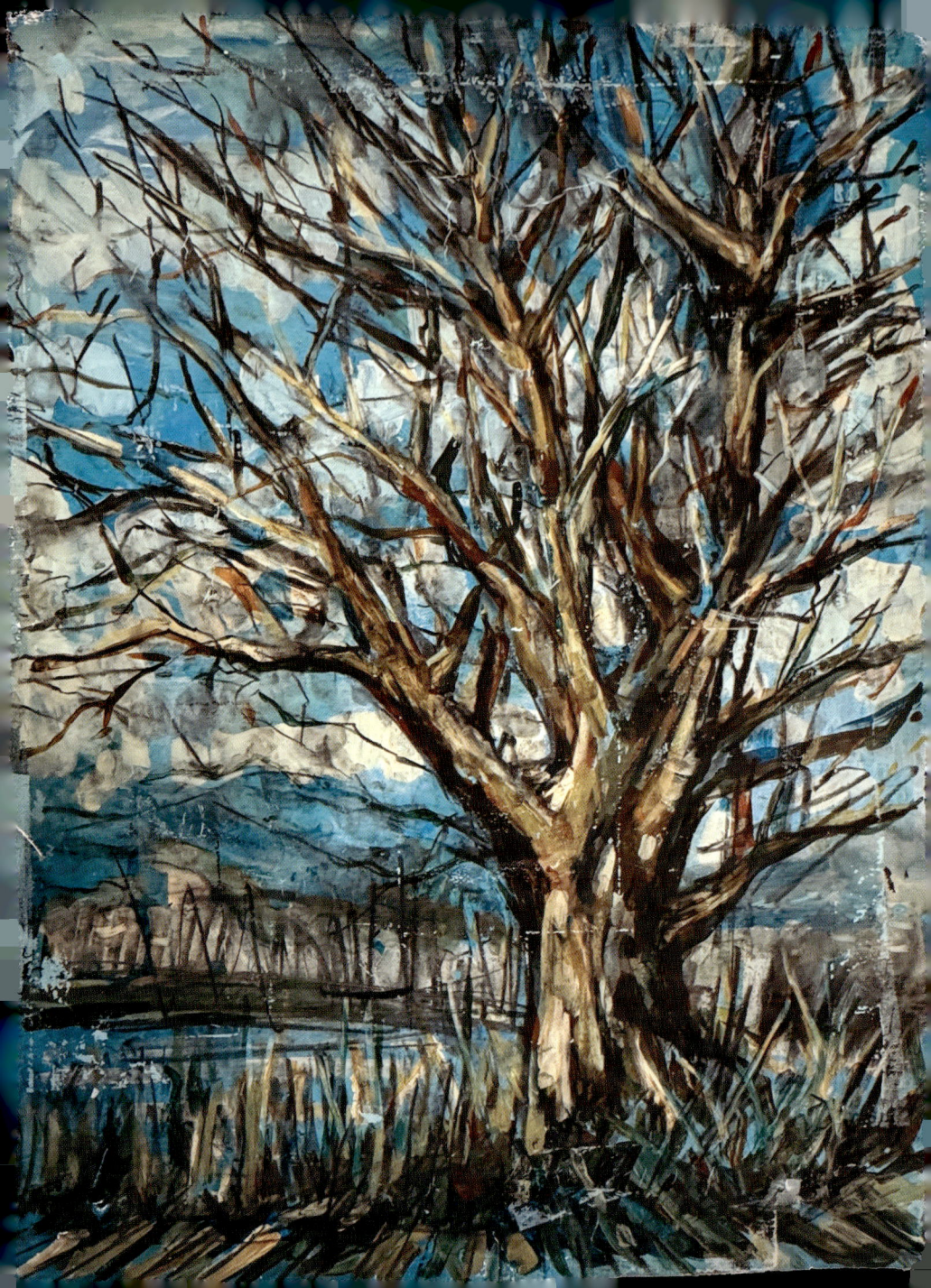

THE FINAL PRINT

This process might feel backward at first, but that's part of the fun. You're layering in reverse, painting from the topmost details down to the background. And in the end, it all pulls together into something surprising, rich, and full of texture. You can still see remnants from a previous print, with little specks and lines of a light blue dappled throughout. There are also some minor wrinkles in the paper, but they don't bother me. They add to the tactile quality of the piece. The tonal qualities of the charcoal drawing remain visible at the top layer of the print, while the brushstrokes underneath add painterly depth.

My fingerprints, smudges, and erasure marks help build shading and add detail to the tree. The Cerulean Blue pickup layer acts like a sky, unifying the entire print and creating contrast against the warmer tones of the tree trunk.

Charcoal drawings let you draw with your whole body, and it is very instinctual. The beauty isn't in perfection, it's in the gesture, the grit, and the unexpected marks that tell a deeper story. The range and depth of mark-making possible with charcoal drawing transfers and the ability to layer and combine drawings make this process incredibly alluring. It merges the expressive energy of drawing with the layered depth of gel plate printing, allowing you to create dynamic, gestural works that retain fine detail while also supporting painterly layers through reverse painting. It's spontaneous, a little messy, and full of character—perfect for artists who want their prints to feel alive, textured, and deeply personal.

NOT JUST CHARCOAL

You can use soft pastels and pan pastels on paper in a similar way to vine charcoal. Their rich pigment and soft texture transfer beautifully to the gel plate. Pastels are a great way to experiment with color right from the start.

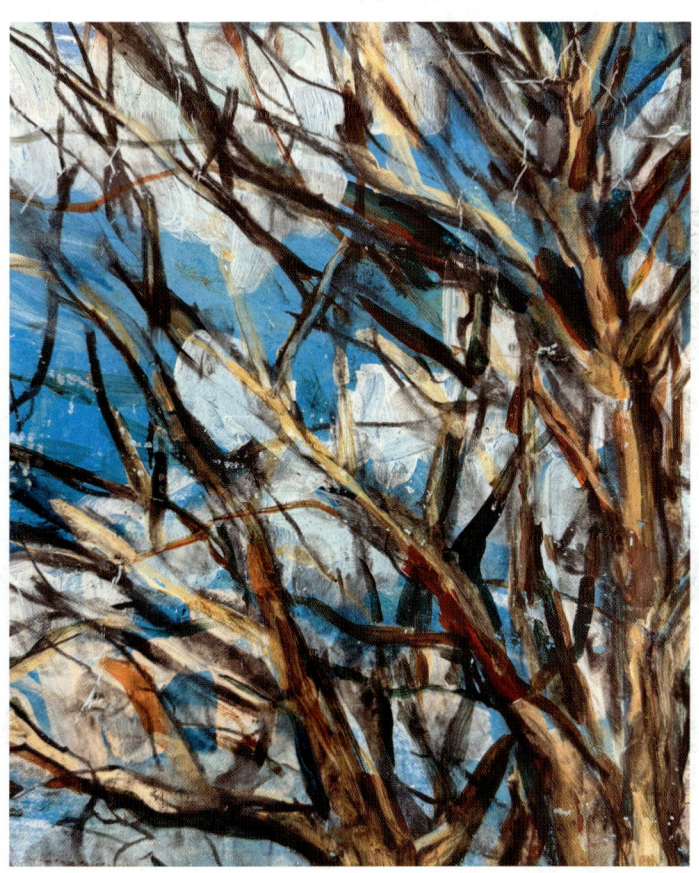

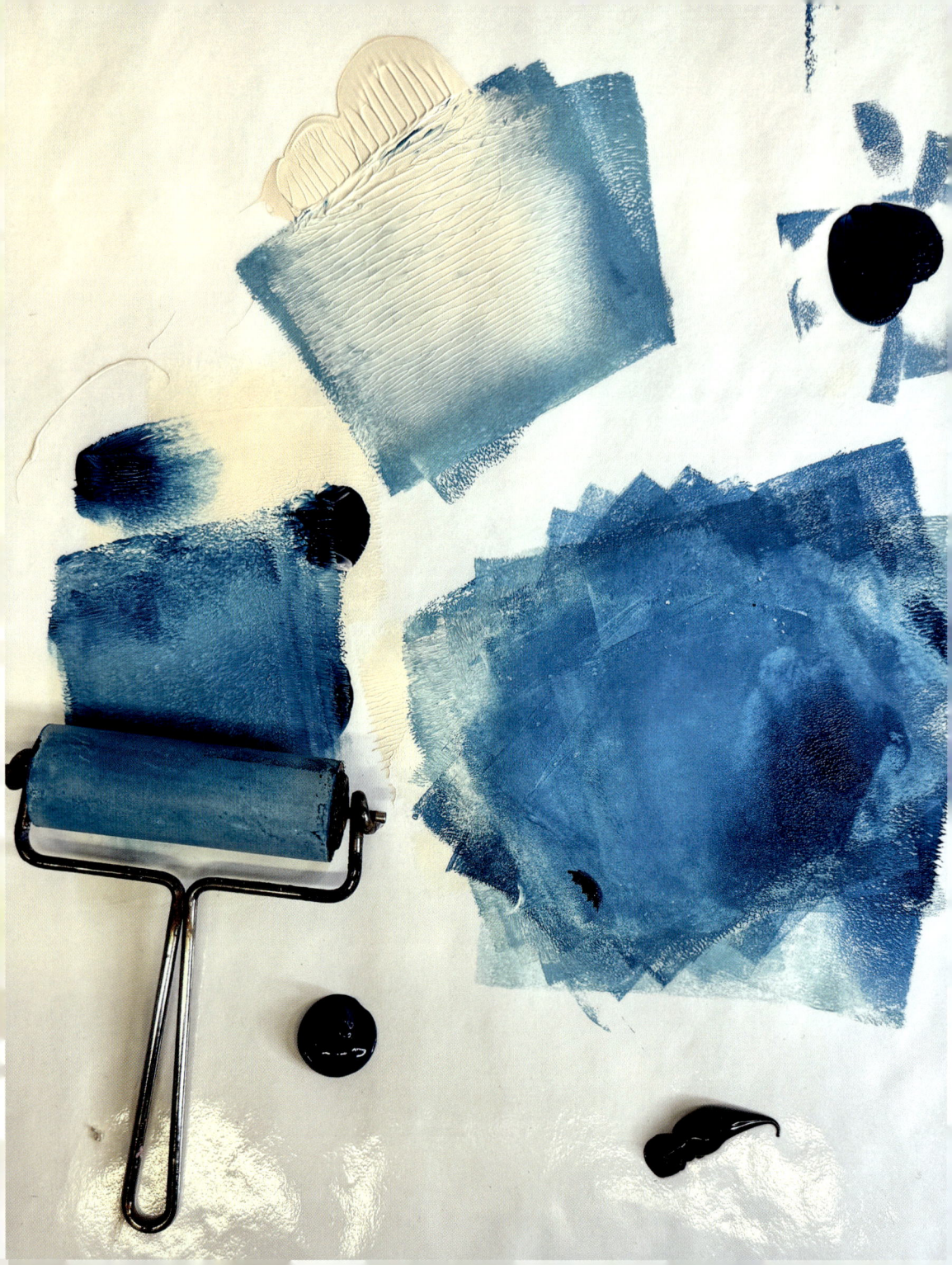

15
PRINTMAKING THAT FEELS LIKE PAINTING

Every pull from the plate adds softness, depth, and those beautiful little imperfections that make a piece feel truly alive. In this chapter, we'll explore how to use painterly techniques to create monotypes. You'll learn how to use color as value and how to combine additive and subtractive methods on the gel plate to build prints with a more expressive, painterly feel.

UNDERSTANDING ATMOSPHERIC PERSPECTIVE

Have you ever gazed at distant mountains and noticed how they fade into blue-gray tones? That ethereal quality isn't your imagination, it's atmospheric perspective at work. As light travels through air, it scatters and softens, making distant objects appear lighter, cooler in color, and less detailed than those up close.

Incorporating atmospheric perspective into your prints mimics how we naturally perceive depth, giving your landscapes a realistic, three-dimensional feel. In this chapter, we'll explore how to create that illusion by combining masks and a value scale.

In this photo I took in Pù Luông, Vietnam, the colors and details are rich and vibrant in the foreground, gradually softening and fading into the distance.

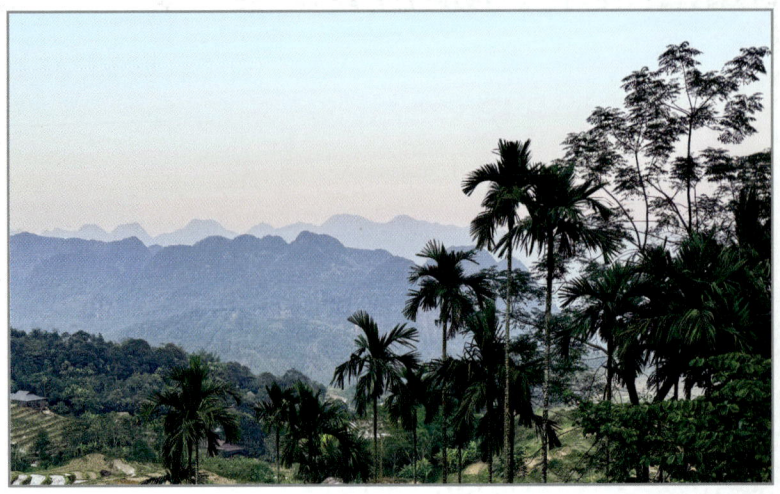

THE IMPORTANCE OF VALUE

In art, value refers to the lightness or darkness of a color, not its price tag! Whether you're working with a full palette or just a few colors, mastering value is key to creating depth and form.

The lightest values (near white) represent distant elements like mountains. The darkest values bring boldness and details to the foreground. Try this: Create your own value scale using one color, white, and black. This scale will help you match tones while you layer your prints.

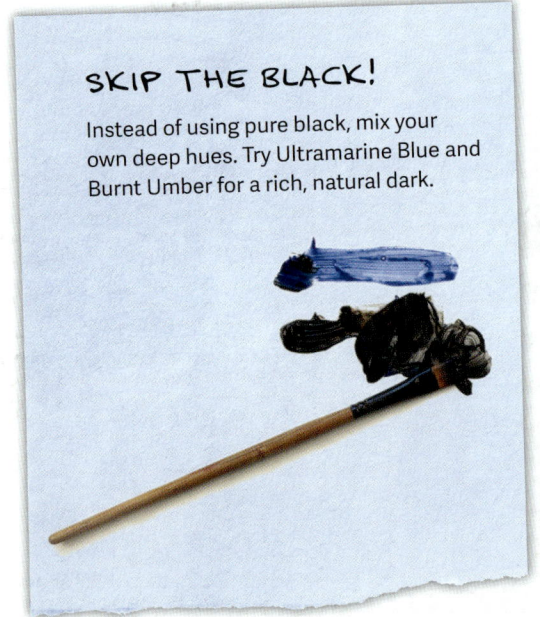

SKIP THE BLACK!

Instead of using pure black, mix your own deep hues. Try Ultramarine Blue and Burnt Umber for a rich, natural dark.

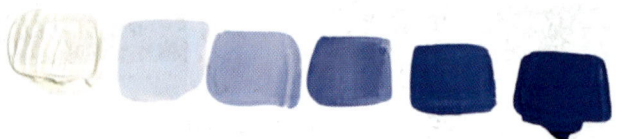

Here is a value scale with whites working their way down to Ultramarine Blue as the darkest value.

BUILDING A LANDSCAPE IN LAYERS

Creating depth in your prints is all about dividing your composition into three zones that mirror the effect of atmospheric perspective:

- **Foreground (Bottom zone):** The darkest tones and boldest shapes. Objects are the most detailed with the sharpest edges, like tangled grasses or a jagged tree trunk.
- **Middle ground (Middle zone):** Mid-range values and softer shapes. Objects are smaller and edges less defined.
- **Background (Top zone):** Lightest values and smallest shapes. Transitions between edges are the softest transitions, like distant hills barely visible through mist.

LANDSCAPING BASICS

Crafting a simple layered landscape is simple—no shovels or rakes required, just masks and paint. I used a few torn pieces of Bristol and my round gel plate. Bristol paper is a powerhouse for DIY masks. It's durable enough to handle the tugging, pulling, and layering of acrylic paint without tearing, even when wet. Yet, it's thin enough to cut or tear into intricate shapes for detailed masks. (Not to mention that I have a ton of scraps lying around, and I prefer to reuse scraps whenever possible.) To make positioning the layers easier, I hinge-registered my paper, allowing me to realign it perfectly on the plate every time (see Chapter 5, "Layer Upon Textured Layer," for more tips).

Using a hinged registration to make sure your prints line up, start at the top of your gel plate with your lightest values for the background and work your way down through the zones and layers. Use masks to block areas you don't want painted. This keeps each layer clean and crisp. Tear your Bristol at an angle for organic, natural looking edges. Gradually go darker as you move down on the plate. Add deeper tones for middle-ground and foreground elements. I finished the example with Ultramarine Blue as my darkest layer.

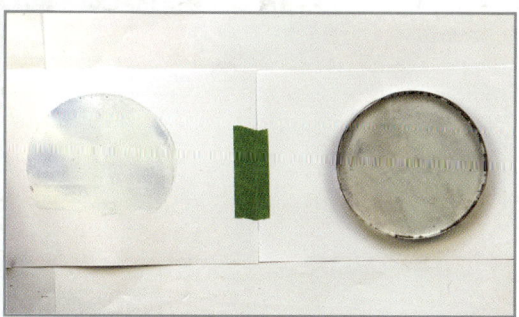

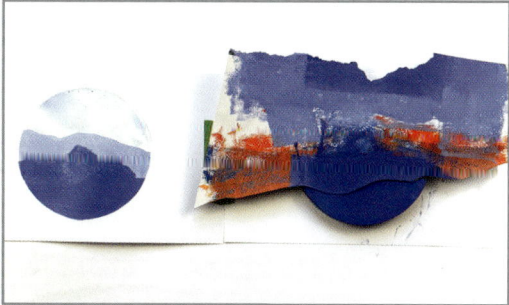

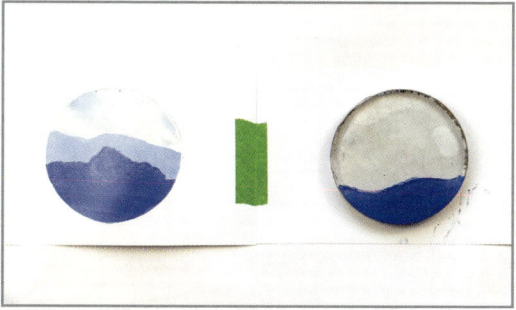

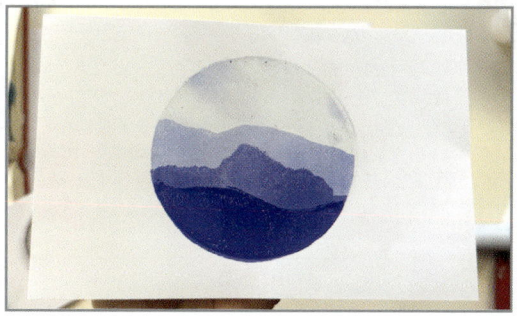

COMPOSITION 101: RULES ARE MADE TO BE... ACTUALLY PRETTY HELPFUL

Great prints begin with some planning. Composition is about finding the perfect spots for everything. If you're not sure where to start, here are a few classic guidelines to help organize your design:

Rule of Thirds: Think of a tic-tac-toe board over your image. The idea is to place focal points along the lines or at the intersections to create a natural flow.

S-Curve: This curvy, flowing shape leads the viewer's eye through an image, like a winding river or a graceful path.

Golden Ratio: Nature's favorite formula, this spiral-based composition (think of a seashell) guides the viewer's eye in a beautifully organic way. You could look up the math behind it or just trust me—it works!

Pyramid Composition: Arranging elements in a triangle shape, with the main subject at the peak, creates stability and a sense of direction, like a visual mountain for the eyes to climb.

Leading Lines: Implied or visible, these lines guide the viewer's eye throughout your print, drawing attention to the focal point. Whether it's a tree branch peeking in from the side or the gentle angles of distant mountain ranges, these elements create a little visual roadmap for your composition print!

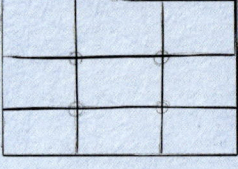

RULE OF THIRDS

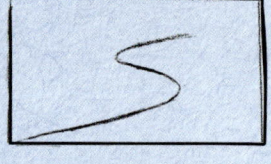

S CURVE

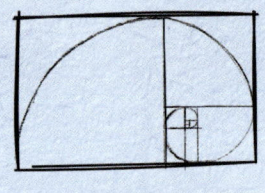

GOLDEN RATIO

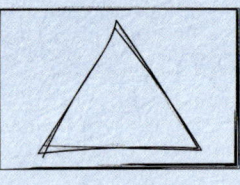

PYRAMID

LAYERING AN ATMOSPHERIC MONOCHROMATIC LANDSCAPE

Now that you've got the basics down, let's level up and create a fully layered monochromatic landscape. First, use Bristol board and painter's tape to set up a hinged registration system. This helps you pull multiple prints on the same sheet without misaligning layers.

Next, create your masks. Preparing your masks ahead of time helps prevent paint from drying out as you work. You will be working in reverse and need to cut away any parts that you want the paint to cover the plate. Place your masks to cover the negative space around objects, leaving the shapes of hills,

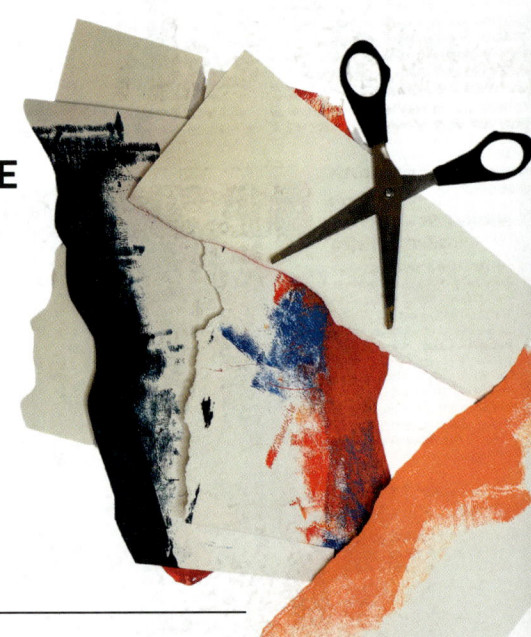

trees, or other elements exposed. Here are some tips for each layer:

- **Background masks:** Tear Bristol board at an angle to create raw, organic edges, perfect for distant hills or mountains. Aim for random, uneven, soft edges.
- **Middle-ground masks:** Use scissors or a craft knife for more detailed shapes like rolling hills or distant trees.
- **Foreground masks:** Focus on cutting out larger, more detailed shapes, such as trees and tall grasses.

Remember, masks are reusable! Flip them or layer them in different ways to add variety to your print.

With your brayer, apply a thin layer of your lightest value to the top of your gel plate. You don't need to cover the entire plate. Make sure you have enough of the plate covered to fill your sky area. Press your paper onto the plate, smooth it down gently, let it sit for a minute, and then lift the paper.

Use your background mask to create the most distant mountain range. Place the mask about a quarter to a third of the way down your plate, letting it gently overlap your sky area to create that dreamy transition between layers. Now, roll out your paint just a touch darker than before. I added a hint of blue to make a deeper valued tint.

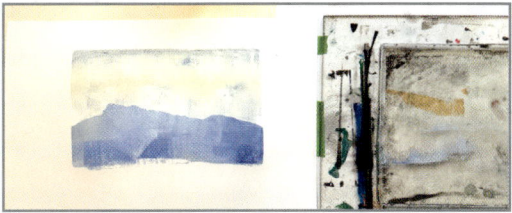

Want more mountains? Keep layering! Mix in a bit less white each time you add a new range to deepen those values gradually. Work your way down the plate like you're building a landscape layer cake!

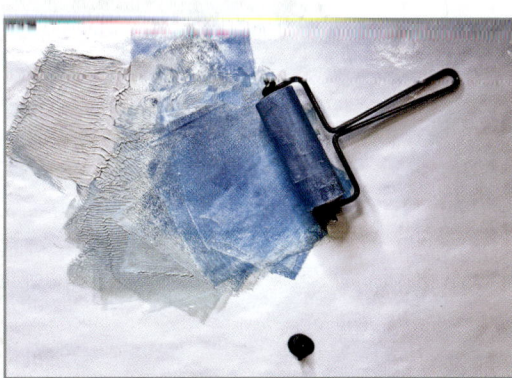

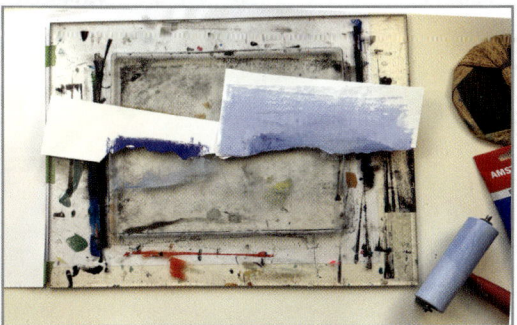

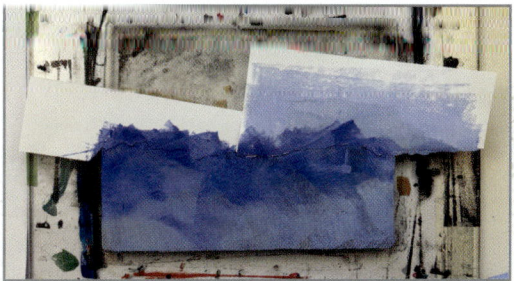

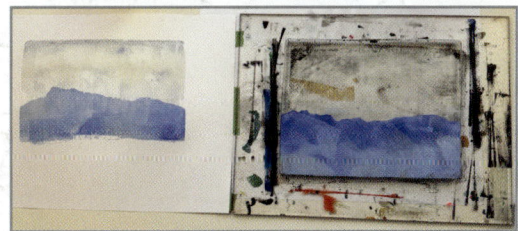

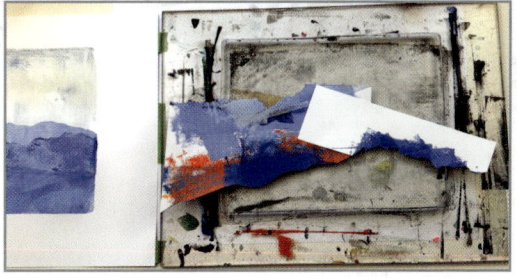

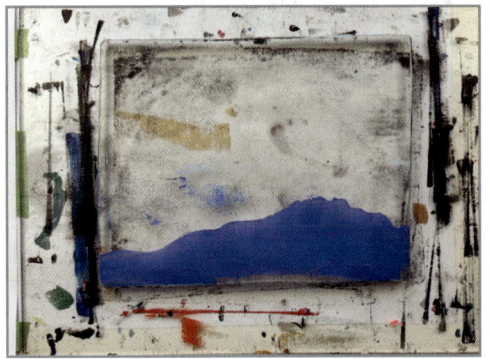

Gradually get darker as you move downward, bring in those middle-ground and foreground masks you crafted. Each overlapping layer adds more depth and drama to your landscape. Have fun with the foreground masks, adding more detail like trees, grasses, or small bushes.

At this point, you can also add small details with your paintbrush. Work quickly, however, before the layer dries.

The final layers might need a bit more drying time because they are layered on top of previous layers that have already dried on your paper. Now that the paper has been printed on a few times, it might not be as flat as before, which makes it harder for the paint to to adhere consistently. Let the paper sit on the plate for at least five minutes. Place some books on top of it to ensure there is even contact between your paper and the gel plate.

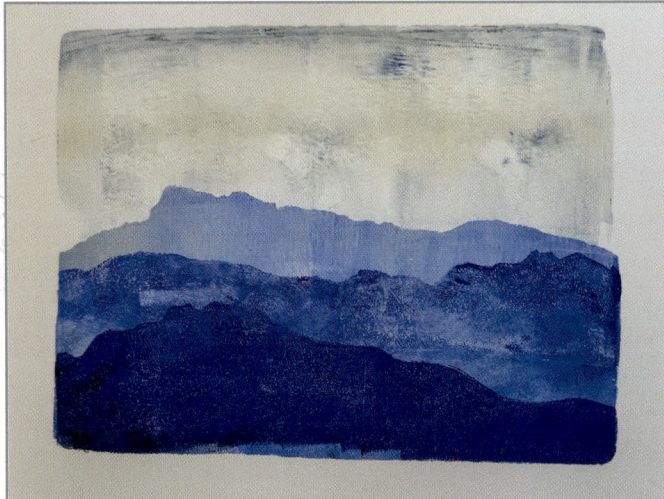

Adding small gradients to each value zone can bring a lovely touch of drama to your landscape! The top part of the zone should be slightly darker than the bottom part. This creates a beautiful effect, almost as if fog is softly rolling over the mountains, enhancing that atmospheric perspective.

Likewise, don't shy away from embracing plate textures. Plate tone and leftover paint from previous prints can create unexpected, organic details in your landscape. So, don't worry about cleaning them off. Let them surprise you and add character!

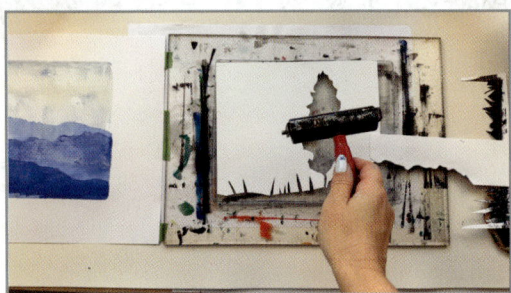
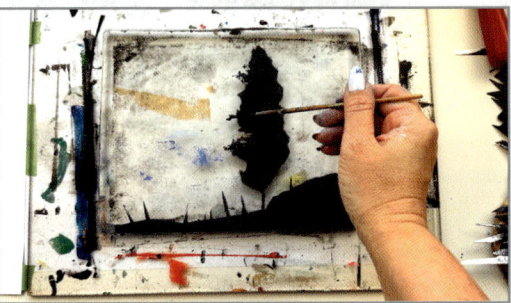

Smaller cutouts from your masks may not fill in with acrylic paint using your brayer. Break out your paintbrush or a sponge and stamp in those little details.

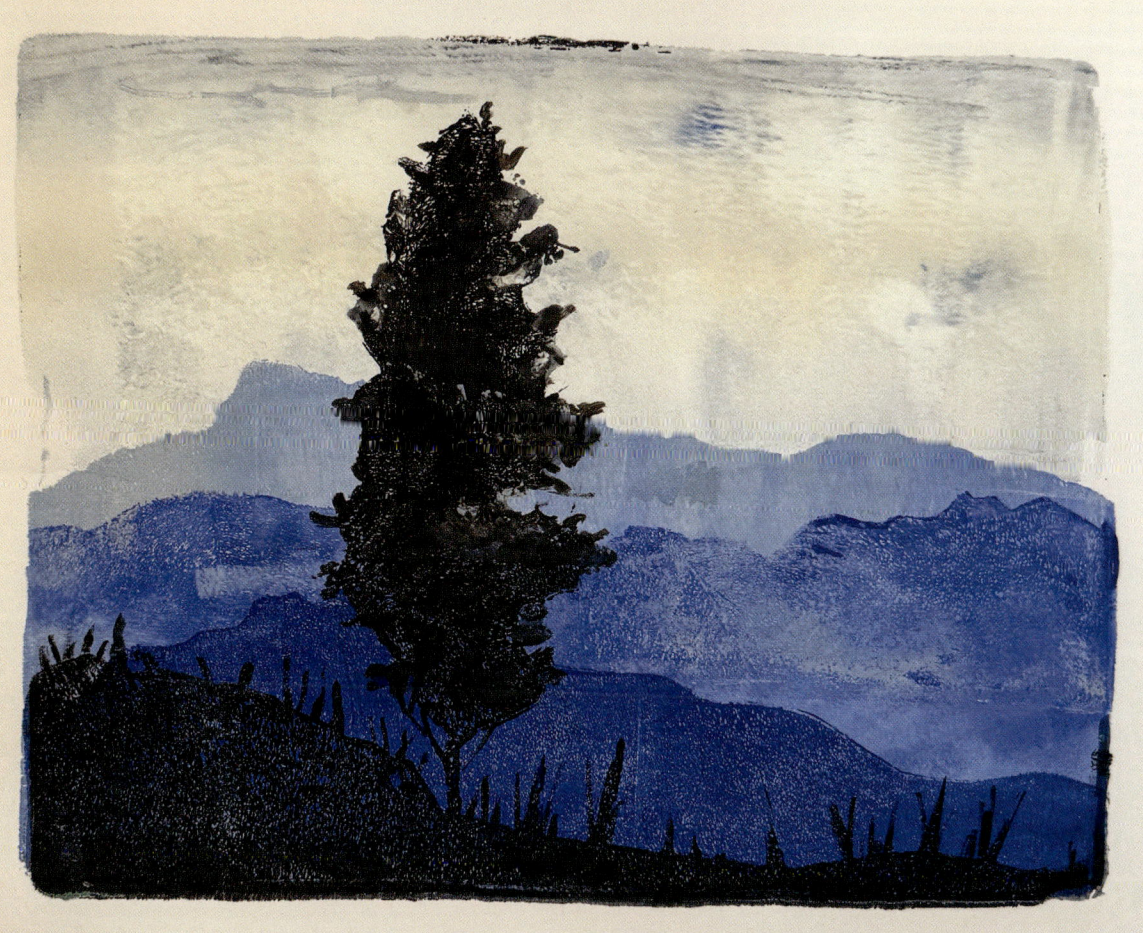

MONOTYPES: A RICH HISTORY AND MY APPROACH

Monotypes have been part of the printmaking world for centuries, and I totally understand why. They're a little unpredictable, a lot of fun, and each one is a true original. Unlike other printmaking methods that rely on repeatable plates, monotypes are one-of-a-kind by design. Every pull is a fresh surprise, which keeps things interesting and occasionally chaotic, but in a good way.

Beyond the stencils and textures or more structured image transfers, monotypes offer a painterly, expressive approach. You'll need to know two main techniques: subtractive and additive. I love blending both, but let's break them down first.

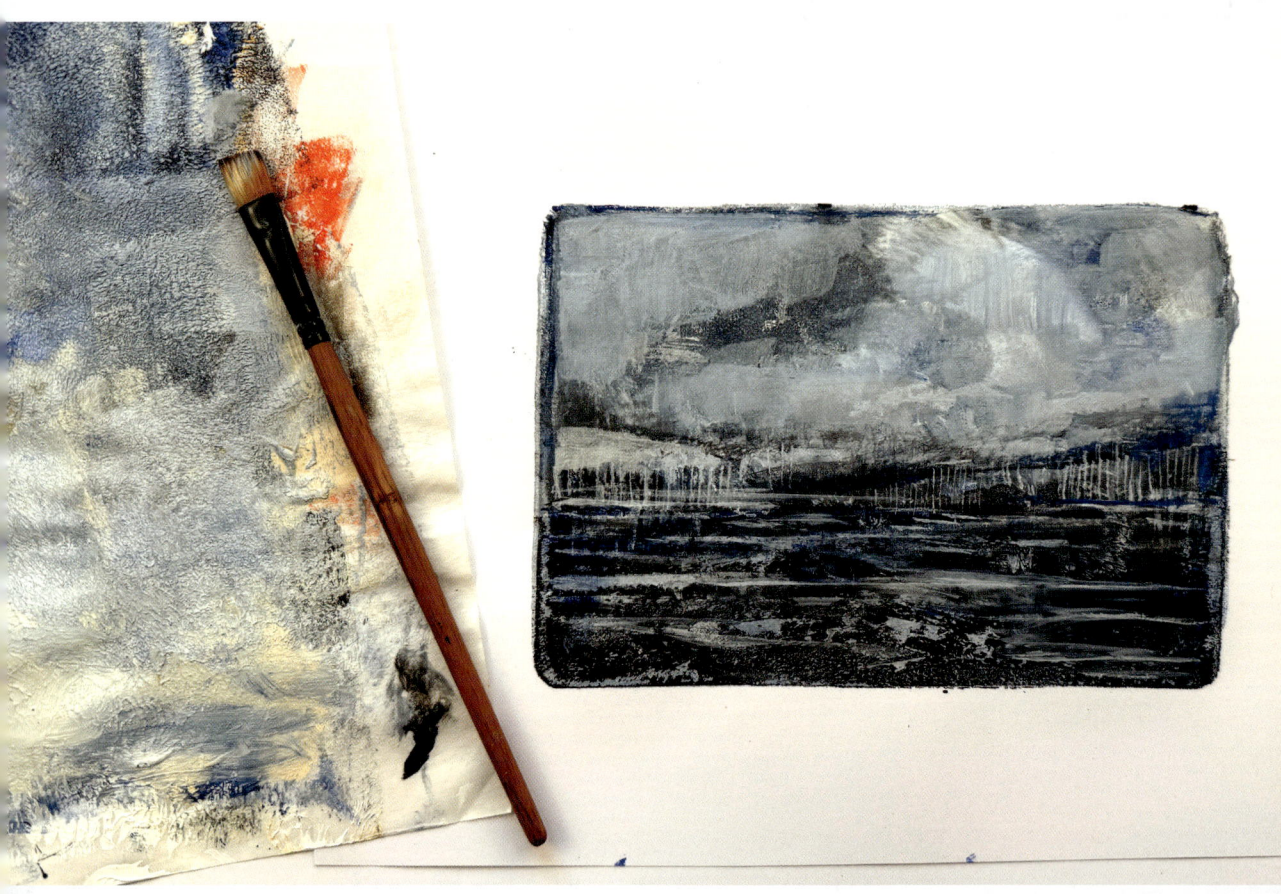

SUBTRACTIVE METHOD: DARK FIELD

The subtractive technique is a lot like reverse painting. You cover the entire plate with a solid layer of paint, and then *remove* areas to reveal your design. Think sgraffito, scratching through a surface to create contrast and light (Chapter 5). It's dramatic and great for atmospheric scenes.

To make the most of this technique, you'll want your paint to stay workable for a while. Acrylic paint dries fast (sometimes *too* fast), so I recommend mixing in a retarder or slow-drying medium. Better yet, try washable etching ink, which stays open longer and gives you time to work. It *will* stain your plate, however, so if that's not your thing, stick to acrylics.

To pull more pigment from the plate, dampen your paper before printing. This gives you beautiful, soft transitions, perfect for dreamy skies or foggy landscapes.

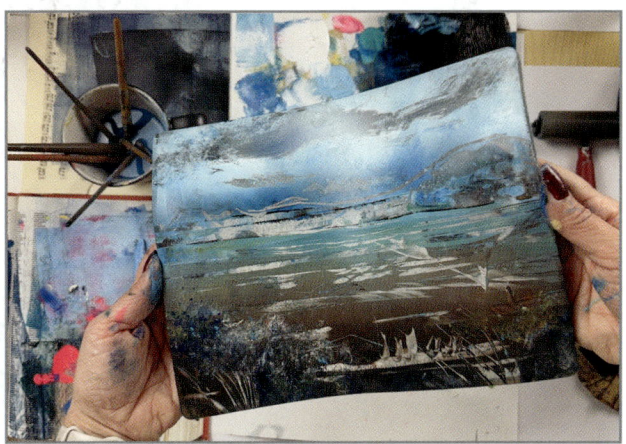

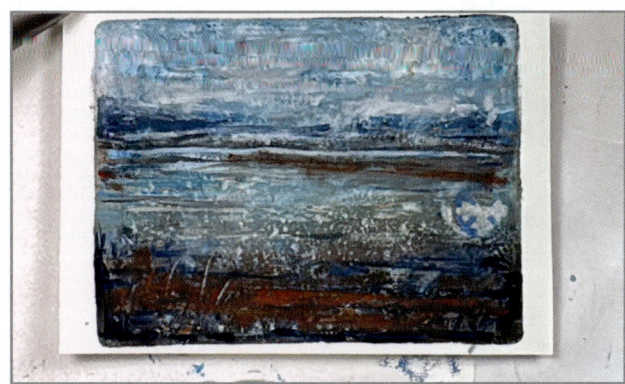

ADDITIVE METHOD: LIGHT FIELD

The additive technique is more like traditional painting, except you're doing it on a gel plate in reverse. You build your image by *adding* paint where you want it. It's fun, intuitive, and very hands-on. But be warned: It's less forgiving than the subtractive method. Every mark you make is a kind of commitment. You can't really undo, so work thoughtfully and layer intentionally. I love using both additive and subtractive approaches together. It's the best of both worlds, letting you build up complexity and texture in a really satisfying way.

STEP-BY-STEP: BUILDING A LIGHT FIELD LANDSCAPE

Let's walk through a print I made using both methods. I used hinged registration for this one, which is super handy for keeping everything aligned while layering. And yes, it took nearly 20 pulls. But don't freak out! They were all quick and mostly wet pulls. No marathon sessions required.

Because I was creating a seascape, the first step was to define where the sky would meet the water. I'm a big fan of the "daily dirty plate" technique, which basically embraces the leftovers from earlier prints. Those bits of residue can add unexpected texture and richness to your new piece. I started by rolling broad bands of color with a brayer to rough in the horizon and water (see below).

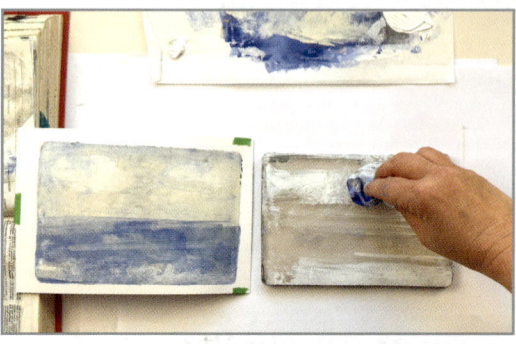

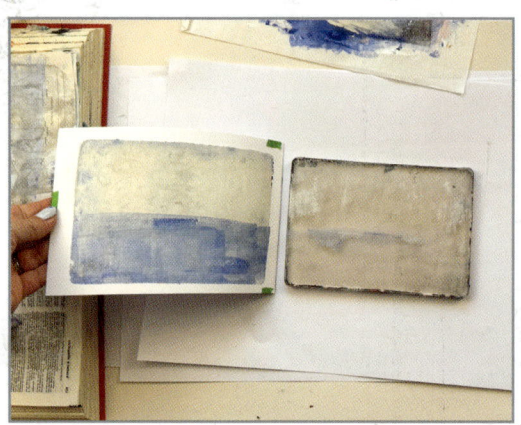

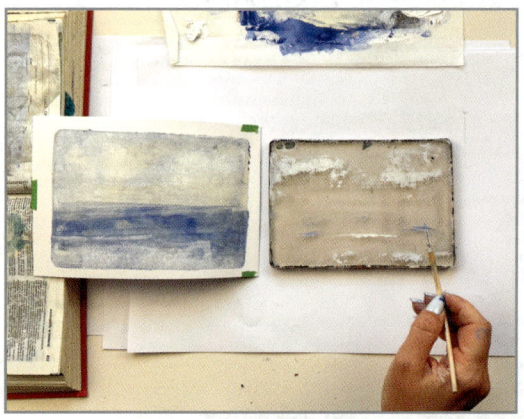

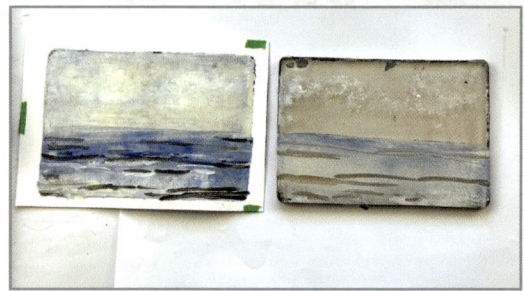

When the base was down, I grabbed some baby wipes and started lifting paint off the plate. This created variations in the sky and soft wave highlights in the foreground. Just a few swipes made the scene feel wind-swept and natural.

To push the movement even more, I painted structured lines with a brush to mimic flowing water. I'm a bit impatient, so I usually lift the print within 30 seconds. Could I wait longer for a more solid transfer? Sure. But honestly, I love the patchy, imperfect bits because they give the print a weathered, organic look.

In the final layers, I added a touch of gel medium to create lovely transparent areas, deepen tones, and gently soften others. It's a subtle move, but it truly helps to balance the bolder sections and adds a delightful sense of depth.

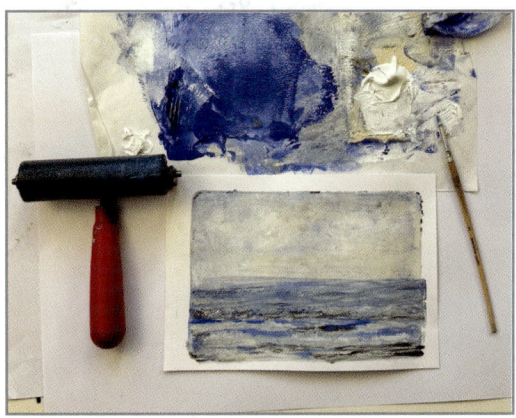

The figure below shows the end result: a layered, moody seascape that feels spontaneous yet intentional. All those quick prints, tweaks, and textures came together to create something totally unique.

The beauty of this process is that every print holds its own surprises. By thinking like a painter, layering values, building atmosphere, and balancing bold moves with subtle shifts you can create landscapes that feel deeply expressive and entirely your own. Everything you practiced in this chapter can also be combined with image transfers to add even more depth and story to your work. And while landscapes are a natural fit for these techniques, they aren't the only option. You can apply the same methods to any other subject matter too.

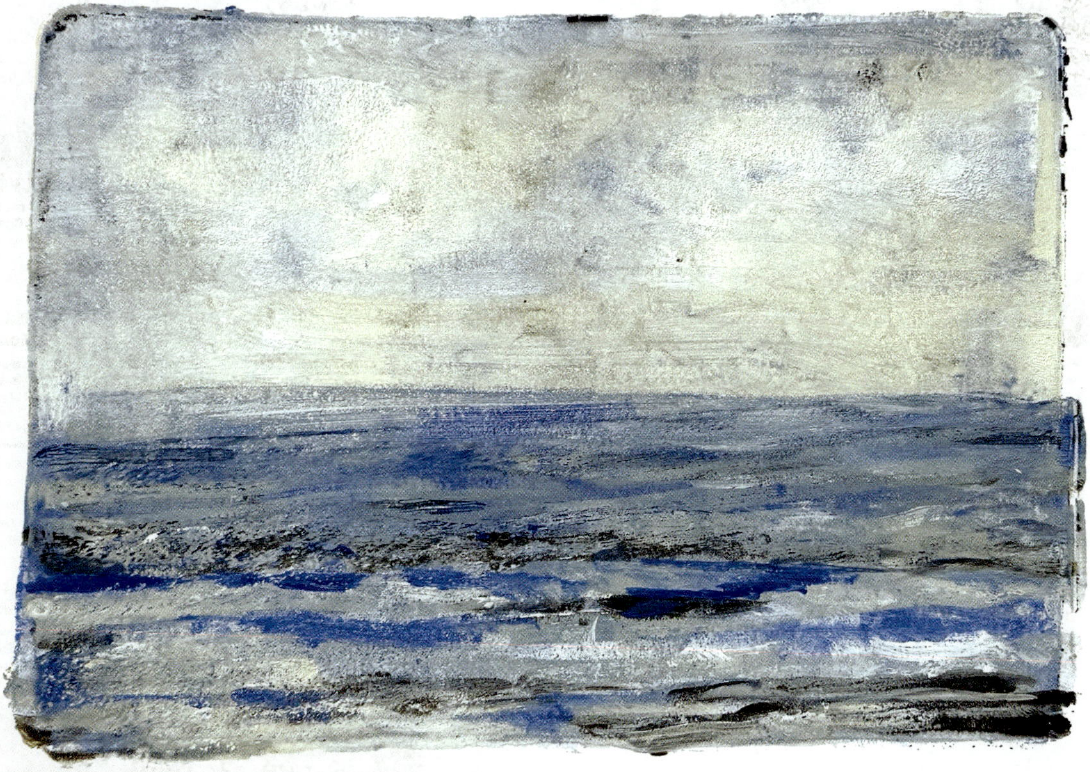

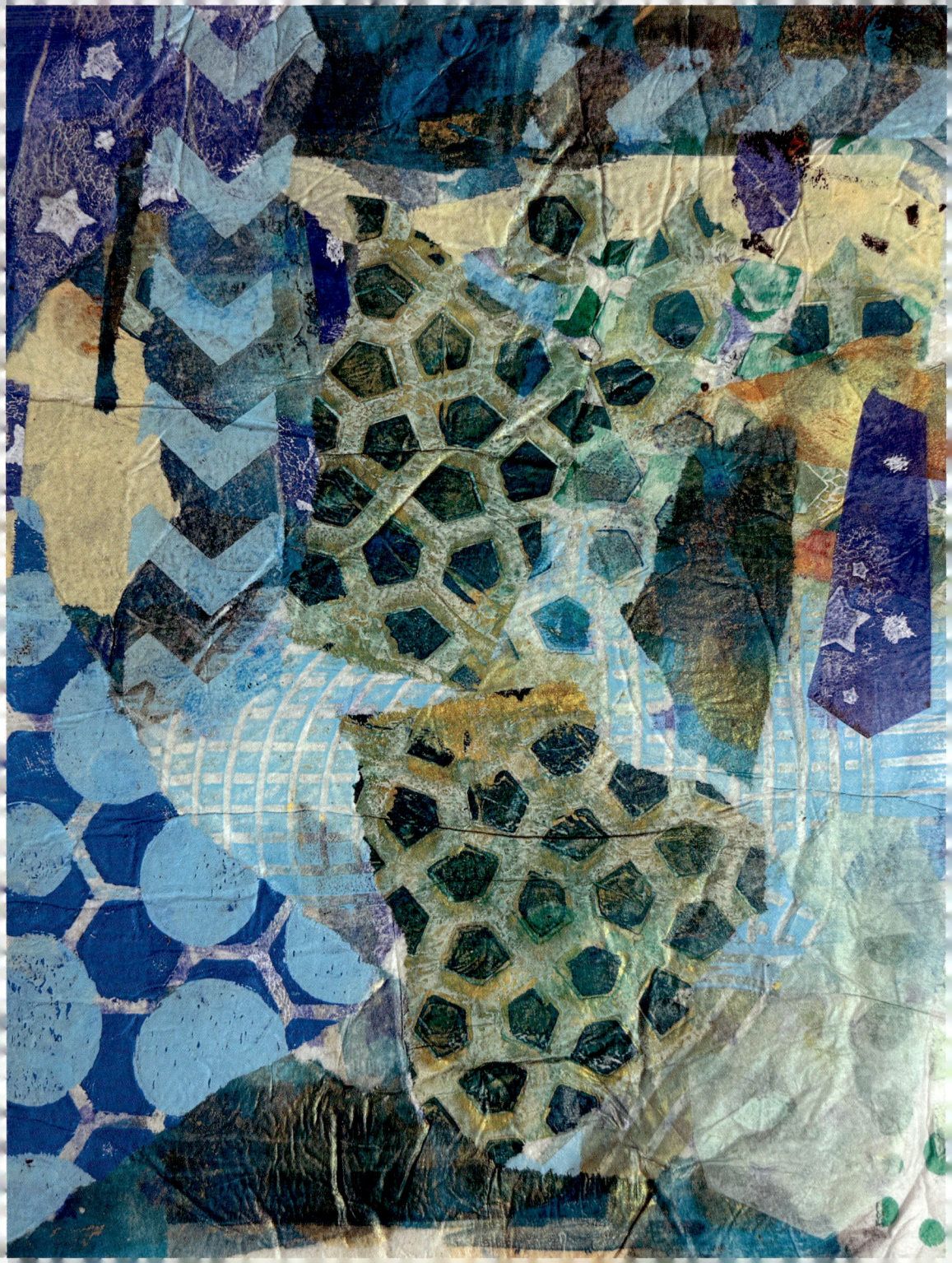

16
COLLAGE AS REVERSE PAINTING

Collage has always had a close relationship with painting. At times, it behaves like it's part of the same conversation, even if in this case it's coming at it from the other side. In this chapter, I want to explore collage as a form of reverse painting. Something that unfolds layer by layer on the gel plate, much like a painting in reverse order.

At its core, this is about working with intention. You're not just gluing papers down. You're constructing a surface that can hold depth, color, history, and tension. Multiple layering techniques can be used, but here we'll focus on one of the most direct and intuitive methods: building collages directly on the plate using gel medium and tissue paper.

REIMAGINING SCRAPS

Building collages directly on the plate enables you to create something entirely new from materials that might otherwise be discarded. In this example, I used nothing more than scraps from earlier prints: small pieces of gel-printed tissue that had been forgotten in scrap piles in my studio. These leftovers became the foundation of a new surface.

I began with a handful of torn tissue papers from previous projects, some printed with stencils and others colored with washes. Using a soft-bristled brush and gel medium, I layered these fragments directly onto the plate, starting with the smallest bits and sealing each piece carefully with additional medium on top.

The goal is to get them as flat and smooth as possible. The smoother the layers, the easier the entire collage will lift from the plate once dry. I typically add some bigger pieces in the last layer to help keep all the pieces attached together.

A collage needs to cure fully before removal. I usually let mine dry overnight or longer, depending on humidity. Once it's fully dry, the result is a richly layered surface that feels like it has grown organically yet is entirely of your making.

What I love about this is the transformation. Pieces that would have ended up in the bin now form something fresh, tactile, full of texture, and ready for a new project.

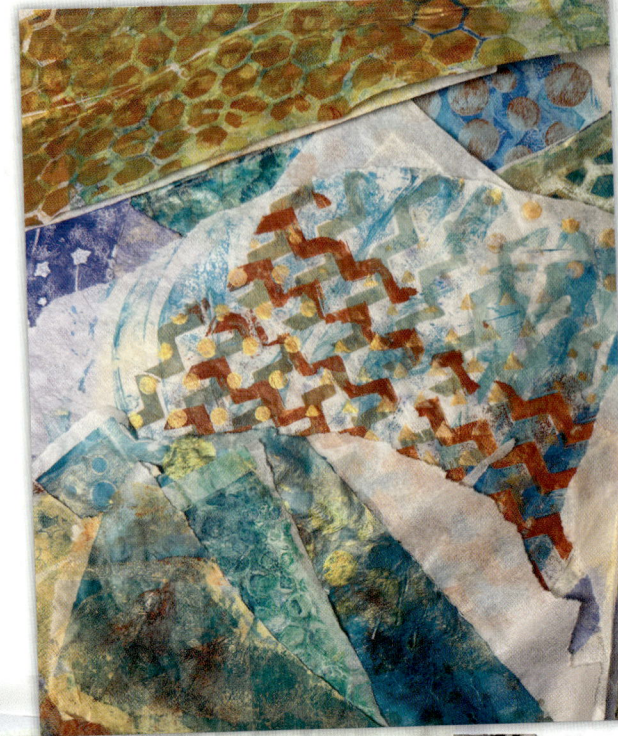

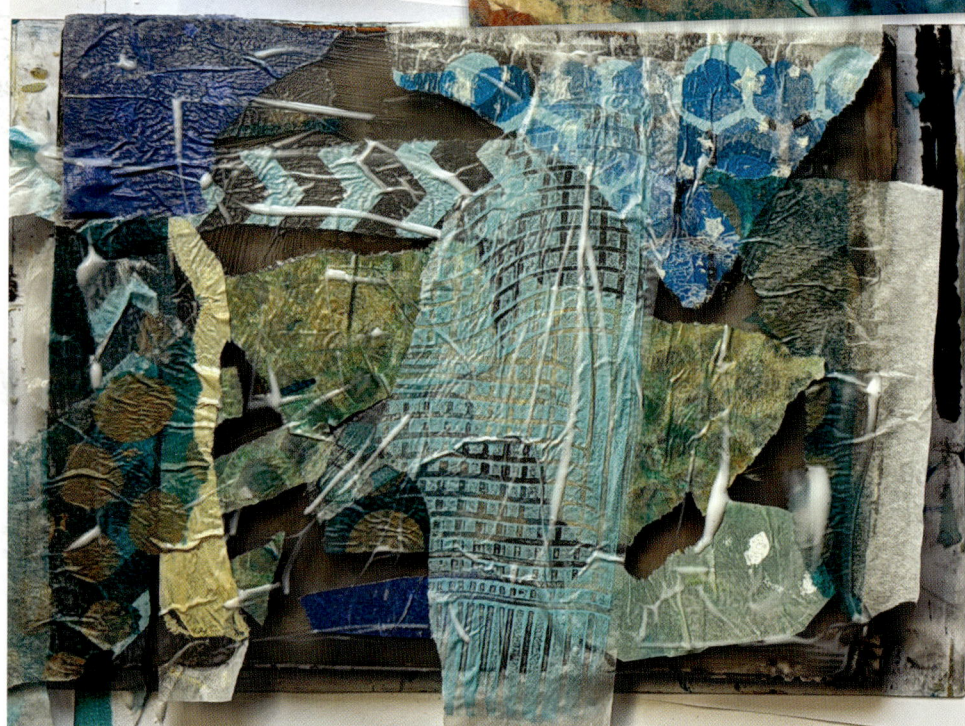

IMAGE TRANSFER WITH COLLAGE REVERSE PAINTING

I originally created this digital illustration of my daughter as inspiration for a painting, but after I printed it out, I knew it should be a gel print with collage. Here are all the steps that I went through to create this multilayered print. I worked on my 16 × 20-inch gel plate, but you can adapt the techniques for smaller formats.

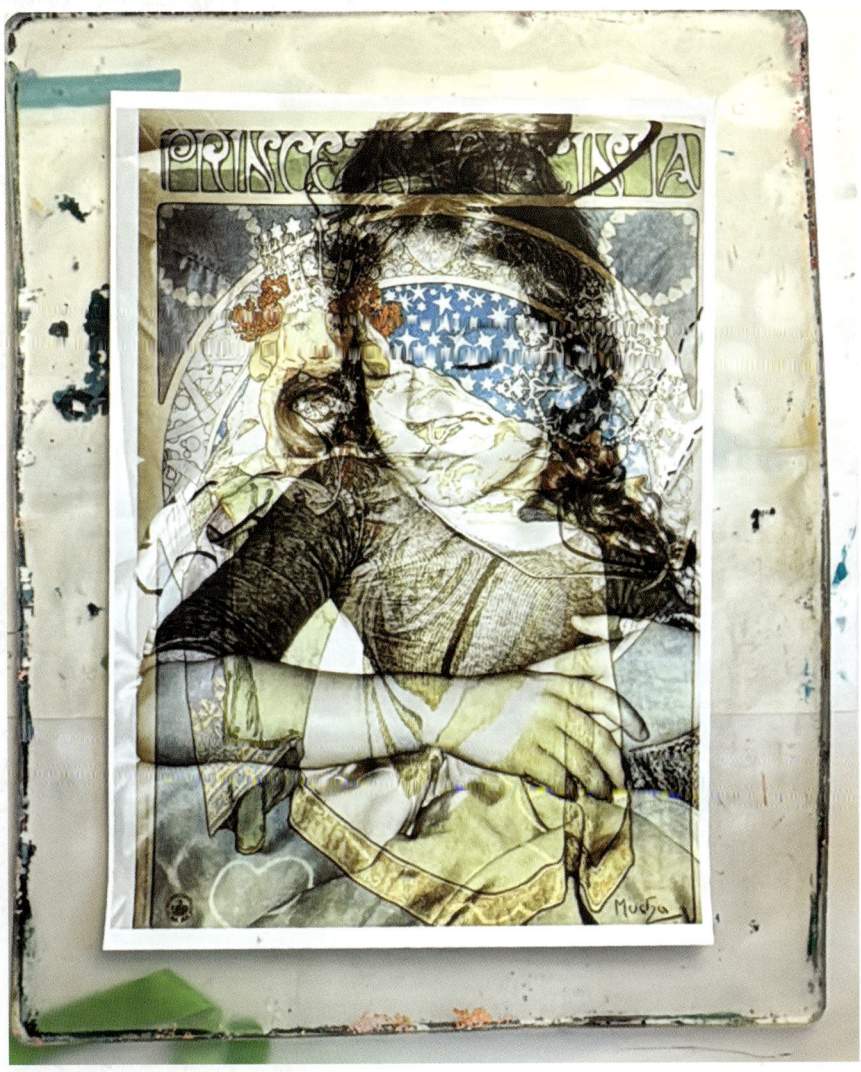

I created this double exposure collage combining a photograph of my daughter with elements from Alphonse Mucha's, 1911 lithograph, *Princess Hyacinth*. I edited it digitally, then converted it to black and white to preserve midtones and emphasize detail.

CHOOSE COLLAGE PAPERS

I typically use wet-strength tissue for this process. It is thin enough to layer and builds beautifully interesting, translucent layers. You can use the prints that you have already pulled or create custom ones that match your vison of the final print. Sometimes I'll make very specific elements, like stars, that I know I want to integrate.

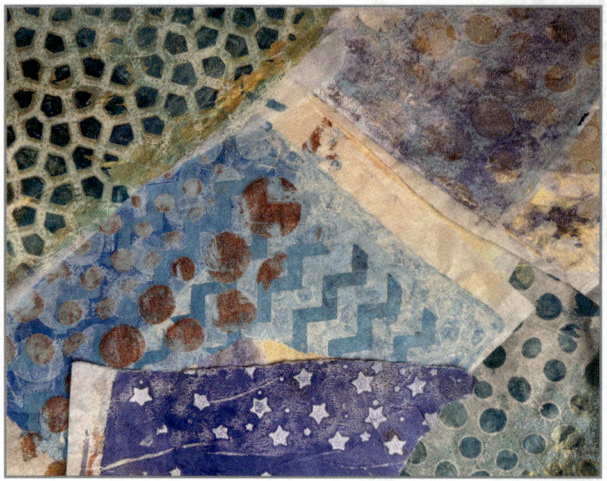

CREATE THE INITIAL TRANSFER

I was not confident my laser print was going to make a good transfer. It was high resolution and fairly high contrast. However, there were a lot of dark areas in the photo. That, combined with the complexity of the image, made me concerned that the image would not be understandable once I transferred it. To lessen the deep-black voids in the transfer, I mixed a little Black Oxide with Phthalo Blue and Viridian Green. This let me paint and build shadows and structure without flattening the image into darkness. Once this layer was dry, I added a thin layer of gel medium and let that dry fully.

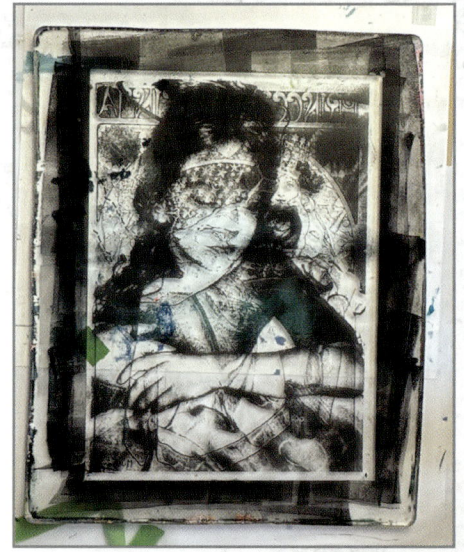

REVERSE PAINT WITH COLLAGE

Apply another thin layer of gel medium in the area you want to collage and place your tissue paper pieces face down into it. Smooth them gently with your brush, then apply another layer of medium on top to fully seal them in place. You can take a structured approach, fitting pieces together like a puzzle, but I usually prefer to go loose and let the layers drift over one another organically.

Each choice affects the final depth. Opaque tissue gives you bold form and contrast, while translucent paper lets other layers shine through. Keep the gel medium moving continuously as it helps the papers fuse into one surface. I went in with a few bits of acrylic paint in the process too for areas where I wanted a slightly more solid look.

You can check your progress by looking underneath the plate. If you're using plexiglass underneath your plate, lift it to get a clearer preview. Try to keep the wet plate from bending or else the layers will start to buckle and wrinkle. Just remember, the final result will still have some surprises.

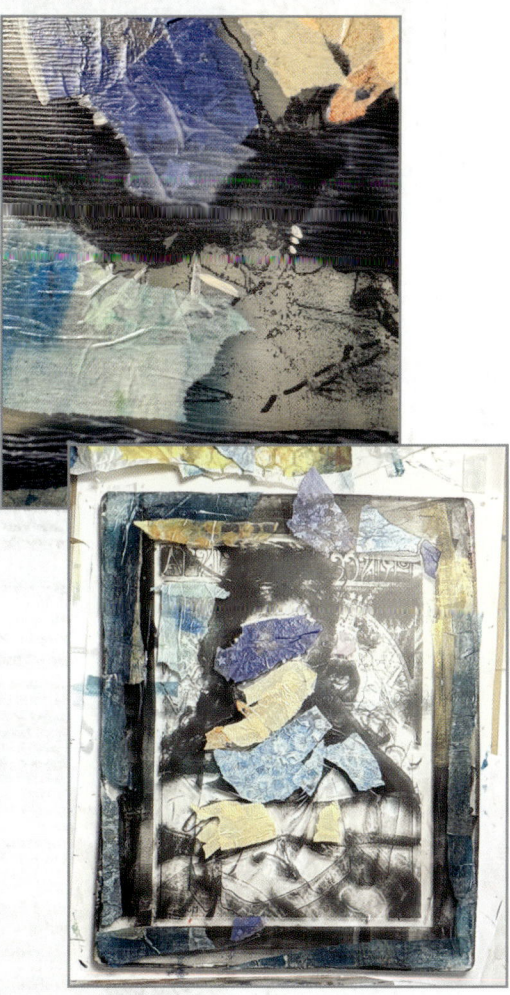

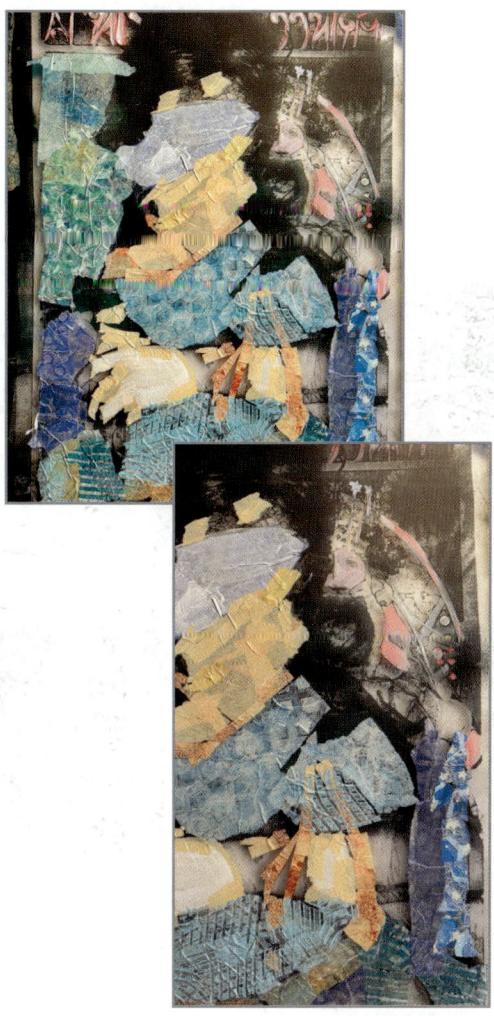

SEAL THE DEAL

Once your collage is complete and fully dry on your plate, it's time to seal the piece with paint. I wanted to ensure that the acrylic paint of the pickup layer was really attaching to the entire surface of the collaged elements. This can be tricky because the tissue will be a bit textured no matter how hard you try to smooth it out. Therefore, I did two pickup layers. I started with a layer of acrylic paint mixed with gel medium, which acts as a binding layer, locking everything together. Then, I applied a final coat of acrylic paint in a fresh color to serve as my pickup layer. I chose a different color to ensure that I could see that it fully covered the surface and I didn't miss any bits.

I used 205-gsm Bristol paper, though heavier papers like 250 gsm can be more forgiving for large works.

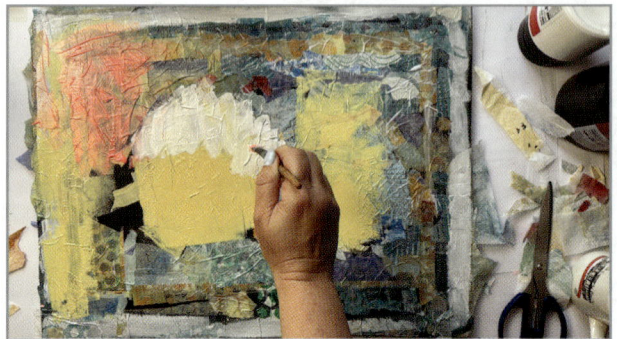

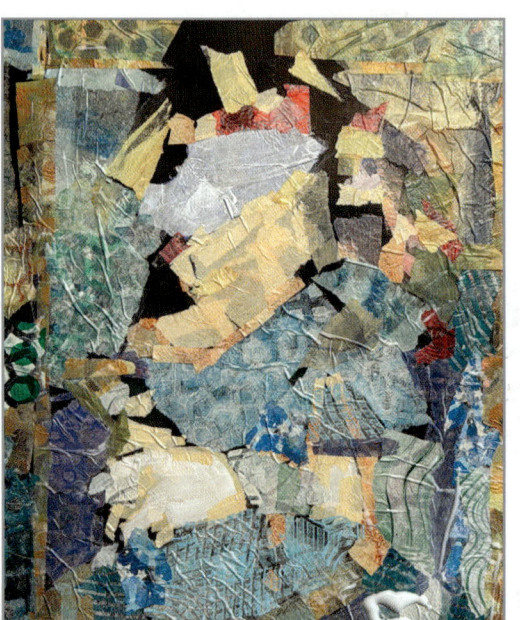

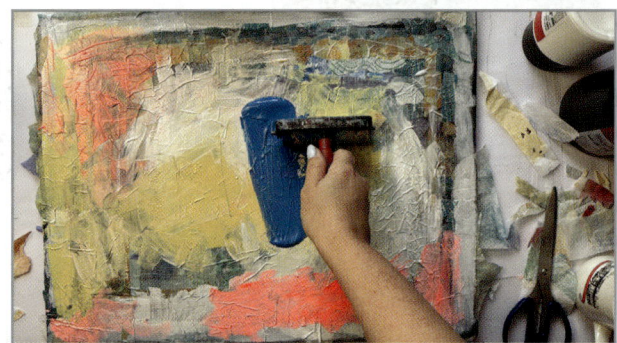

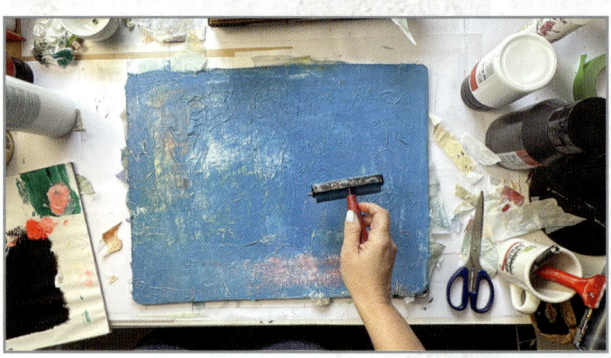

Lay the paper down evenly, and press it firmly with your hands, smoothing outward from the center. You want to ensure every bit of the Bristol is touching every bit of the paint and that they have firm contact. Then, stack a few books on top for consistent pressure and leave it to rest for 24 hours. This waiting period is crucial.

PULL THE PLATE

After lifting the books, I gave my print another 12 more hours to dry. You'll know it's ready when the back of the paper no longer feels cool to the touch. Only then should you flip the plate and begin slowly peeling it away from the paper. Work slowly and pull the plate from multiple directions to gradually release the print from the plate. Carefully loosen the edges before lifting. If any tissue papers didn't fully adhere, you can reapply them with a bit of gel medium.

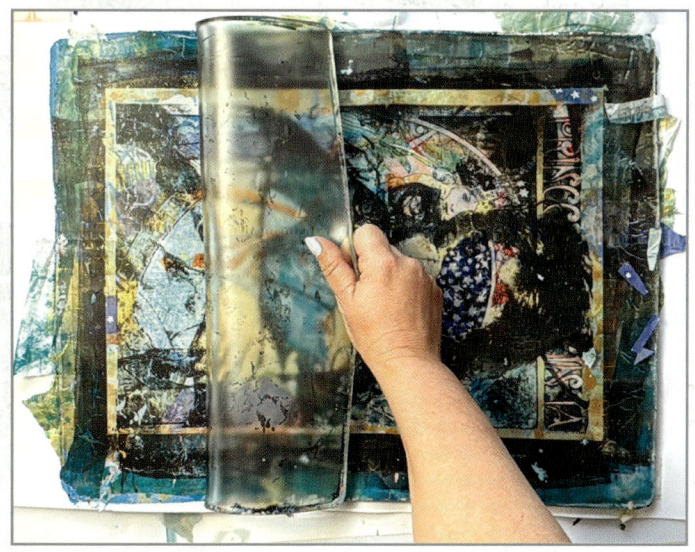

APPLY FINISHING TOUCHES

Look over the surface. Do any areas need to be fixed? Do the colors feel balanced? You might choose to enhance details with more tissue, a bit of hand-painting, or selective edits to the edges. I added a bit more collage on the front of the print to bring out details and colors that were blocked by the darker bits of the image transfer.

Sometimes I trim my prints. Other times, I leave them raw with torn borders visible. That rough edge holds the history of the process. There's a visual tension between the tightness of the collage and the openness of the unfinished border.

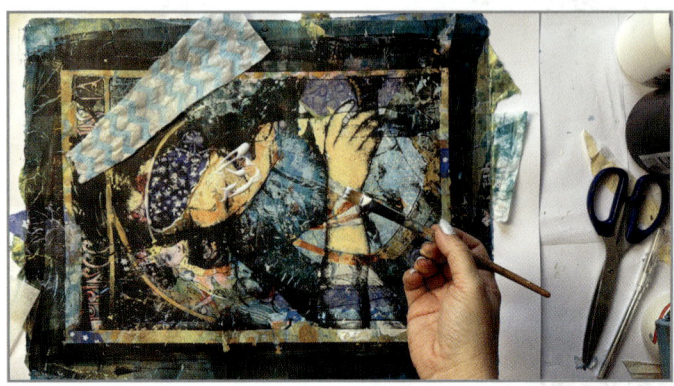

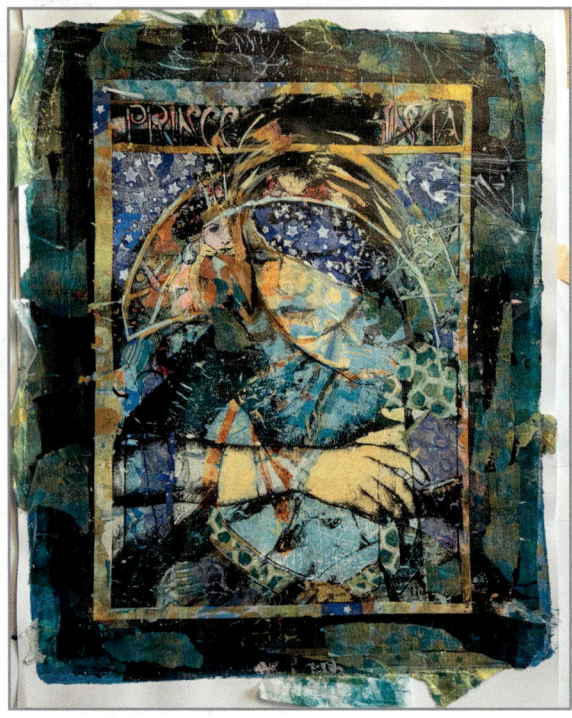

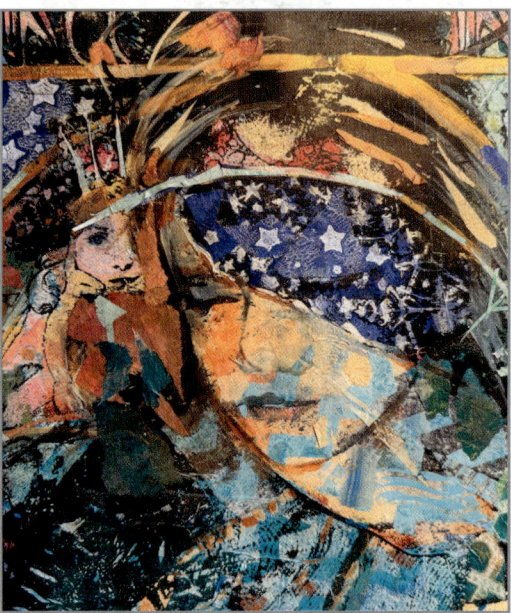

Above: In this detail, you can see the additional layers of gel printed tissue that I added on top of the print, mainly in the hair, the blue zigzags across the face, and some other details to lighten the print.

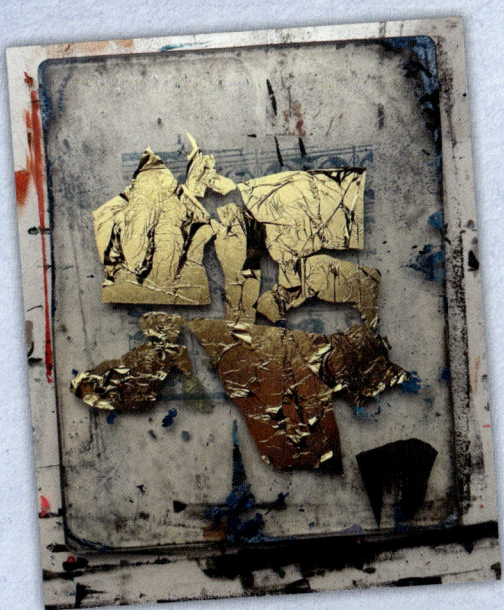

ADD MORE SPARKLE

The stickiness of the gel plate also allows for materials beyond paint and paper. Gold leaf, in particular, works beautifully with this process.

Because the plate naturally holds the gold leaf without the need for sizing adhesive or gel medium, it becomes a perfect surface for reverse gilding. Try sprinkling a bit of gold leaf between your transfer layer and reverse painting layers. It doesn't have to be pristine. Start with something distressed. That texture helps you understand how the material behaves. The result is a subtle shimmer that catches light.

A PLATE OF POSSIBILITIES

Creating collages on the gel plate opens up new possibilities for creativity. It facilitates reinvention and repurposing; what was once cast aside becomes the foundation for something greater. This process is not swift, and perfection is rarely achieved on the first attempt. If you allow it the time it needs and approach it with care and curiosity, however, you'll find that the plate is more than a way to copy—it embodies possibility.

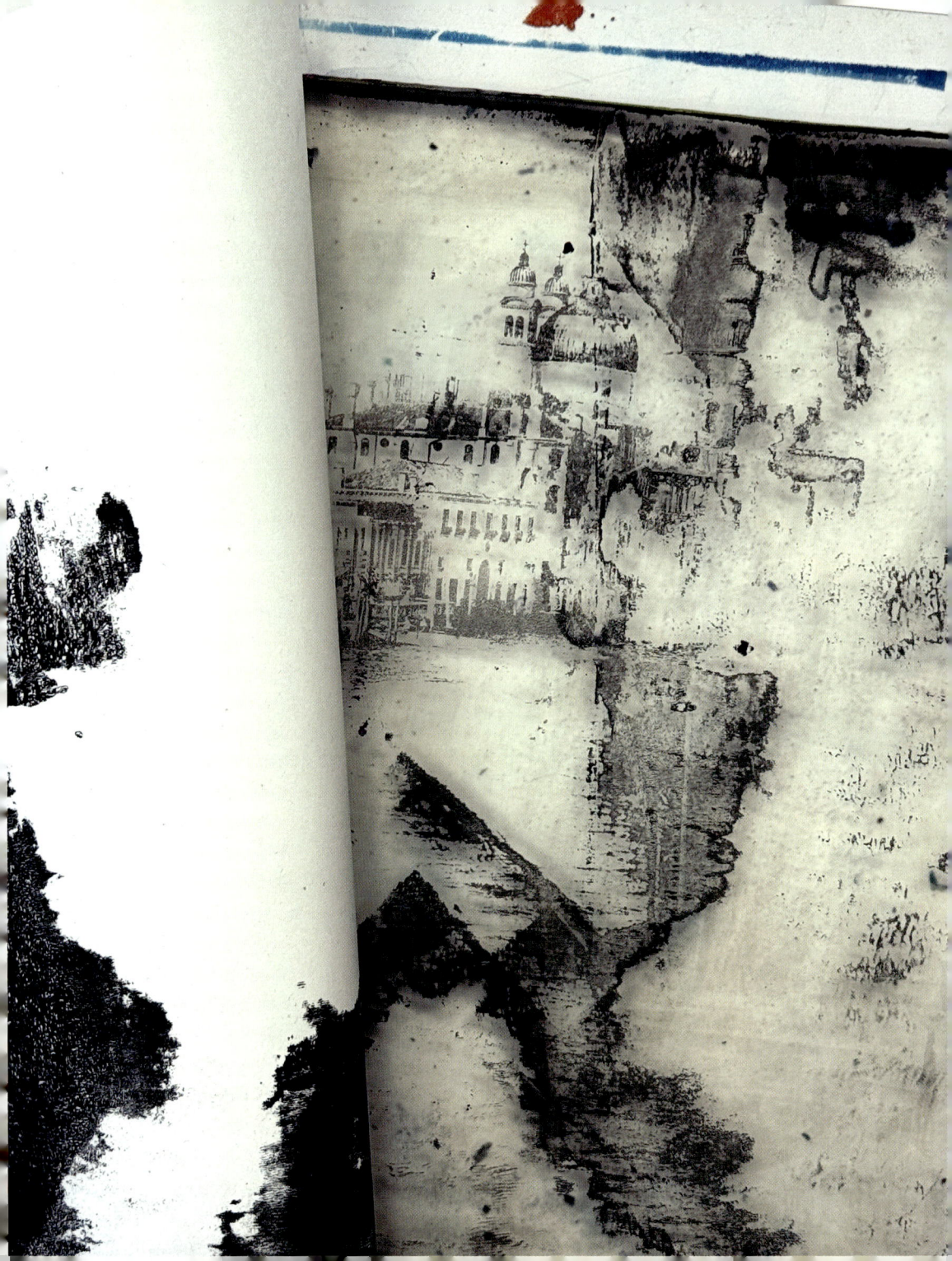

17
MASTERING MISHAPS

Gel plate printmaking is as much about exploration as it is about technique. Ever got that sinking feeling while pulling a print because it wasn't turning out quite the way you had imagined? You're definitely not alone. From faint transfers and patchy layers to torn paper or stubborn areas that refuse to lift, these challenges are all part of the experience.

This chapter is meant to walk you through those moments and offer ways to troubleshoot the most common frustrations. I've been there myself, feeling annoyed, confused, and on the verge of launching my brayer across the studio. But over time, with trial, error, and a bit of curiosity, I found approaches that helped me push through the mess.

What follows is a collection of practical solutions, tested tips, and insights I've gathered after plenty of less-than-perfect pulls or, how I learned to stop worrying and love the gel plate.

PATCHY, FAINT, OR NO IMAGE TRANSFER

It's frustrating to pull a print and find the image barely visible or completely missing. This usually happens because of too little paint, the wrong type of paint, low toner density, poor contrast in the image, or too much pressure during transfer.

When it comes to paint, balance is everything. Instead of applying paint directly to the plate, use a palette or even a second gel plate to help control the amount. Roll out your paint until it's smooth and thin. If it feels thick or sticky, your print will likely suffer.

Roll in multiple directions and lift the brayer slightly at the end of each pass to help spread the paint more evenly. I often roll excess paint off onto an old book page or scrap sheet.

Uneven areas in a print are typically the result of excessive paint, uneven rolling, or inconsistent pressure. Keep rolling until your paint feels evenly distributed. If the brayer is dirty or paint is clumping on one side, clean it well before continuing.

Cheaper brand paints and craft paints might work great on the gel plate for stencils and even reverse painting, but they often fall short in the image transfer process. They are typically too thin. Let's say you switched to Amsterdam Black Oxide and you are still struggling. If the paint is staying on your plate, then you are probably adding too much paint to the plate. If it all lifts up on to your paper, it is either too thin or you don't have enough toner printed on your laser print to create a resist.

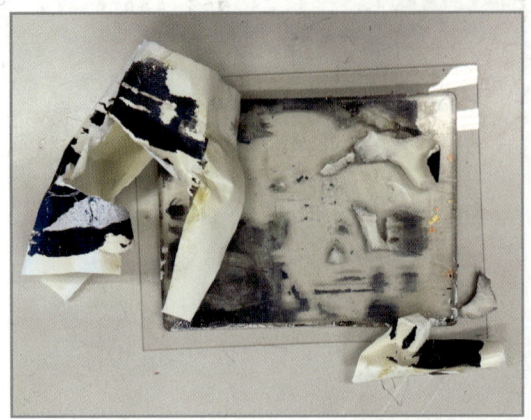

To boost toner density, begin with high-resolution images (300 dpi or higher) and adjust your contrast so the blacks are deep and the whites stay bright. Adding a halftone filter can help concentrate toner. Switching your image mode from grayscale to CMYK (even if you're printing in black and white) can help your printer lay down more toner, as well. If your printer has an Eco mode (or similar), be sure to turn it off. That feature is meant to save toner, which works against us here. Your printer might have different settings that could lay down more dense layers of toner.

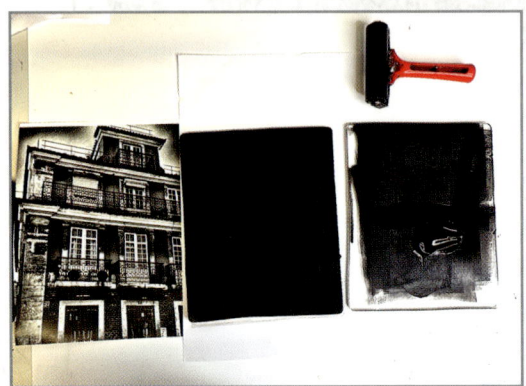

If your prints still feel too light, try double-printing. It will lay down twice as much toner. It's a tricky method, because some printers pull paper unevenly, and misalignment can lead to blurry results. Or if you are like me, no matter how many attempts, you still load the paper in the wrong direction, leading to accidental double exposures.

Paper choice also plays a big role. Standard 80-gsm printer paper usually works well for transfers, though if you're double-printing, try going a bit heavier, like 100 to 160 gsm. Avoid glossy, coated, or heavily textured papers, which can stick to the plate. When applying the laser print to the plate, use light, even pressure. Press slowly and make sure every part of the surface makes contact.

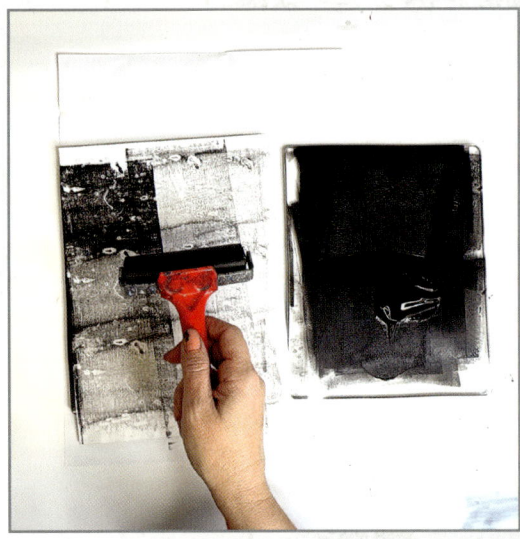

PAPER TEARING, STICKING, OR WRINKLING

When paper tears during image transfer, it usually means the paint dried too much before lifting. Try removing the paper after 3 to 10 seconds rather than letting it sit too long. Once the paint bonds too tightly with the fibers, it starts to act like glue.

If your pickup layer causes tearing or sticking, your paper might be too delicate. This can easily happen when using tissue paper, charcoal paper, or anything with a soft fiber structure. Mixed-media paper or Bristol board tends to hold up much better. If a section does tear and stick to your plate, a light spritz of water and gentle rubbing can help lift it off without damaging your plate.

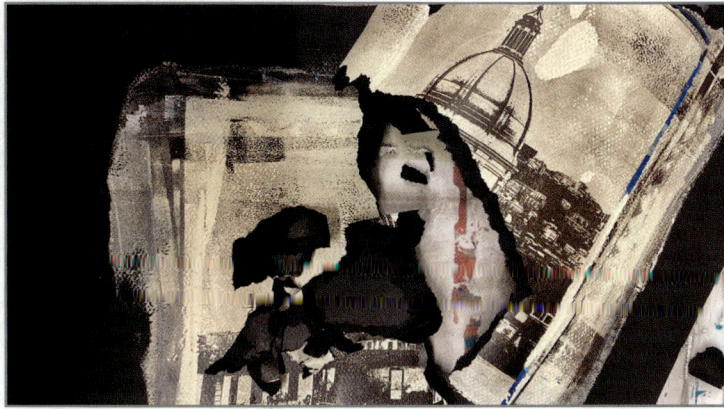

Black charcoal paper is fairly soft and didn't have the strength to handle being pulled off of the gel plate.

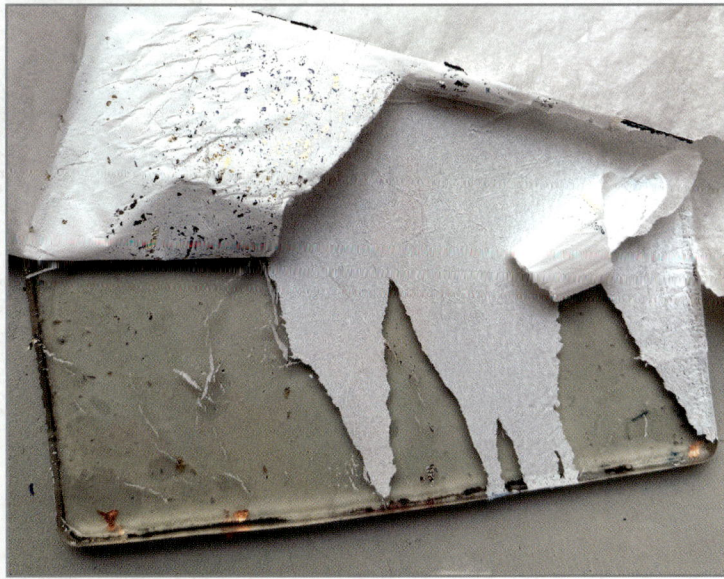

Tissue paper is great for wet pulls, but it has a hard time withstanding the gel plate grip.

Wrinkles usually show up when you use too much paint or when your paper is too absorbent. I enjoy working with Canson paper, but depending on the paint's thickness and humidity levels, it sometimes warps. To flatten wrinkled prints, sandwich them between heavy books for 30 to 90 minutes. If the conditions are especially damp, let them sit overnight to flatten. I forgot to put books on this print; the paper wrinkled immediately and then dried that way. As a result, the lift layer worked only on the parts where the paper was still touching the gel plate.

If you find your plate feels overly sticky all the time, it might be worth trying another brand. Some plates naturally have more tack to them, which can affect how paper lifts or sticks.

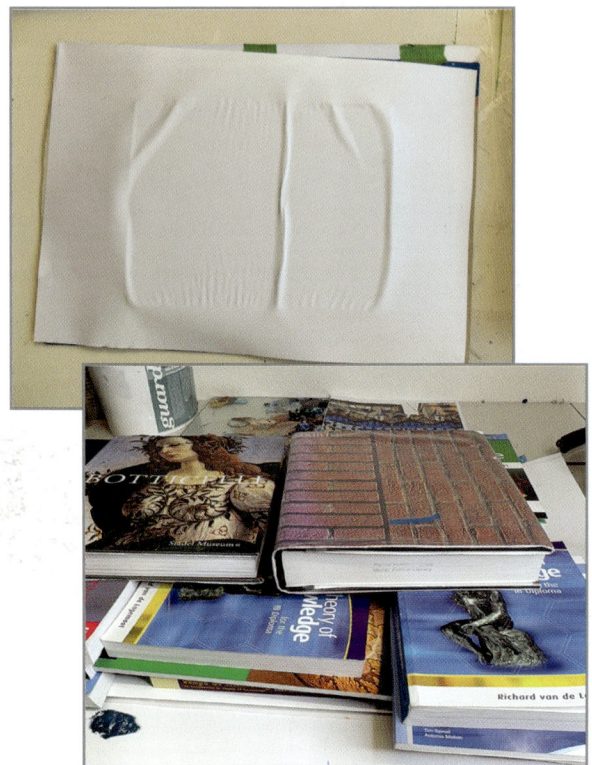

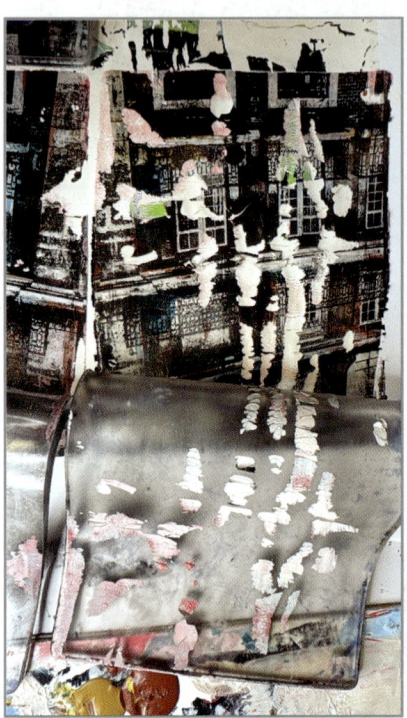

STUCK PRINTS THAT WON'T LIFT

When part of your print sticks to the plate while you are lifting, don't panic. If the paint is still a bit damp, you can lay the paper back down and press it with a heavy book. Letting it sit for a few more minutes may help the layer pull more fully. If the paint has already dried, try lifting from a different direction. If it still refuses to budge, add a light layer of gel medium to both the plate and the stuck area, press the paper back down, and let it dry under weight. This trick often does the job.

If large portions of the print remain on the plate after pulling up your final layer, chances are your pickup layer was too thin or dried out too quickly.

POOLING, BEADING, CRACKING, OR PEELING PAINT

When paint pools into tiny droplets instead of spreading smoothly, it usually means something is off with either the paint itself or the surface of your plate. Start by asking a few quick questions. Is your paint too watery? Are you using a very thin or inexpensive brand that's been heavily diluted? If you've already adjusted your paint and it's still happening, the plate may be the issue.

This kind of beading is especially common with new gel plates. Often, there's a slight residue left over from manufacturing that can repel paint. Washing the surface with mild dish soap can help remove it. Another option is to apply a thin layer of gel medium on top of your image transfer to prime the plate before painting. This added layer gives the paint something to grip, helping it lay down more evenly.

That said, not every instance of pooling needs to be corrected. In fact, some of the most intricate, lace-like textures come from this exact effect. If the pattern feels interesting, let it stay. It might lead you somewhere unexpected. When I use watercolor markers on my plate, pooling is inevitable even with gel medium, but it adds to the texture.

Cracking paint is a different issue. It often happens when paint is applied too thickly or if the plate is bent while the paint is still drying. I've had this happen with spray paint, and while unintentional at first, I started bending the plate deliberately to achieve a crackled effect.

If your paint is peeling off of your gel plate while you are spreading it, then it might be drying too quickly. Remember that the brayer not only puts down paint but has the ability to lift it as well. This can happen when you have some partially dried paint on your plate. It might also be your pressure with the brayer. Use a light touch if you think this is happening because your plate is gripping the paint too much. Perhaps you need to condition the plate with a bit of mineral oil.

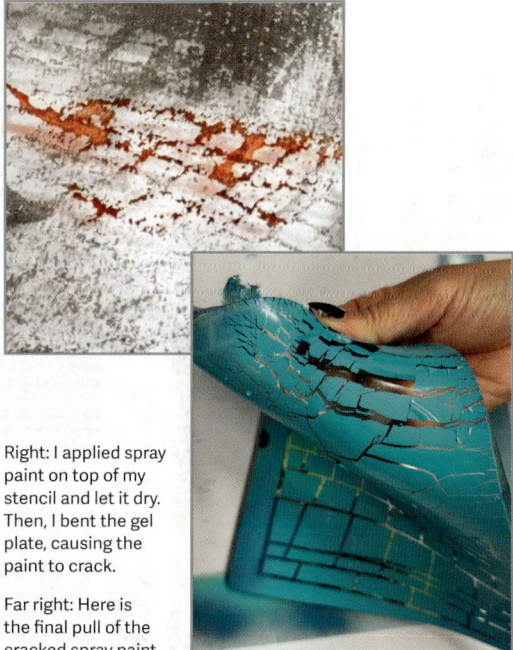

Right: I applied spray paint on top of my stencil and let it dry. Then, I bent the gel plate, causing the paint to crack.

Far right: Here is the final pull of the cracked spray paint.

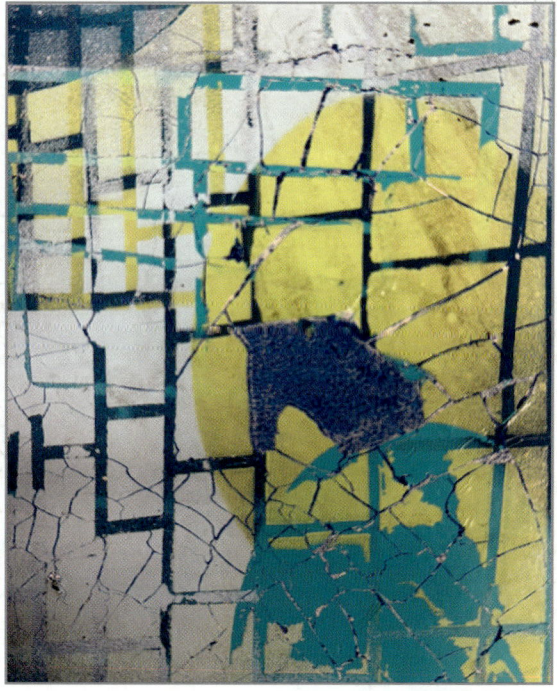

MARKS ON YOUR PRINTS

Circular spots or ghost-like textures are often watermarks that develop after storing a wet plate against plastic or acetate. Cleaning your plate with dish soap or baby oil can help reduce them. They usually fade with repeated use, but if they continue to show up in your prints, you can touch up those areas with a bit of paint later on.

Built-up paint on your brayer can lead to messy results. Texture on your brayer can lead to uneven application and even streaks in your prints. It's easy to fall behind on cleaning when you're in the middle of a creative flow. Aim to have a roll-off sheet nearby to keep the brayer clean while you are working. A quick wipe with a baby wipe also helps remove wet paint. What about when the paint dries on your brayer? Try soaking your brayer in orange-based cleaner or Murphy's Oil Soap. The same cleaning trick also works well for your stencils.

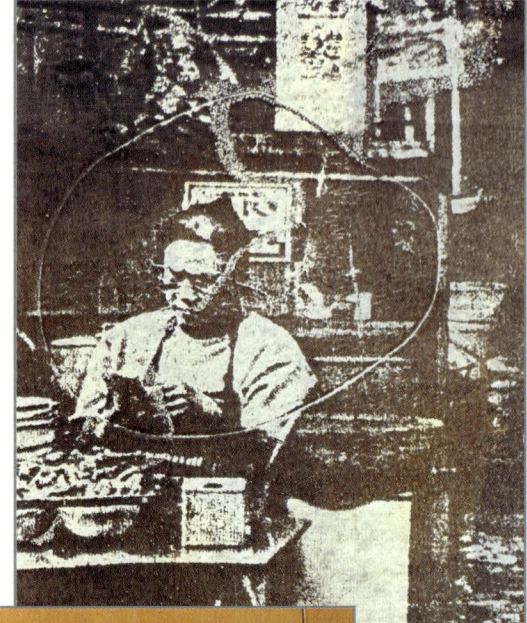

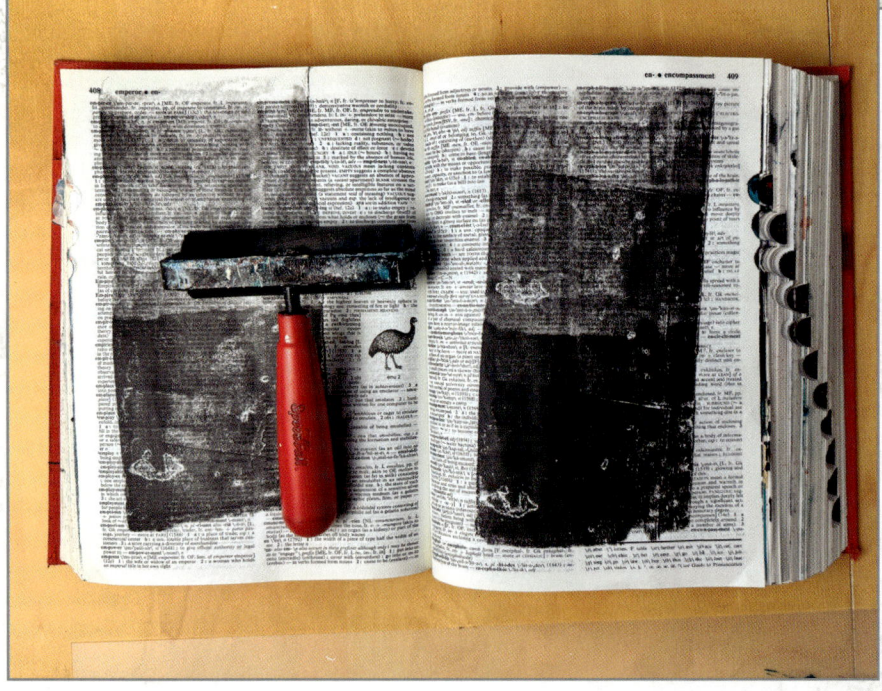

STILL STRUGGLING?

Take a more scientific approach. Each combination of paint, plate, and paper behaves differently. Keeping a log can help you notice patterns and refine your approach. Track things like:

- Paper types and weights
- Printer settings
- Paint brands
- Drying times
- Humidity or temperature
- What didn't work and what fixed it

Over time, you'll develop your own customized set of notes that will serve you better than any instruction manual.

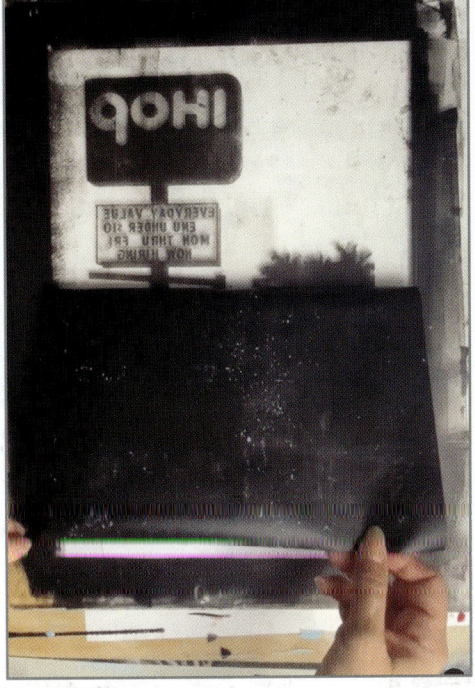

PRESS ON

The best way to learn is through making. That includes making prints that go wrong. Every mistake teaches you something about how these materials interact. What starts as a mistake can often lead to something better. A so-called failure might introduce a new texture, shape, or direction you hadn't considered. The key is to stay open, keep experimenting, and let those imperfect results guide you in an unexpected direction. Some of the most satisfying prints I've made were total accidents.

So, give yourself permission to let go of expectations. Stay curious. Keep layering, lifting, printing, and adjusting. Eventually, something clicks, and that print you almost gave up on becomes one of your favorites.

Roll up your sleeves. Take a deep breath. Press on. You've got this!

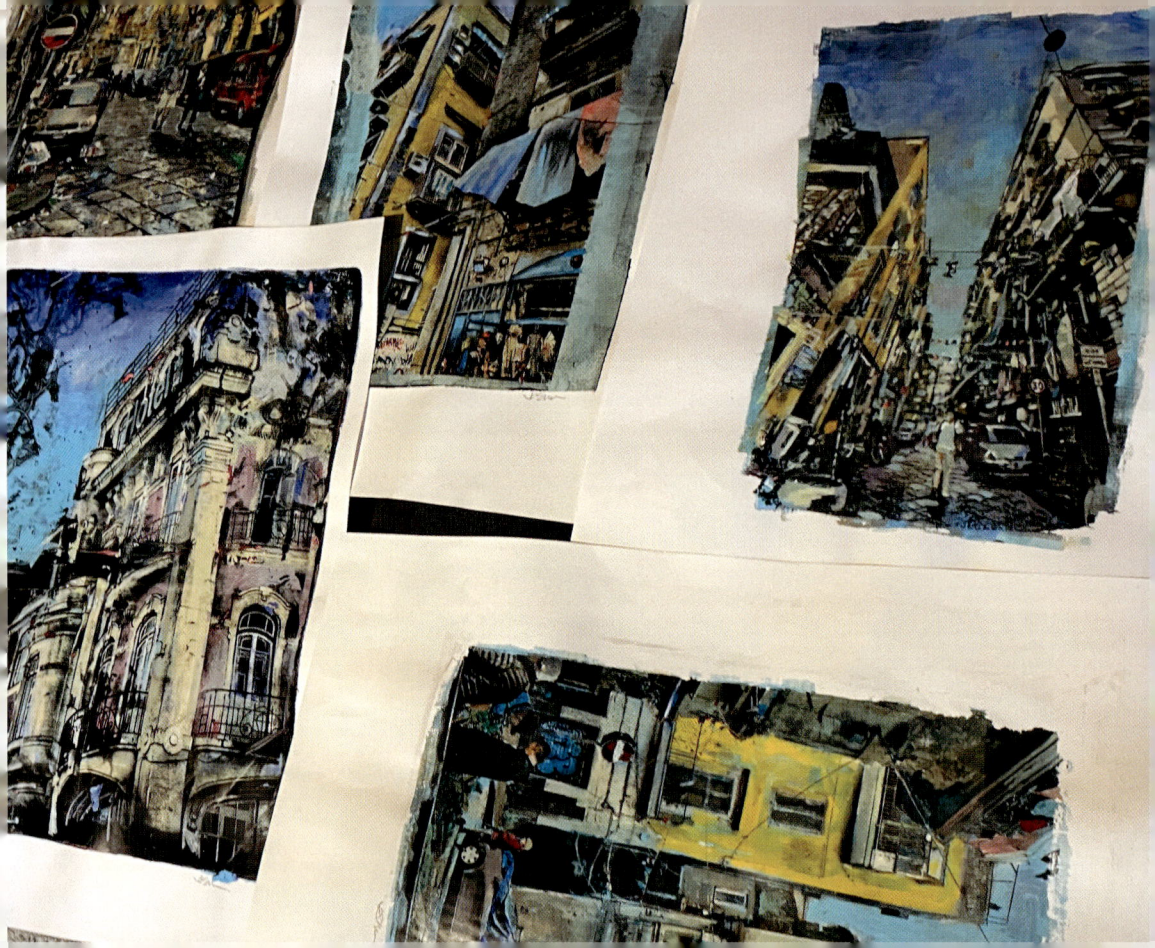

18

CREATIVE WAYS TO USE YOUR GEL PRINTS

You know the moment when you pull a print from the plate, lay it out, and really look at it? You're wowed by the great colors, rich textures, and incredible patterns. But then... reality sets in. Although the print is beautiful, it may not be quite wall worthy.

WHAT'S NEXT?

So, what do you do? Let it disappear into the drawer with the rest, or see it for what it *could* be?

Not every print demands a frame. Some evolve into something more interesting when you let go of that expectation. When you rework, deconstruct, or build on top of them, those in-between pieces that you were unsure about can end up driving your most inventive work.

Prints tend to fall into three loose categories:
- Wall Worthy
- Hidden Gems
- Recyclables

Each opens up different creative possibilities. Take a closer look.

WALL WORTHY

Wall-worthy prints are your immediate winners, the ones that deserve to be framed and shown off.

When I create a gel print that I really love (the kind that immediately makes me think, "Yes, this is the one!"), I tend to frame it, leaving a nice border around the edges to give the eyes a place to rest. This gives me some flexibility with how they are presented. A great alternative, however, is to mount the print on a wood panel for a clean, modern look. I often opt for a cradle board, which is a wooden panel with a frame attached to the back to help keep it from warping and make it easier to hang.

Before mounting your print on a wood panel, first prep the panel with gesso to keep the acids and impurities of the wood from staining your image. Next, paint the sides whatever color fits your print's vibe. It is easier to do this step before mounting your print, because you

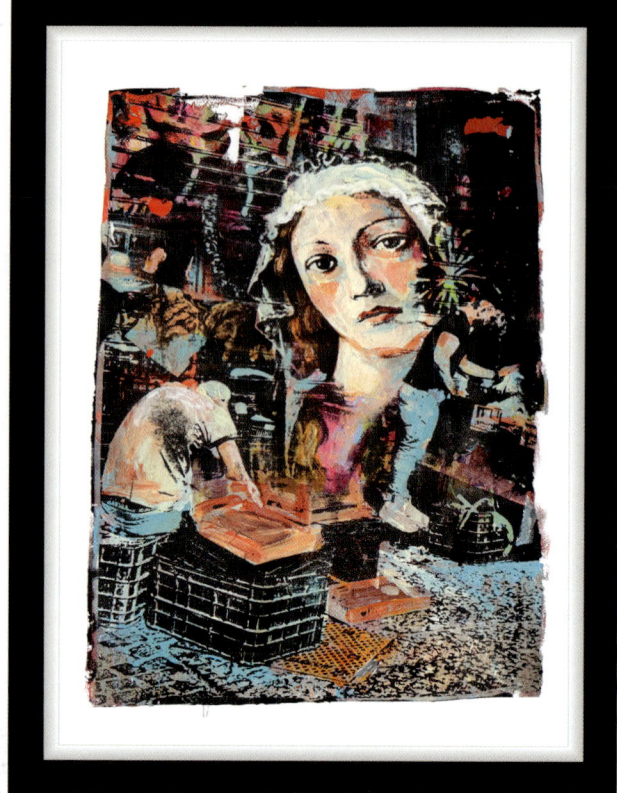

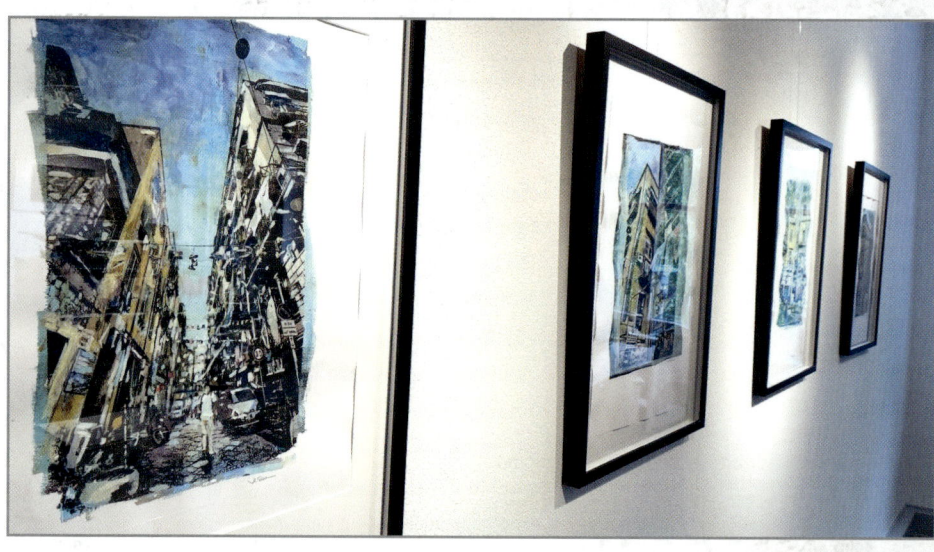

can be a bit sloppier with your brushstrokes without the worry of getting paint on your artwork. I choose a light wash of gold to complement my image.

I don't obsess over measurements. Instead, I cut one edge perfectly straight along the print using a paper trimmer or craft knife, then trim an adjoining edge square. Once that corner's crisp, I glue it down using gel medium, starting from that clean corner so I know everything will line up flush. I apply the medium to both the wood panel and the back of the print, pressing it down flat to remove bubbles. To help with this step, you can use a small rubber squeegee or something firm but flexible. Make sure that no gel medium is on the surface of the print because you will need to stack some books on it to prevent warping while drying.

After drying overnight, I use a very sharp blade and trim the remaining sides directly on the panel, keeping the knife flush against the wood. It gives me clean, exact edges without stressing over measurements. Glide and steadily glide the blade along the excess with the cradle board face down on your workspace. Once the gel print is fully adhered, dried, and trimmed flush to the panel, I make sure the print surface is clean, then I apply gel medium over the entire print and edges in a few coats, ensuring that they are all sealed. Now it is ready to be hung on your wall.

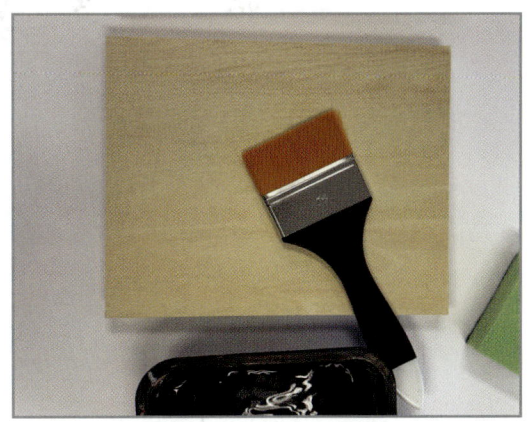

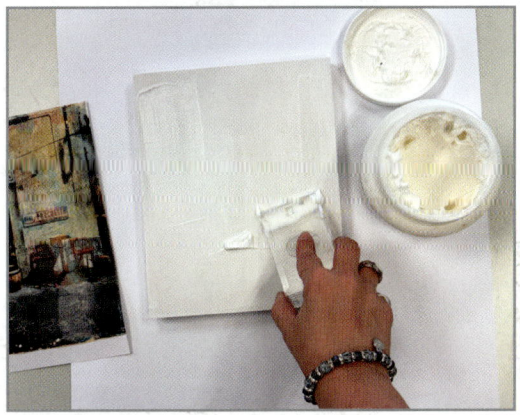

I couldn't find my plastic squeegee, so I repurposed this plastic card holder. It worked fairly well.

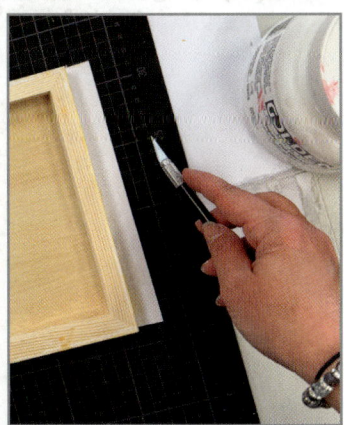

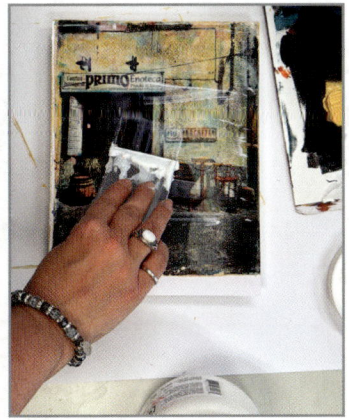

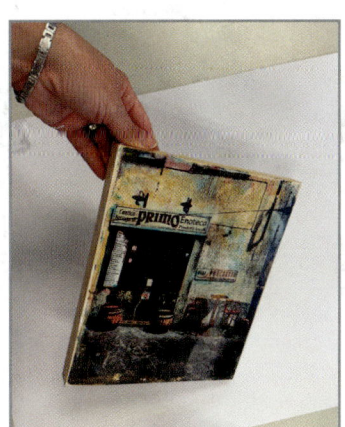

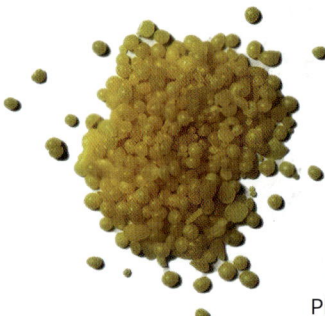

Sometimes I will opt for beeswax coating over the mounted print. It gives the piece a soft, velvety finish with a warm, encaustic-like glow. It also adds a protective layer that makes the colors feel even richer. Plus, I just love the slightly vintage, dreamy vibe beeswax brings to the whole piece. I use natural beeswax pellets and melt them slowly in an electric griddle. Using a natural bristle brush, I lightly apply a thin layer of melted wax over the entire surface, working fairly quickly because it sets fast. Yours might look a little cloudy or uneven at first, but don't panic.

After the wax cools for a few minutes, grab a clean cloth or soft rag and buff the surface in gentle circles. This is the fun part where the magic happens. The dull wax starts to polish up and glow.

The more layers you add, the more textured the encaustic effect you will create on your print. Make sure to let each layer cool and give it a light buff before adding the next layer. If you want to add even more dimension, you can even press botanicals or color pigments into the layers.

A QUICK NOTE ON ADHESIVES

Some adhesives might seem convenient, but don't hold up over time. PVA glue tends to create a cloudy haze. Glue sticks often lack staying power, and rubber cement yellows and becomes brittle. If you want both a strong bond and archival quality, gel medium is the best option. I typically opt for the satin finish.

HIDDEN GEMS

Some prints don't quite hold together as complete pieces, but within them are fragments that deserve a second look: hidden gems. An edge might carry an unexpected texture, a strip of color might harmonize in a way that feels fresh, or a section might have just the right layering to catch your eye. These elements become raw material for more intentional and focused work.

You might find them resurfacing in collages, sketchbook spreads, or layered mixed-media pieces. What they offer isn't about preserving the original, but rather it's about reshaping it and sparking your imagination. By treating these fragments as a starting point, they lead you somewhere new, opening up creative paths that a finished piece might never have revealed.

COLLAGE

Collage offers one of the most versatile ways to work with gel prints. If you're just beginning, consider starting with a grid format. Cut your prints into even squares; 2 × 2 inches is a manageable size. Then arrange them across a page. The uniformity provides structure while the variations within each square introduce rhythm and surprise. The figures below show an example that I am working on in my scrap paper dictionary.

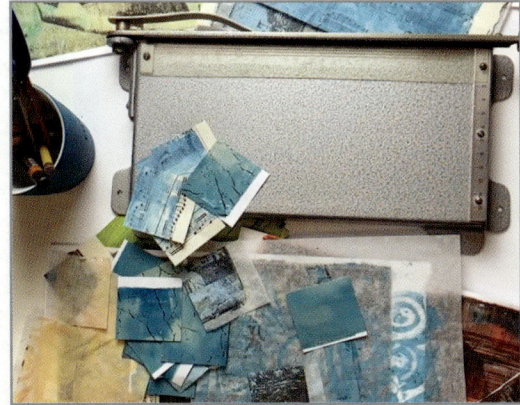

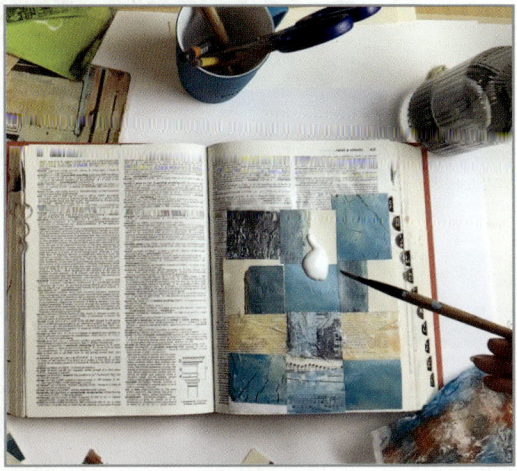

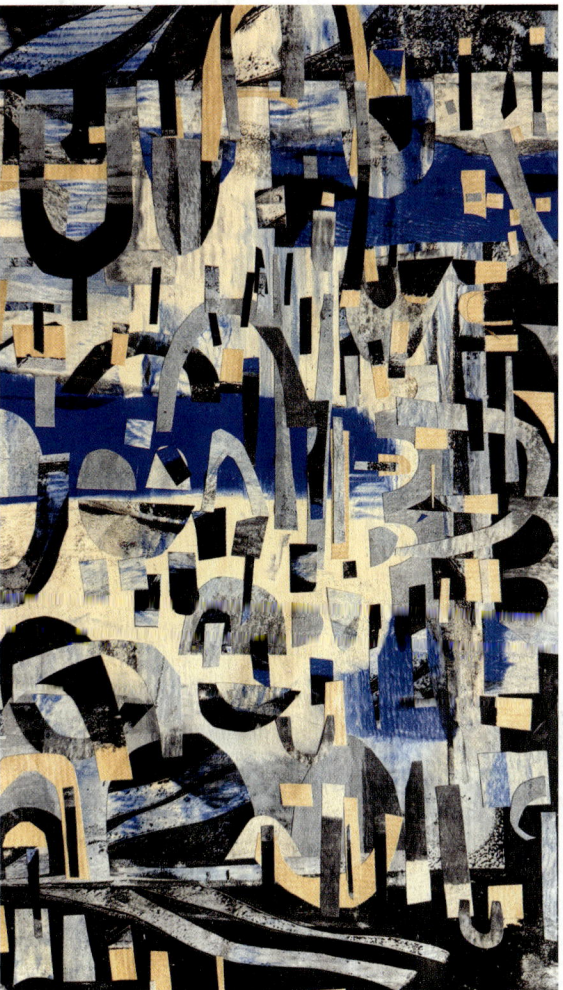

To glue your pieces in place, use a soft brush to apply a thin, even layer of gel medium to your surface, to the back of each piece, and then over the top once everything is arranged. This final layer helps seal the collage and creates a cohesive finish.

As you develop your own approach, begin layering more strategically. Try placing transparent tissue prints over more opaque pieces to build visual depth. Mixing textures, overlapping forms, and adjusting the opacity of layers allows you to create complexity and guide the viewer's eye across the composition.

This collage came from a mix of experimental prints and plate-cleaning sheets. I cut a variety of shapes—some geometric, some organic—and arranged them over a base print. Most of the color palette stayed within a range of blues, which helped unify the composition and allowed me to play more freely with scale and shape. A final layer of satin glazing medium sealed the print and gave it a nice finish.

Among the materials I reach for, tissue paper is my favorite for gel print collages. Its transparency and delicacy make it perfect for layering and blending. In one landscape composition, I used dark blue gel prints on Bristol paper for the foreground and placed them over soft, tissue-based layers to create a sense of depth and atmosphere.

In another example, I printed a light blue circle with a small round gel plate. I then layered tissue paper on top to suggest light and distance, using transparency to imply depth.

You can also create your own artist book by repurposing an old or discarded book as a substrate. Look for books with thick, durable pages. Children's board books work especially well for this because of their sturdy, nonabsorbent surface. Before you begin, use

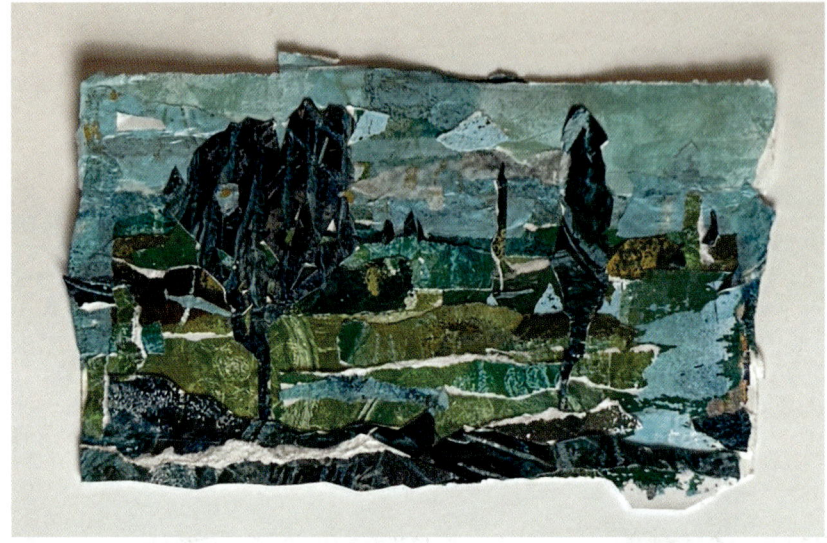

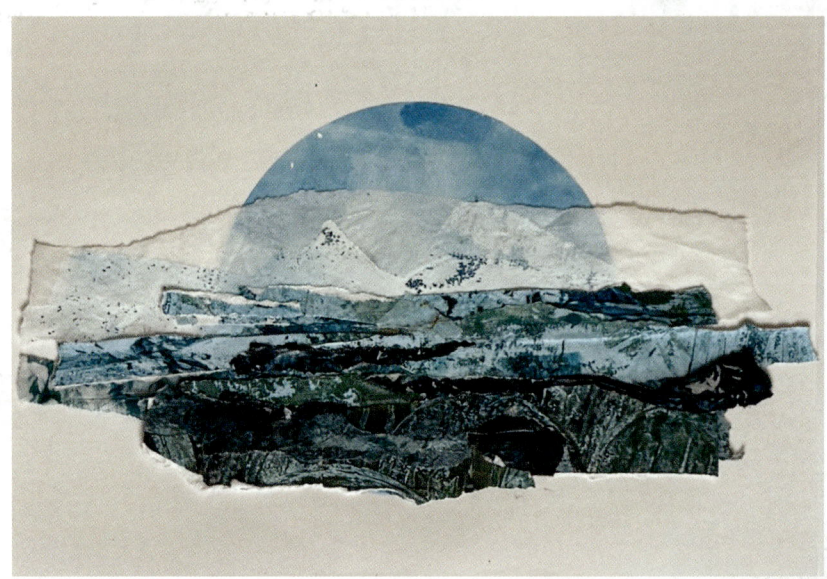

a piece of sandpaper to gently scuff the glossy finish. This gives your gesso or gel medium something to grip onto.

From there, you have options. You can prime the pages with gesso or a layer of gel medium, then print directly onto them, or you can build up a collage directly on the surface. Either way, work one spread at a time and allow each set of pages to dry thoroughly before moving on.

To help smooth your papers and ensure strong contact with the surface, use your small rubber squeegee. Once everything has dried completely, you can use a sharp craft knife to trim away any paper overhang or clean up the edges.

This process turns something forgotten into a tactile, layered object that holds both image and form and something you can return to, flip through, and continue to build over time. It may give you ideas for how to layer, combine colors, and work on your composition skills in the process.

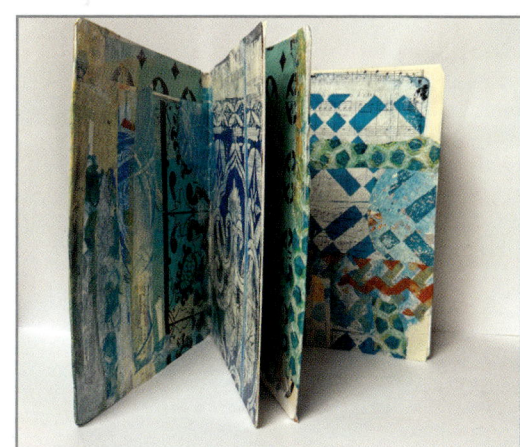

HANDMADE BOOKS

Gel prints work beautifully as covers for handmade books. Whether you're binding a sketchbook, assembling a travel journal, or creating an accordion fold book, the layered surfaces and painterly qualities of gel prints add character and texture before you even open the first page. I make these small travel books with watercolor for myself and my children when we travel. I start by making a small signature (a group of pages folded together) out of scrap watercolor paper that is always near my paper cutter. They are lightweight enough to carry around on our adventures and easy to pull out when the time beckons. They make great memories for our travels.

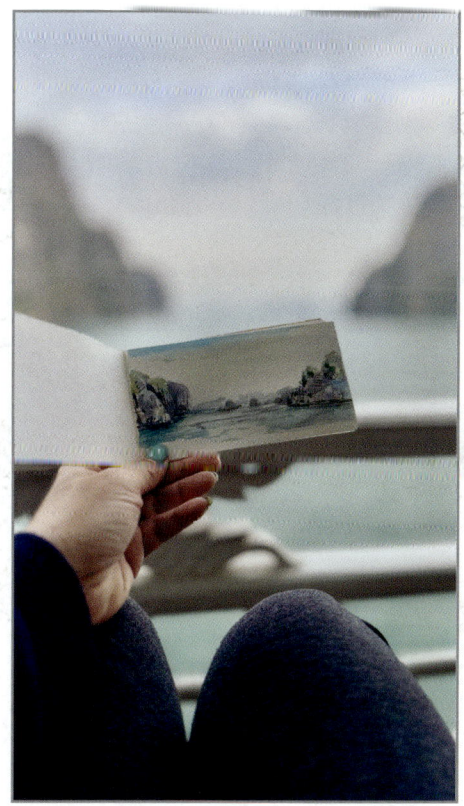

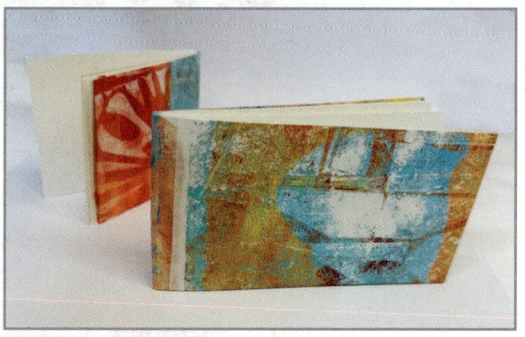

ART JOURNALING ON GEL PRINTS

Gel prints make for great art journaling inspiration. They already carry layers, color, and texture, which makes facing the blank page less daunting. Use full pages as backgrounds, tear them into shapes and reposition them, or highlight certain sections with drawing materials. I love using the random textures of the gel print to create doodles and zentangles. I like to call this technique advanced doodling.

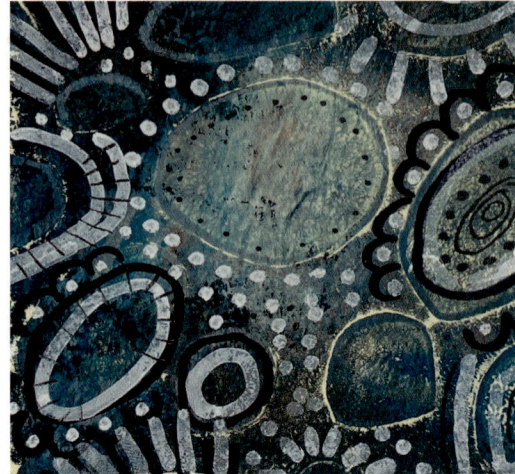

Below: This is one that I am currently working on. The image transfer was from a photo of tile in Lisbon, Portugal, and the print is perfect for creating a structure for me to build on the shapes and patterns with a black pen and a white paint marker.

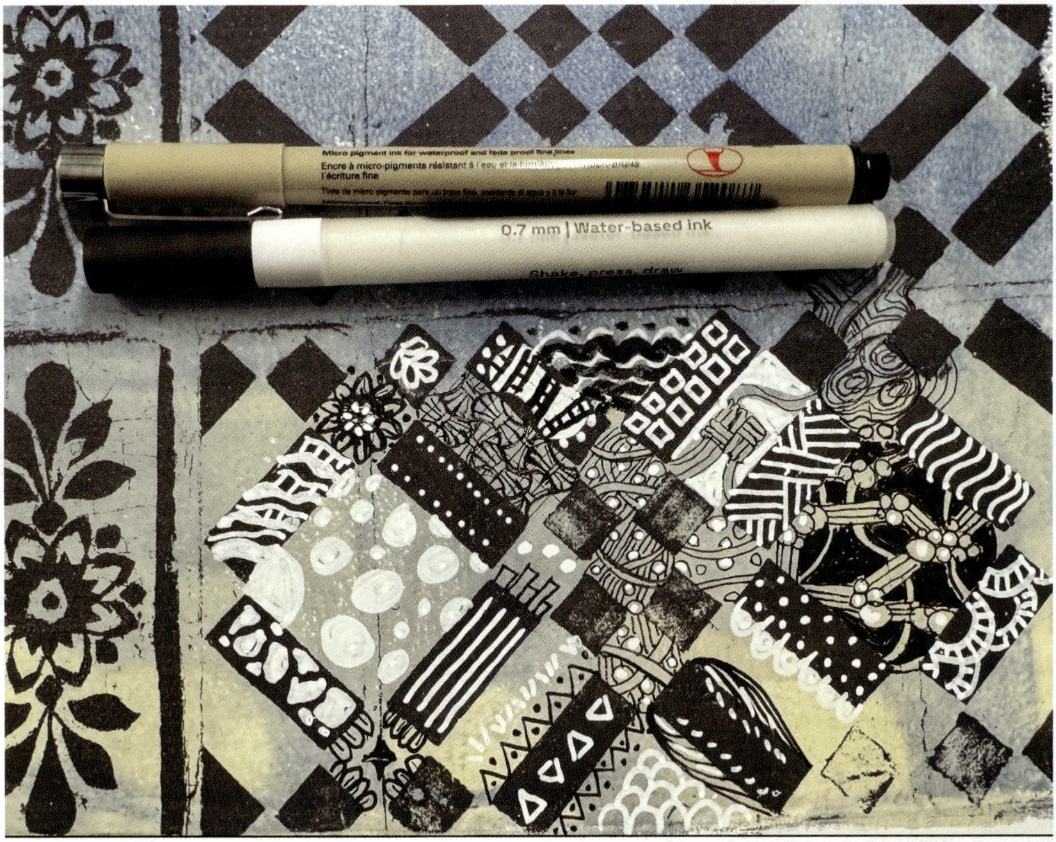

EVERYDAY USE

Gel prints don't have to live only in your studio practice. They translate well into everyday objects. You can use larger prints as wrapping paper or fold smaller ones into cards. Try cutting them into bookmarks or tags. They also work beautifully when glued to boxes, wooden panels, or small household items. You even can lay clear packing tape on your gel prints to create a sealed finish for bookmarks.

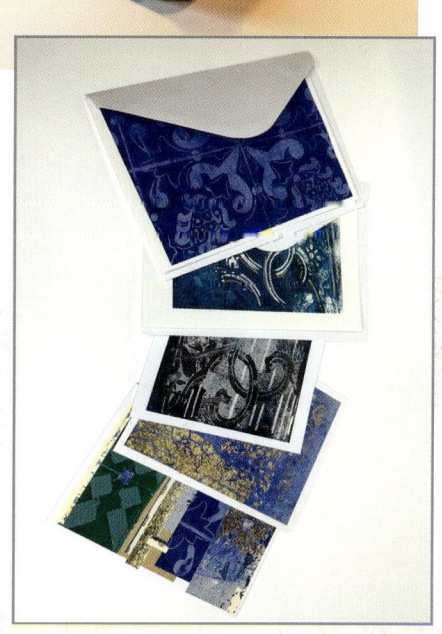

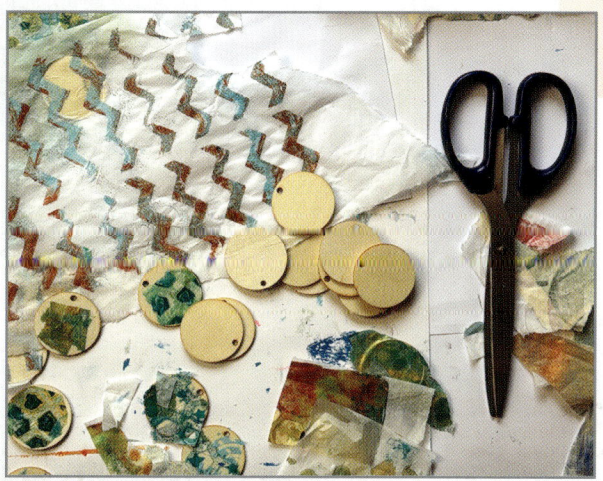

RECYCLABLES

Don't trash your bad prints! Recycle them by printing on them again. The underlayer introduces color and texture that interacts with the new print in surprising ways. Remember this example? I printed a Naples street scene on top of a botanical print, and you can still see the earlier shapes and tones coming through in a subtle but important way.

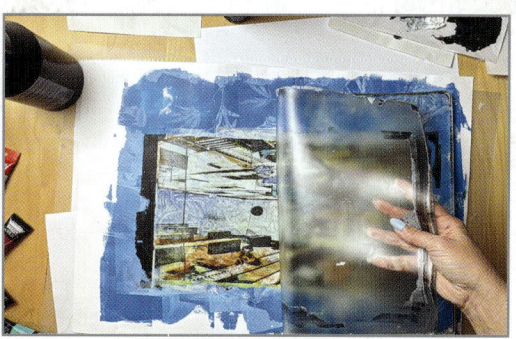

I keep all of these so-called failures around for reprinting or even for other projects. I have a stack of low-contrast prints from various workshops that I have done. They make great surfaces for sketching, especially when you want something more interesting than a blank page. When I went to Vietnam, I packed several of these. This drawing from Hạ Long Bay in Vietnam began with a pen sketch of the iconic land formations growing out of the water. I then layered in colored pencil on top. The gel print served as a lovely underpainting for this work.

And when all else fails, use those prints as tools. They work well as brayer-cleaning sheets or as protective layers when testing out a new idea. Just because something didn't work the first time doesn't mean it's finished.

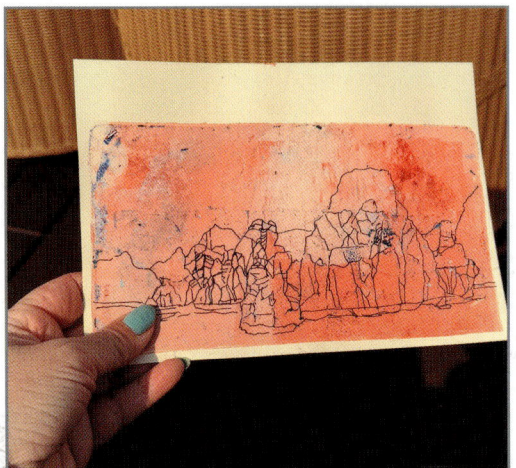 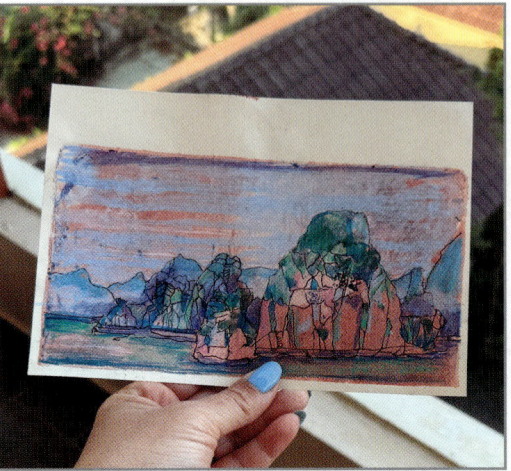

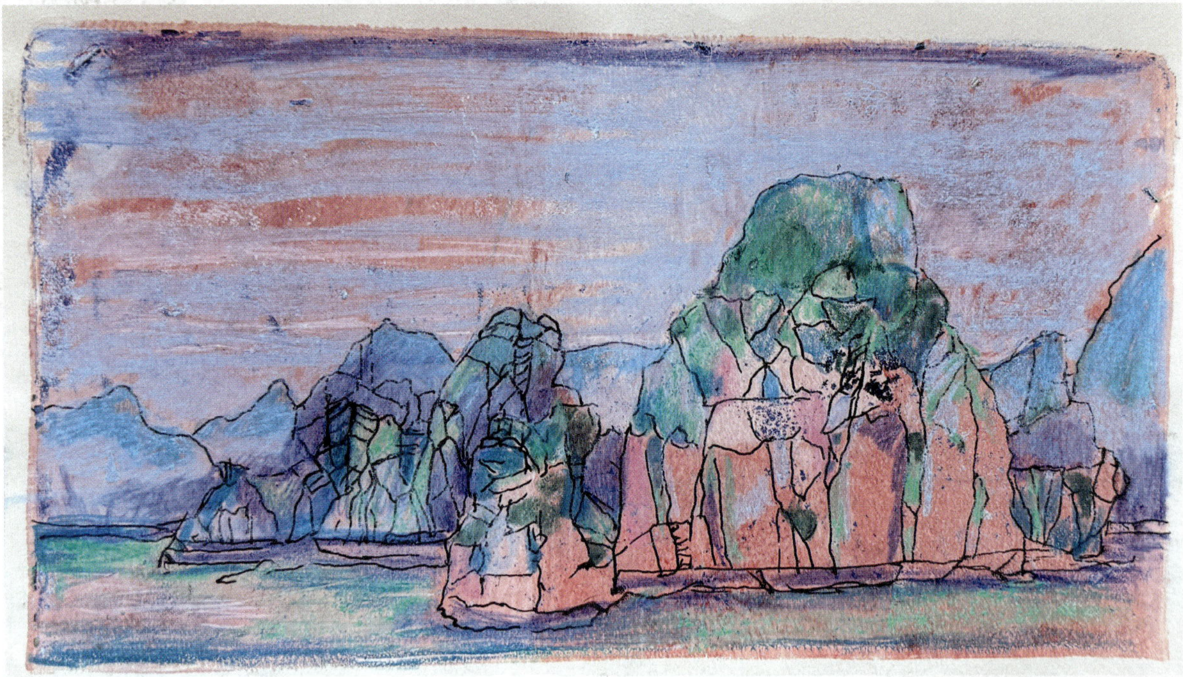

FINAL THOUGHTS

Gel printing exists in a space between control and chance. Each layer, each pulled print, is part of an ongoing process, something that builds over time rather than landing in one final, perfect result. The pieces that feel incomplete still offer a foundation. They're part of the conversation between the material and the maker.

So don't hesitate to work back into them. Cut them up, draw on top, glue them into books, or cover them with something new. They don't have to be precious to be useful. Your discarded prints might just become the most generative part of your practice.

This process rewards intuition and adaptation just as much as technical skill, inviting you to respond in the moment rather than only following fixed rules. Let each print, successful or not, become part of your visual thinking.

Keep exploring, stay curious, and trust your materials to lead you somewhere unexpected and worthwhile.

Happy Printing!

ART TEACHER'S GUIDE: TEACHING GEL PLATE PRINTMAKING IN THE CLASSROOM

Here is a practical guide designed for art educators who want to bring gel plate printmaking into their classroom. I used this with grades 6–12, though it can be adapted for younger or older students too.

START WITH THE BASICS

Students are often immediately drawn to the feel of the gel plate. After all, it's got this weirdly irresistible, jelly-like texture that begs to be poked. I lean into that excitement. Begin by explaining what a gel plate is and give a demonstration of how to lift a texture print. They will be captivated by the process. Try to set the tone that this is about process, not perfection. It's about exploring, discovering what happens, and leaning into happy accidents. Letting go of perfection is hard for a lot of students. It is about teaching resilience and creative thinking throughout the printmaking process.

Once students get comfortable with layering and lifting prints, you can introduce more creative techniques. Teach students how to paint directly on the plate. This means they'll need to think in reverse. Start simple: flowers, geometric shapes and patterns

work well. Encourage them to choose their own designs and color palettes. This gives them freedom and helps shift the focus from product to process.

Next, you can introduce resist techniques. Start with oil pastels drawn directly onto paper. Again,

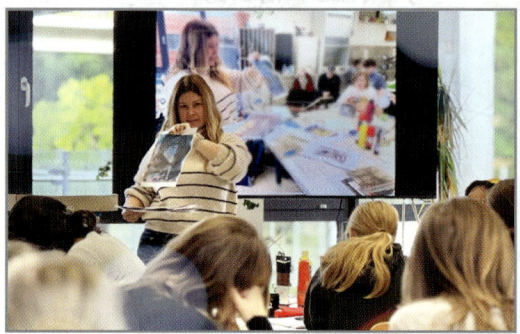

quick, abstract shapes or patterns work great. Then show them how to transfer that drawing onto the plate. Once they understand the idea, introduce resist techniques using magazines transfers (I keep a stack of donated *Vogue* magazines in the classroom). Let them practice. It can be frustrating at first. That's okay! Encourage peer-to-peer sharing. Watching how others use the plate or solve problems helps build community and creativity.

TEACHER TIPS & TRICKS

Use old textbooks as roll-off sheets. The students love rolling their brayers out in the textbooks, which also helps them keep the brayers cleaner. If your school budget allows, stock a variety of plate sizes. They can use the smaller plates for quick experiments or while waiting for bigger plates to dry.

Store plates flat on acetate or plexi sheets.

Number your brayers and plates (on the plexi) and assign each student a number. It helps you keep tabs on which brayers and plates are returned spotless and others that needed a bit more attention.

Let students clean their plates with baby wipes or packing tape (they'll love the tape peel!).

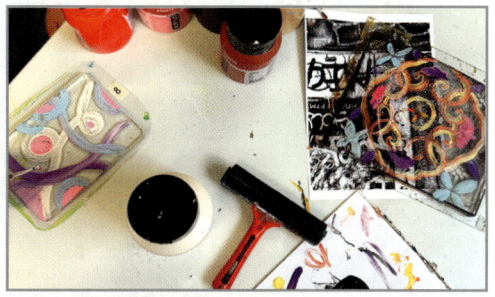

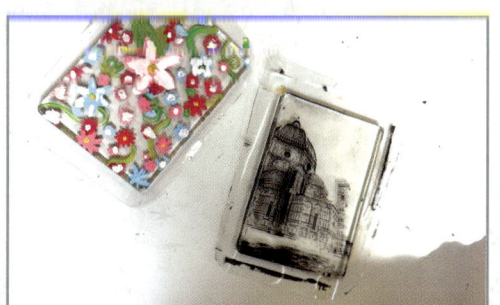

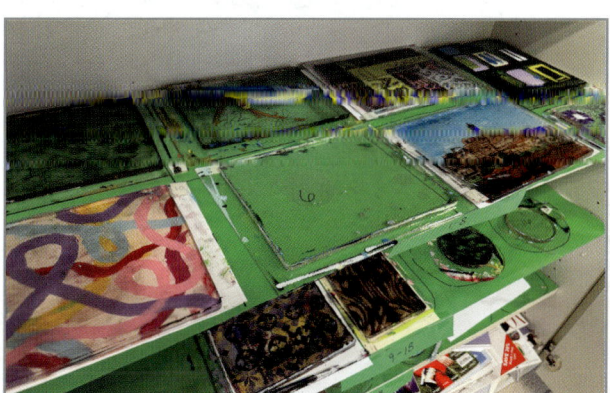

BEYOND THE BASICS

They progress to laser print image transfers next beginning with high-contrast, black-and-white laser prints that you have tested. Let them practice with these until they get the hang of how much paint to use, how long to wait, and how to brayer correctly.

Once they've figured out the basics, they can edit and print their own photos. This gives them a huge sense of ownership and pride when they pull a successful transfer of their own work. Emphasize process over perfection. Teach students to reprint over "failures," collage with scraps, and repurpose what doesn't go as planned.

For students who aren't ready to use their own photos, laser-printed pages from adult coloring books (especially mandalas and bold geometric designs) are a great middle ground. They're high-contrast and easy to transfer, and they let students keep experimenting while reinforcing the process.

What starts as playful printing becomes a space for real growth. With every layer pulled, students learn to trust the process, embrace surprises, and stay curious. In the end, the gel plate is about taking risks, exploring freely, and finding beauty in the unexpected. In the classroom, it becomes a way to build resilience through hands-on creativity.

ACKNOWLEDGMENTS

Thank you to the community of artists I've met through social media and my gel printing courses. Your passion, curiosity, and generosity keep me experimenting and inspired. Big love to Gelli Arts for fueling my obsession with this medium. To my amazing colleagues and students at Frankfurt International School, thank you for cheering me on and never judging my perpetually paint-splattered, chipped manicure. And the biggest, thank you to my family near and far, for their endless support in all my creative pursuits even when I took over the kitchen and turned it into an art studio so I could cook dinner and make art at the same time. You are my everything, and I couldn't have done this without you.